Contents

List of figures

Preface

When I was an undergraduate in the 1960s at the Australian National University in Canberra, I decided to attend a conference organised by the Australasian Association of Philosophy. The main theme of the conference, which was to be held at the University of Queensland in Brisbane, was mind in relation to body. Being a student, I had little money. I came to the conclusion that the only feasible way for me to travel to the conference was by hitch-hiking. In those days hitch-hiking was not a dangerous thing to do and drivers were quite willing to pick up hitch-hikers as freeloading passengers.

At that time the journey by road from Canberra to Brisbane was some 700 miles. For the whole of the last 200 or so miles I was fortunate to obtain a lift from a lorry driver returning to the cane fields of northern Queensland. The driver was large, sunburnt and wore a red baseball cap. One of the courtesies expected from a hitch-hiker was that he or she be prepared to chat with the host driver. This courtesy seemed especially apposite when the driver was a long-distance lorry driver who otherwise had to travel for long periods without any company other than his radio. My driver soon discovered that I was a student travelling to a conference about the mind. So he said, 'So, mate, you're a philosopher? A student of the mind? Well, then, could you tell me what it is that you fellers say about the mind?'

I regret to say that I answered very badly. My memory seemed suddenly to be a store without goods. The lectures that I had attended and the books that I had read seemed to have left no trace. I fear that the man in the red baseball cap left me at the turn-off to the university campus with a rather poor opinion of me as a student of the mind. Some thirty years later I am still a student of the mind. This book is my attempt to give a better answer to the man in the red baseball cap.

Acknowledgements

I would like to thank the following for their help, advice, criticism or encouragement when writing the text of *Matters of the Mind*: Charles Benson, David Berman, Jack Copeland, Brendan Dempsey, Hugh Gibbons, Pat Hartigan, Ray Houghton, Raymond Keene, Maureen Lapan, Paul O'Grady, Joseph Pheifer, Ullin Place, Diane Proudfoot and Elizabeth Valentine. I am also indebted to the Committee of Deans at Trinity College Dublin for their award to me of a research grant from the Arts and Social Sciences Benefaction Fund. However I owe two special debts of gratitude; first, to my friend and former colleague, John Gaskin, who has given me invaluable criticism, unstinting encouragement and shrewd advice, chapter by chapter, year by year, on the whole typescript. Second, to my most indefatigable, dependable and amiable research assistant, Brian Garvey.

Without the timely help of Piaras Walsh and Norton Disk Doctor, there would have been no typescript to be printed from the computer disks. Without the perceptive suggestions, shrewd advice and generous encouragement from Jackie Jones and the splendidly exacting copy-editor Ann Vinnicombe, as well as Carol Macdonald and James Dale, of Edinburgh University Press, there would be no book.

(1995) Museum of the History of Psychological Instrumentation; Princess Elizabeth of Bohemia © The Bodleian Library; Sigmund Freud © The Associated Press Ltd.; Article from the *Irish Times* © *Irish Times*; photograph of John B. Watson reproduced with permission from the Psychology Department, Furman University; B. F. Skinner © Nina Leen/TimePix; Moritz Schlick, c. 1920 © AKG London; photograph of Wittgenstein reproduced with permission from Trinity College Library, Cambridge; drawing of Gilbert Ryle by Hubert Andrew Freeth reproduced by courtesy of the National Portrait Gallery, London; two plates from *The Expression of the Emotions in Man and Animals* (third edition) by Charles Darwin, 1998, HarperCollins; *Le Penseur* by Auguste Rodin © musée Rodin (photo Jérôme Manoukian); Luigi Galvani, 1737–1798, Tab. II, dissection of a sheep © Wellcome Library, London; lithograph of Luigi Galvani © Wellcome Library, London; portrait of Pierre-Paul Broca (1824–1880) © Wellcome Library, London; the brain's hemispheres, neurones and cut corpus callosum from Atkinson et al.: *Introduction to Psychology*, 1993, Harcourt Brace Jovanovich; photograph of Charles Sherrington reproduced with permission from Visual Image Presentations; Wilder Penfield © Montreal Neurological Institute; Penfield's experiment on the brain from *The Excitable Cortex in Conscious Man*, 1958, Liverpool University Press; Roger Wolcott Sperry receiving his Nobel Prize for medicine © Hulton Getty; photograph of Karl Lashley © Harvard University Archives; photograph of J. J. C. Smart © J. J. C. Smart and Liz Smart; photograph of Patricia Churchland © Lisa Lloyd; Ludwig Wittgenstein (1889–1951) (portrait by the Austrian artist Professor Otto Zeiller) with kind permission of Trinity College, Cambridge; Pascal's calculating box taken from *Oeuvres de Blaise Pascal*, vol. 4, 1779, reproduced by kind permission of the Board of Trinity College, Dublin; Leibniz's calculator taken from *Leibnitii Opera Omnia*, vol. 3, 1768, reproduced by kind permission of the Board of Trinity College, Dublin; Charles Babbage (1792–1871), Charles Babbage's Difference Engine and Lady Lovelace © The Science Museum/Science & Society Picture Library; Jacquard Loom and punch card taken from *The Art of Weaving* by Clinton G. Gilroy, 1845, reproduced by kind permission of the Board of Trinity College, Dublin; The ENIAC computer © The Smithsonian Institution; '39 die in computer cult suicide' by Tim Cornwell, *The Independent*, 28 March 1997 reprinted with permission from Historic Newspapers; photograph of Kenneth Craik reproduced with permission from the Psychology Department, University of Cambridge; photograph of Alan Turing by Elliott & Fry reproduced by courtesy of the National Portrait Gallery, London; The Turing Test from *Mindwaves* edited by Colin Blakemore and Susan Greenfield © Blackwell Publishers; photograph of Hilary Putnam © Hilary Putnam and Ruth Anna Putnam; *Blade Runner* still: BFI Films: Stills, Posters and Designs; photograph of Jerry Fodor reproduced with permission from the Philosophy Department, Rutgers University; Execution of Louis XVI © Bibliothèque Nationale de France; sleep experiments © Lou Manna; schematic diagram of the brain reconsciousness reprinted by permission from *Nature* 375: 121–123 (1995) Macmillan Magazines Ltd.; EEG readings re-dreams from *The Human Mind Explained* by Susan Greenfield (Henry Holt, New York); photograph of Thomas Nagel reproduced with permission from Thomas Nagel; picture of a bat taken from Conrad Gesneri's *History of Animals*, Book III, 1635, reproduced by kind permission of the Board of Trinity College, Dublin; photograph of David Chalmers reproduced with permission from R. R. Jones; 'Teenager sees colour after life in black and white' by Jojo Moyes, *The Independent*, 22 October 1997 reprinted with permission from Historic Newspapers; photograph of Colin McGinn reproduced with permission from Colin McGinn; photograph of assembly workers reproduced courtesy of Ford Motor Company; Samuel Johnson from *Johnsoniana: Or a Collection of Bons Mots*, London, J. Ridley, 1776, from the Early Printed Books collection of Trinity College, Dublin Library; photograph of John Searle reproduced with permission from John Searle; photograph of Richard Rorty reproduced with the kind permission of Richard Rorty; aerial view of Oxford © Chris Donaghue, The Oxford Photo Library; Charles Darwin reproduced courtesy of the Department of Library Services, American Museum of Natural History; photograph of a dog from *The Expression of the Emotions in Man and Animals* (third edition) by Charles Darwin, 1998, HarperCollins; stamp with portrait of Descartes © French Post Office.

Chronology of Modern Philosophy of Mind

Year   Important events in the history of modern philosophy of mind and in cognate subjects

1890   William James's *Principles of Psychology* and C. Lloyd Morgan's *Animal Life and Intelligence* are published. The philosopher-psychologist Christian von Ehrenfels publishes his paper, 'On Gestalt qualities' and so begins Gestalt psychology.

1892   William James publishes his *Psychology: Briefer Course*.

1894   C. Lloyd Morgan publishes *An Introduction to Comparative Psychology*. This book, together with his previous one, introduced the idea of 'trial and error learning' in animals, which in turn was to be an important influence on behaviourism.

1895   Sigmund Freud and Josef Breuer publish the first work on psychoanalysis, *Studies on Hysteria*. Publication of Friedrich Nietzsche's *The Anti-Christ*.

1896   Henri Bergson's *Matter and Memory* is published. Psychiatrist Franz Müller-Lyer publishes his paper, 'Concerning the Theory of Optical Illusions: On Contrast and Confluxion'.
Oswald Külpe establishes his psychological laboratory at the University of Würzburg.

1897   First volume of Havelock Ellis's *Studies in the Psychology of Sex* is published.

1898   Psychologist Edward Lee Thorndike, using mazes and his 'problem box', performs some of the first controlled experiments on animal learning and publishes his results in *Animal Intelligence*.
First edition of G. F. Stout's influential *A Manual of Psychology*.

1899   Aspirin, as a drug to cure headaches, is introduced.

1900 Publication of Freud's *The Interpretation of Dreams*, and Wilhelm Wundt's *Comparative Psychology*.

1901 Freud's *The Psychopathology of Everyday Life* is published.

1903 Professor of Physiology at the Military Medical Academy of St Petersburg Ivan Pavlov, whose work influenced the early psychological behaviourists, is awarded the Nobel Prize for his research on digestion. J. B. Watson publishes his Ph.D. dissertation at the University of Chicago, entitled *Animal Education*. G. E. Moore publishes his influential article, 'The Refutation of Idealism'.

1904 Chicago psychologist cum philosopher James Angell publishes his *Psychology: An Introductory Study of the Structure and Function of Human Consciousness*, an important text of the early, pre-behaviourist, 'psychology as the study of mind as related to behavioural functions' school of psychology.

1905 In answer to a request from the French Ministry of Education, psychologist Alfred Binet, in collaboration with Theodore Simon, devises the first standardised ('intelligence') test to discover 'defective' primary-school children.

1906 The founding father of the science of psychology, the German Professor of Philosophy at the University of Leipzig, Wilhelm Wundt, retitles as *Psychological Studies*, the journal he had originally founded, in 1881, as *Philosophical Studies*.
Pavlov publishes, in Russian, the results of his work on conditioned reflexes. Physiologist Charles (later Sir Charles) Sherrington publishes an account of his work on spinal reflexes, the control of muscles and the relationship between the voluntary and involuntary nervous system, in *The Integrative Action of the Nervous System*.
Two physiologists, the Italian Camillo Golgi, and the Spaniard Ramón y Cajal, are awarded the Nobel Prize for their work on the structure of the nervous system. William James delivers the Lowell Lectures in Boston, which are published the following year under the title *Pragmatism*.

1907 The psychiatrist Pierre Janet delivers a series of lectures at Harvard University, published under the title *The Major Symptoms of Hysteria*.

Publication of Bergson's *Creative Evolution*.

1908 The publication by the British psychologist William McDougall of *An Introduction to Social Psychology*, one of the seminal works in social psychology. The psychiatrist cum neurologist Kurt Goldstein gives one of the earliest, detailed, clinical descriptions of the startling behavioural effects of cerebral hemispheric disconnection caused by damage to the *corpus callosum*.

Posthumous publication of Nietzsche's *Ecce Homo*.

1909 Freud delivers a series of lectures on psychoanalysis at Clark University, Massachusetts, later published as *Five Lectures on Psycho-Analysis*.

E. B. Titchener publishes his *Lectures on the Experimental Psychology of the Thought Processes*.

1910 Wilhelm Wundt publishes the first volume of his massive ten-volumed *Folk Psychology*.

J. B. Watson writes a popular account of his recent work, 'The New Science of Animal Behaviour', for *Harper's* magazine.

1911 The sixth and final edition of Wilhelm Wundt's *magnum opus*, the two-volume, *Principles of Physiological Psychology*, is published.

Publication of psychologist William McDougall's *Body and Mind*.

1912 With the publication of his seminal paper, 'The Experimental Study of the Perception of Motion', Max Wertheimer puts Gestalt psychology on a firm foundation.

1913 Publication of Edmund Husserl's *Ideas – General Introduction to Pure Phenomenology*, and psychologist J. B. Watson's seminal behaviourist paper, 'Psychology as the Behaviorist views it'. The term 'neuropsychology' is first used in an address by Sir William Osler at the opening of the Phipps Clinic at the Johns Hopkins Hospital.

Freud publishes *Totem and Taboo*. James Mark Baldwin publishes his *History of Psychology*, tracing the development of psychology from Aristotle to 'the present time'.

1914   Psychologist E. B. Holt publishes *The Concept of Consciousness*.

1915   Ferdinand de Saussure, the 'father of modern linguistics', publishes *Course in General Linguistics*.

1917   The first pictures of a living brain are taken with x-rays. Psychologist Wolfgang Köhler publishes the results of his celebrated studies of the behaviour of anthropoid apes on the island of Tenerife in *The Mentality of Apes*. Publication of Moritz Schlick's *General Theory of Knowledge*.

1919   Henri Bergson publishes *Spiritual Energy* (though its English translation in the following year is entitled *Mind-Energy*).

1920   Carl Jung's *Psychological Types* is published. J. B. Watson publishes his article 'Is Thinking merely the Action of Language Mechanisms?'

1921   Max Wertheimer, Kurt Koffka and Wolfgang Köhler found the journal, *Psychological Research*, the house journal of the Gestalt school of psychology.
The American linguist and anthropologist Edward Sapir publishes *Language*.
Bertrand Russell publishes one of the important early texts in modern philosophy of mind, *The Analysis of Mind*. Using ideas from psychological behaviourism and from depth psychology, Russell jettisons his previous dualism in favour of a 'neutral monism'.
Ludwig Wittgenstein publishes the *Tractatus Logico-Philosophicus*, the only book of his published in his lifetime.

1922   Psychiatrist Hermann Rorschach first develops 'ink-blot tests' as a diagnostic device for distinguishing personality types and personality disabilities. Psychologist Edward Chace Tolman publishes his article, 'A New Formula for Behaviorism'. In this article he attempted to include cognitive states and purposiveness into a 'non-physiological behaviourism'.

1923   Neuropsychologist Karl Lashley publishes 'The Behavioristic Interpretation of Consciousness'. Psychologist Jean Piaget publishes *The Language and Thought of the Child*, and in effect begins the modern subject of developmental psychology.

1924   First edition of J. B. Watson's *Behaviorism*.

1925 Publication of John Laird's *Our Minds and Their Bodies*, and C. D. Broad's *The Mind and its Place in Nature*.

1927 Publication of Martin Heidegger's *Being and Time*.

1929 Psychiatrist Hans Berger invents the electroencephalogram.
Lashley publishes *Brain Mechanisms and Intelligence*.
E. G. Boring publishes the first edition of his *History of Experimental Psychology*.
Publication of A. N. Whitehead's *Process and Reality* and of C. I. Lewis's *Mind and the World-Order*.

1930 Lashley publishes his article, 'Basic Neural Mechanisms in Behavior'.

1931 Husserl publishes *Cartesian Meditations*, Rudolf Carnap his article, 'Psychology in the Language of Physics', and G. F. Stout *Mind and Matter*. John Anderson reads his paper, 'Mind as Feeling', to a meeting of the Australasian Association for Psychology and Philosophy. John Dewey publishes *Philosophy and Civilization*.
Schlick's seminal article 'The Turning Point in Philosophy' is published in the first volume of *Erkenntnis*, the 'house journal' of the Vienna Circle.

1932 Psychologist Frederick Bartlett publishes *Remembering: A Study in Experimental and Social Psychology*. In the year in which he shared the Nobel Prize for physiology or medicine with Sir Charles Sherrington, Lord Adrian publishes an account of his work on the nervous system in *The Mechanism of Nervous Action: Electrical Studies of the Neurone*.
In Vienna, Kurt Gödel produces his 'incompleteness theorems' about mathematics. Rudolf Carnap publishes his article 'The Elimination of Metaphysics through the Logical Analysis of Language', and Gilbert Ryle reads 'Systematically Misleading Expressions', the manifesto of Linguistic Analysis, to the Aristotelian Society in London.
H. H. Price publishes *Perception*.

1933 Psychologist E. G. Boring publishes *The Physical Dimensions of Consciousness*. Wittgenstein dictates *The Blue Book* to his students.

1934 Wittgenstein dictates *The Brown Book* to two of his pupils – three typed copies are made. John Wisdom publishes *Problems of Mind and Matter*, and G. H.

Mead *Mind, Self and Society: From the Standpoint of a Social Behaviorist*. Karl Popper publishes *The Logic of Scientific Discovery*.

1935   Carl Hempel publishes his paper, 'The Logical Analysis of Psychology'.

1936   Two pharmacologists, the Englishman Sir Henry Dale, and the German Otto Loewi, are awarded the Nobel Prize for their discoveries relating to the chemical transmission of the nerve impulse.
A. J. Ayer publishes *Language, Truth and Logic*.

1937   Psychologist, Lev Vygotsky's *Thought and Language* is published, posthumously, in Russian.

1938   Electroconvulsive therapy (ECT), or the deliberate induction of an epileptic-like convulsion in a patient suffering from mental illness, by means of a jolt of electricity to the brain, is employed for the first time. Psychologist B. F. Skinner publishes *The Behavior of Organisms*, which gives an account of his early work on 'operant conditioning' (or 'behaviour operating on the environment' conditioning). Carl Jung publishes *The Interpretation of Personality*.

1940   R. G. Collingwood publishes *An Essay on Metaphysics*.

1941   C. I. Lewis's paper, 'Some Logical Considerations Concerning the Mental,' appears in *The Journal of Philosophy*.

1943   Psychologist Kenneth Craik publishes *The Nature of Explanation*, in which he postulates that the brain may make use of models which in turn provide humans with their forward-planning capacities. Jean-Paul Sartre publishes *Being and Nothingness*.

1944   Howard Aiken of Harvard University, with the help of the International Business Machines Corporation (IBM), develops the first fully automated calculating machine (called the 'Automatic Sequence Controlled Calculator'). The American physiologists Joseph Erlanger and Herbert Gasser are awarded the Nobel Prize for their work on differentiating the functions of different types of nerve fibres.
Alfred Tarski publishes his paper 'The Semantic Conception of Truth and the Foundation of Semantics'.

1945   Publication of Maurice Merleau-Ponty's *The Phenomenology of Perception*.

1946 The first electronic computer (the 'Electronic Numerical Integrator and Calculator' or ENIAC) is built, by a team led by John Eckert and John Mauchley, in collaboration with John Von Neumann, in the Electrical Engineering School of the University of Pennsylvania in the United States.
Publication of Sartre's *Existentialism and Humanism*.

1948 Mathematician Norbert Wiener invents the term 'cybernetics' when he publishes *Cybernetics, or Control and Communication in the Animal and the Machine*. Alfred Kinsey publishes *Sexual Behaviour in the Human Male*.

1949 The Portuguese neurologist, Antonio Moniz, is awarded a Nobel Prize for his therapeutic use of prefrontal brain leucotomy.
The Australian psychiatrist John Cade uses lithium to treat depression. Neuropsychologist Donald Hebb publishes *The Organization of Behavior: A Neuropsychological Theory*. Gilbert Ryle publishes *The Concept of Mind*.
Simone de Beauvoir publishes the first great modern text of feminism, *The Second Sex*.

1950 Mathematician Alan Turing publishes his article, 'Computing Machinery and Intelligence'. Psychologist James Gibson publishes *The Perception of the Visual World*. Lashley publishes his paper, 'In Search of the Engram'.
W. V. O. Quine attacks the venerable distinction between analytic and synthetic propositions in his paper, 'Two Dogmas of Empiricism'.

1951 Psychologist George Humphrey publishes *Thinking: An Introduction to its Experimental Psychology*, and ethologist, Nikolaas Tinbergen, publishes *The Study of Instinct*. Publication of Jean-Paul Sartre's *The Psychology of Imagination* and of Ryle's essay, 'Feelings'.

1952 Nobel Prize-winning neurophysiologist Roger Sperry publishes his classic paper 'Neurology and the Mind–Brain Problem', arguing that a great deal of human behaviour, including voluntary behaviour, can be explained in terms of the coordination of innate patterns of neural connections.

Alan Turing delivers a BBC radio broadcast on machine intelligence.

1953   Francis Crick, James Watson and Maurice Wilkins discover the structure of DNA (deoxyribonucleic acid), the transmitter of genetic information. Publication of B. F. Skinner's *Science and Human Behavior*. Posthumous publication of Wittgenstein's *Philosophical Investigations*.

1954   Publication of Piaget's *The Construction of Reality in the Child* and Gilbert Ryle's *Dilemmas* (his Tarner Lectures at Cambridge in 1953).

1955   J. L. Austin delivers the William James Lectures at Harvard, which are posthumously published as *How to do Things with Words*.

1956   U. T. Place publishes 'Is Consciousness a Brain Process?', a seminal paper in the development of the mind–brain identity theory.
Gilbert Ryle edits the published version of a series of lectures about analytic philosophy, broadcast on BBC radio, entitled *The Revolution in Philosophy*.

1957   The neurophysiologist Wilder Penfield gives an account of his work in eliciting memories and sensations by the implantation of electrodes into the human brain, in his Sherrington Lecture at the University of Liverpool. The lecture is published later as 'The Excitable Cortex in Conscious Man'.
Linguist cum philosopher Noam Chomsky publishes *Syntactic Structures*, Peter Geach *Mental Acts* and Elizabeth Anscombe *Intention*.
The American psychologist Abraham Maslow publishes *A Philosophy of Psychology*, which is held as the inaugurating event of the movement called humanistic psychology.

1958   Neurophysiologists David Hubel and Torsten Wiesel begin their pioneering work on the visual cortex of the brain.
Posthumous publication of von Neumann's Silliman Lectures at Yale University in 1956, under the title *The Computer and the Brain*. Publication, posthumously, of Wittgenstein's *The Blue Book* and *The Brown Book*. Publication, by economists, Herbert Simon and colleagues, of *Elements of a Theory of Problem Solving*,

and by R. S. Peters of *The Concept of Motivation*. Ryle's lecture, 'A Puzzling Element in the Notion of Thinking', is published.

1959   Marvin Minsky and John McCarthy set up the MIT Artificial Intelligence Project. Norman Malcolm publishes *Dreaming*. Noam Chomsky's review of B. F. Skinner's *Verbal Behavior* appears. Peter Strawson publishes *Individuals*, which puts forward a 'double aspect' theory of mind, and J. J. C. Smart his paper, 'Sensations and Brain Processes'.

1960   Hilary Putnam publishes his seminal functionalist paper 'Minds and machines'.

1961   Psychologist Donald Broadbent publishes *Behaviour*. Michel Foucault publishes his *History of Madness*.

1962   David Armstrong publishes *Bodily Sensations*. William Kneale delivers the Arthur Stanley Eddington Memorial Lecture, entitled 'On having a Mind'. The anthropologist Claude Levi-Strauss publishes *The Savage Mind*.

1963   John Eccles, Alan Hodgkin and Andrew Huxley obtain the Nobel Prize for their work in discovering the electrochemical mechanisms associated with the nerve cell membrane.
The journal *Neuropsychologia* is founded. Publication of Anthony Kenny's *Action, Emotion and Will*, Sydney Shoemaker's *Self-Knowledge and Self-Identity*, and J. J. C. Smart's *Philosophy and Scientific Realism*. Donald Davidson presents his paper, 'Actions, Reasons, and Causes', at a meeting of the American Philosophical Association. Paul Feyerabend produces what is probably the earliest statement of 'eliminative materialism' in his essay 'Materialism and the Mind–Body Problem'.

1964   Roger Sperry publishes a popular account of the theoretical significance of his 'split-brain experiments' in regard to lower vertebrates, in his essay 'The great cerebral commissure'.

1965   The American neurologist Norman Geschwind publishes his classical two-part paper on behavioural neurology, 'Disconnexion Syndromes in Animals and Man'.

1966   The work of the Russian neuropsychologist Alexander Luria, on the psychological effects of brain traumas, becomes widely known and influential with the publication in English of his monumental text *The Higher Cortical Functions in Man*. Warren McCulloch produces *Embodiments of Mind*, a seminal work in 'artificial intelligence'.

Publication of Konrad Lorenz's *On Aggression* and Jacques Lacan's *Writings*.

1967   Neurophysiologist Michael Gazzaniga publishes an overview of the 'split-brain experiments' in regard to epileptic humans, which he conducted together with Sperry, in his essay 'The Split Brain in Man'.

The Harvard psychologist Ulric Neisser publishes his book *Cognitive Psychology* and thereby, in effect, founds the modern subject of cognitive psychology. Putnam publishes his paper, 'The Mental Life of some Machines'.

Publication of Jacques Derrida's *Speech and Writing* and of the magisterial, eight-volume, *Encyclopedia of Philosophy*, edited by Paul Edwards.

1968   Chomsky publishes *Language and Mind*, an extended version of his Beckman Lectures at the University of California at Berkeley in 1967.

Publication of Armstrong's *A Materialist Theory of the Mind*. Davidson delivers his paper 'Mental Events' as part of a lecture series at the University of Massachusetts.

1969   Psychologist D. O. Hebb, publishes his essay 'The Mind's Eye'. Daniel Dennett publishes *Content and Consciousness*.

1970   The Society for Neuroscience is founded. By the end of the 20th century, it had more than 26,000 members.

1971   The work of the Englishman Godfrey Hounsfield and the South African Allan Cormack leads to the construction of the first CAT (computer axial tomography) brain scanner.

Christopher Longuet-Higgins, in his commentary on the Lighthill Report, introduces the term 'cognitive science'. Davidson reads his paper 'Psychology as philosophy' to a Royal Institute of Philosophy Conference, and 'The Material Mind' at a conference in Bucharest. Dennett's paper 'Intentional Systems', is published.

1972   Psychologists David and Ann Premack publish a brief account of their work with chimpanzees in 'Teaching

Language to an Ape'. Armstrong publishes his paper 'Materialism, Properties and Predicates'.

1973   Bernard Williams publishes a collection of essays, *Problems of the Self*. Putnam reads his paper 'Philosophy and our Mental Life', as part of a symposium on 'Computers and the Mind' at the University of California at Berkeley.

1974   Thomas Nagel publishes his essay 'What is it Like to be a Bat?'

1975   Shoemaker's article 'Functionalism and Qualia' is published.
Putnam publishes a volume of collected essays, *Mind, Language and Reality* and Jerry Fodor *The Language of Thought*.

1977   Armstrong's essay 'The Causal Theory of the Mind', is published.

1978   The founding, in America, of a new interdisciplinary journal, *Behavioral and Brain Sciences*, that ranges from 'molecular neurobiology to artificial intelligence and the philosophy of mind'.
Dennett's collection of essays *Brainstorms: Philosophical Essays on Mind and Psychology*, is published.

1979   A collection of papers written by Ryle in the first half of the 1970s is posthumously published as *On Thinking*. Nagel publishes a collection of essays, entitled *Mortal Questions*, and Paul Churchland *Scientific Realism and the Plasticity of Mind*.

1980   Davidson publishes a collection of essays, entitled *Essays on Actions and Events*, and Richard Rorty publishes *Philosophy and the Mirror of Nature*.
John Searle publishes his article 'Minds, Brains and Programs' in *Behavioral and Brain Sciences*.

1981   Paul Churchland publishes 'Eliminative Materialism and the Propositional Attitudes'. Publication of Fodor's *Representations* and, in *Scientific American*, his article 'The Mind–Body Problem'.

1982   The collection *Neuropsychology after Lashley*, edited by J. Orbach, is published. The posthumous publication of psychologist David Marr's book *Vision: A Computational Investigation into the Human Representation and Processing of Visual Information*

and of Gareth Evans's book *The Varieties of Reference*.
Colin McGinn publishes *The Character of Mind* and
Frank Jackson his article, 'Epiphenomenal Qualia'.

1983   Psychologist Philip Johnson-Laird publishes *Mental
Models*, John Searle *Intentionality*, Stephen Stich *From
Folk Psychology to Cognitive Science*, Fodor *The
Modularity of Mind* and McGinn *The Subjective View*.

1984   John Searle delivers the BBC Reith Lectures, which are
published in the following year as *Minds, Brains and
Science*.
Derek Parfit publishes *Reasons and Persons*.

1985   Clinical neurologist Oliver Sacks publishes a series of
essays arising out of his case work at the Albert Einstein
College of Medicine in New York, entitled *The Man
Who Mistook His Wife for a Hat*. Gerald Edelman
delivers his paper 'Neural Darwinism' to the 20th Nobel
Conference at Gustavus Adolphus College, Minnesota.

1986   The 'connectionist bible', *Parallel Distributed Processing*,
edited by J. L. McClelland, D. E. Rumelhart, and the
PDP Research Group, appears.
Nagel publishes *The View From Nowhere* and Patricia
Churchland *Neurophilosophy: Toward a Unified Science
of the Mind/Brain*.
The neurologist Lawrence Weiskrantz publishes
Blindsight.

1987   Dennett publishes *The Intentional Stance* and Fodor
Psychosemantics.

1988   The Human Genome Project, with the aim of mapping
the complete sequence of DNA (all human genes), is
established in Washington.
The new, anti-depressant 'wonder drug' Prozac becomes
available.
Putnam publishes *Representation and Reality*.

1989   Fodor delivers the Donnellan Lectures, entitled 'Problems
of Content in Philosophy of Mind', at Trinity College,
Dublin. McGinn publishes his essay 'Can we solve the
Mind/Body Problem?' and his book *Mental Content*.
Publication of Roger Penrose's *The Emperor's New
Mind*.

1991   Dennett publishes *Consciousness Explained* and McGinn
The Problem of Consciousness.

1992   Publication of Searle's *The Rediscovery of the Mind*,

Owen Flanagan's *Consciousness Reconsidered* and Fodor's *A Theory of Content and Other Essays*. Edelman publishes *Bright Air, Brilliant Fire: On the Matter of the Mind*.

1994   The first interdisciplinary Tucson conference on consciousness is held at the University of Arizona at Tucson, USA. The appearance of the first issue of the interdisciplinary *Journal of Consciousness Studies*, which includes articles by Francis Crick, Roger Penrose, Stuart Hameroff and Benjamin Libet.
Publication of John McDowell's *Mind and World*, Robert Brandom's *Making It Explicit* and of the neuroscientist, Antonio Damasio's, *Descartes' Error: Emotion, Reason and the Human Brain*.

1995   The first issue of *Consciousness Research Abstracts* appears. The Oxford brain scientist, Susan Greenfield, publishes *Journey to the Centers of the Mind*.

1996   Publication of David Chalmers's *The Conscious Mind*.

1997   The Russian grandmaster and world chess champion Gary Kasparov is defeated by the chess-playing computer 'Deep Blue' in a six-game chess challenge in New York.
Publication of Steven Pinker's book in evolutionary psychology, *How the Mind Works*.

1998   Through work done by the neuroscientist Brian Salzberg at the University of Pennsylvania, one episode of the BBC television series on *The Human Body* includes images, magnified 10,000 times, of a nerve impulse associated with a single neuron whose activation, in turn, is associated with 'a passing thought'.

1999   A team of artificial life researchers at the British Telecom, Martlesham Heath Laboratories, Ipswich, England, inaugurate the project 'Soul Catcher 2025' aimed at developing a computer chip which could be implanted behind a person's eye and so record that person's complete lifetime visual sensations.
A team of biomedical engineers, at the Dobelle Institute and the Columbia-Presbyterian Medical Centre in New York, has been able to restore some sight to a blind person by means of a miniaturised video camera, direction finder, and computer programmed to discriminate outlines, connected to that person's visual cortex via an artificial optic tract of electrodes.

CHAPTER ONE

The Twilight of the 'Two Worlds' View

The soul clapped hands

We are all familiar with the image of John Brown's body mould'ring in the grave while his soul goes marching on, and many of us will have read in Charles Dickens's *The Old Curiosity Shop* about poor little Nell's body lying in solemn stillness upon her little bed while her soul, that little bird, first nimbly stirred and then took flight from its earthly cage. Many of us will also have attended a funeral in which the presiding minister, reading from the burial service in *The Book of Common Prayer*, will have declared that 'forasmuch as it hath pleased Almighty God of his great mercy to take unto himself the soul of our dear brother here departed, we therefore commit his body to the grave'. It is part of western culture that we humans are made up of a soul or spirit which inhabits a body and that upon the death of the body the spirit will depart. Perhaps the most beautiful passage illustrating this traditional belief is contained in an anecdote about William Blake, as related by a contemporary to his nineteenth-century biographer, Alexander Gilchrist:

> At the commencement of 1787, the artist's [William Blake's] peaceful happiness was gravely disturbed by the premature death, in his twenty-fifth year, of his beloved brother [Robert]: buried in Bunhill Fields the 11th February. Blake affectionately attended him in his illness, and during the last fortnight of it watched continuously day and night by his bedside, without sleep. When all claim had ceased with that brother's last breath, his own exhaustion showed itself in an unbroken sleep of three days' and nights' duration. The mean room of sickness had been to the spiritual man, as to him most scenes were, a place of vision and of revelation; for Heaven lay about him still, in manhood, as in Infancy it 'lies about us' all. At the last solemn moment, the visionary eyes beheld the released spirit

1

ascend heavenward through the matter-of-fact ceiling, 'clapping its hands for joy' – a truly Blake-like detail. No wonder he could paint such scenes! With him they were work'y-day experiences.[1]

While they would not have claimed to have seen departing souls clapping their hands with joy at being at last freed from the confines of their earthly bodies, in the last decades of the nineteenth century and the first decades of the twentieth century, most philosophers and psychologists would have held a view that was not very different from Blake's. They would have held an academically sanitised and suitably secularised version of this dualism of soul and body, though, by then, they would have referred to the dualism as that between mind and body. Many, perhaps most people, who are untainted by any acquaintance with contemporary philosophy or psychology, would still see things in this same dualistic way today.

The story told in the first half of this chapter is the story of how the *fin-de-siècle*, academic, secular versions of this dualism of mind and body had been given their basic shape by the work of Descartes. In the second half of the chapter, the story told is of how the Cartesian[2] orthodoxy was called into question in a fundamental way in both philosophy and psychology in the early

Figure 1.1 A dualistic vision: William Blake's *The Soul Hovering over the Body Reluctantly Parting with Life*.

Figure 1.2
The father of modern dualism about mind and body, the French philosopher and scientist, René Descartes.

decades of the twentieth century. The bulk of the book, however, is the story of what, after much turbulent debate over the last sixty years, has been put in place of this Cartesian and common-sense orthodoxy. Now, however, it is time to begin the story by referring briefly to Descartes and to how he came to set the agenda for the modern debate about mind and body.

René Descartes (1596–1650) was an extraordinarily gifted seventeenth-century French mathematician, physiologist, physicist and philosopher. His initial interests were in mathematics. While still in his twenties he invented analytical geometry, whereby positions in space can be plotted by reference to three artificially-fixed lines or axes laid out at right angles to each other in three dimensions, and meeting at a point, the *origin point*. The link lines or 'coordinates' running from the position to be plotted to these axes are still known as *Cartesian coordinates*. A little later on, in his physiological phase, given the resources of his time, he hypothesised remarkably accurately about the physiological mechanisms involved in various organs and systems of the human body. In particular he made contributions to the physiology of the human eye and the human digestive system and to the study of limb reflexes in man and animal. He wrote an important work on meteorology (the study of weather) and, on account of that work, he is often credited with putting forward the first correct explanation of the nature of rainbows. In propounding his revolutionary ideas about scientific knowledge and scientific method, wittingly or unwittingly he laid the foundations for investigations in empirical psychology for the next three hundred years. Yet, with something approaching extreme perversity, Descartes is now best remembered through the fact that most twentieth-century accounts of mind define themselves in opposition to what they take to be Descartes's account. In the history of ideas, Descartes is like the great soccer player who is only remembered nowadays as the player who missed a penalty shot in the 1998 World Cup.

To understand Descartes's account of mind, it is necessary to understand something of his approach to scientific method, because, in effect, his account of the former arose as a by-product of his account of the latter. In regard to the latter, his account of scientific method, his aim was to provide a doubt-proof foundation and a secure method for that paradigm of the objective approach to knowledge that we now call science. In this context the phrase 'objective approach' calls upon two senses of the term 'objective'. First, it refers to the gaining of information about the world via careful *disinterested observation* which can be replicated by other disinterested observers and which, at least in more modern eras, can be bolstered by experiments under laboratory conditions. In short, it refers to the scientific approach. Second, it refers to the fact that the object of such careful observation is '*a world out there*' and so objective in relation to any subject observing it. Descartes believed that he could provide this doubt-proof foundation for science by setting himself the project of making sure that the very process of observation itself, which was at the core of his account of an objective scientific method, was immune to sceptical doubt about its data. Otherwise, how could we be sure that our senses are not deceiving us? If we can be gulled by optical illusions with comparative ease, such that we see a stick in water as bent or a heat haze in the desert as a lake, perhaps we should not rely on our senses for the authority of our *scientia* or 'strict knowledge' of the world or anything else.

Somewhat unexpectedly, Descartes did not set out upon this project by seeking a way of ensuring that the knowledge we gain of the world from our senses was immune to illusion. Rather, more boldly, he immediately proposed a firm foundation for all our knowledge, whether of the world or of anything else. He suggested that this firm foundation, indeed a rock solid one, could and should be erected upon the indubitable knowledge we had about the objects and events of our interior world, the world of each person's own consciousness. In a sense he was saying that, previously, philosophy had got things back to front. Every other form of knowledge, including of the very existence of an external world, was at best a reliable inference, at least ultimately, from the indubitable knowledge of the contents of consciousness gained by this subjective route of self-consciousness.

Descartes believed that he could demonstrate that this was the correct approach to finding a foundation of exact and certain knowledge by engaging in a strategic ploy which later commentators called his 'method of universal or radical doubt'. The ploy began with the attempt to see whether one could doubt everything, absolutely everything. If one found that in fact there was something one could not doubt, then this could become the firm foundation for the whole structure of human knowledge. As we shall see, however, Descartes encountered great difficulties in moving from his claim of having discovered an indubitable foundation to his reconstruction of even the ground floor of the skyscraper of human knowledge.

Descartes's discovery of that 'something' which could not be doubted by anyone, and which was to be his firm foundation for all knowledge, is most clearly and dramatically announced in his *Discours de la Méthode* (*Discourse on the Method of Rightly Conducting Reason and Reaching the Truth in the Sciences*) of 1637. Originally the *Discourse* was the introduction to a collection of essays on mathematical and scientific topics (the *Optics*, about the refraction of light through lenses, *Meteorology* and *Geometry*), which were to display the new mathematically based methods of scientific enquiry. In section IV of the *Discourse*, Descartes wrote:

> But immediately upon this [adoption of the strategic ploy of doubting everything] I noticed that while I was trying to think everything false [to doubt the truth of everything], it must needs be that I, who was thinking this (*qui le pensais*), was something. And observing that this truth 'I am thinking (*je pense*), therefore I exist' was so solid and secure that the most extravagant suppositions of the sceptics could not overthrow it, I judged that I need not scruple to accept it as the first principle of philosophy [that is, the 'indubitable foundation'] that I was seeking.[3]

In his reply to the *Second Objections* (objections made by various writers to another of his works, the *Meditations*),[4] the argument, 'I am thinking, therefore I exist', was written in Latin as *Cogito ergo sum* and that version has subsequently assumed fame. Many philosophers have smeared much ink on a great deal of paper wondering whether the *Cogito* argument is valid or whether, for example, Descartes should have written 'Some thinking (the doubting) is going on at this moment, therefore there exists, at least at this moment, a thought' or 'If the thinking is that *I* am thinking, then there is, at least at this very moment, a subject that thinks it thinks.' The *Cogito* is also a staple of the stock pot for that thin gruel called 'Lecturer's Witticisms'. One spoonful should suffice to satisfy curiosity: 'You can't, of course, substitute "I am, therefore I think", for the *Cogito*, for that would be to put Descartes before the horse.' Be that as it may, Descartes himself believed that, with the *Cogito*, he had discovered the indubitable foundation for all knowledge and proceeded to build upon it.

Descartes pointed out that the indubitable facts of self-consciousness, such as that I am now thinking, for example, are clear and distinct and immediate presentations of consciousness. You do not have to observe them or argue for them; they just confront you in your own stream of consciousness. You cannot escape knowing about them. This, suggested Descartes, was a clue to the essence of consciousness, which in turn was the essence of mind. For Descartes, our mental life was one and the same thing as our interior subjective waking (or else dreaming) conscious life.

Somewhat curiously, at least from the perspective of our time,

Descartes was less certain about the existence of the physical world. In our age, most people, if they think at all about such things, are dedicated above all to affirming the undeniable existence of the physical world which we observe with our senses, and about which the natural sciences provide us with such astonishing details. Given his initial strategy, Descartes now felt the need to invoke a connection or to build a bridge between our immediate and indubitable knowledge of objects and events in our stream of consciousness (his foundation for all knowledge) and our knowledge of the physical world as mediated by our senses. The connection or bridge that Decartes proposed, namely God, was something that would have little appeal to many in our more agnostic age. If, Descartes argued, we had clear and distinct ideas in our consciousness, and so a very strong conviction, to the effect that we are now perceiving our own bodies or perceiving some object or event in the physical world, then God must have allowed these ideas so to present themselves in such a vigorous way to our consciousness. If this exceedingly strong and most pervasive of convictions was illusory, then the very allowance of such a deceitful state of affairs at the heart of our mental life implied that God himself must be deceitful. This would imply that God was not perfect, which, in turn, would imply that there was, strictly, no God at all.

Descartes, of course, needed and duly produced a separate argument for the existence of God. However his argument for God's existence does not seem to be any stronger than the foregoing invocation of God as a philosophical *deus ex machina* who ultimately puts the firmness into knowledge's firm foundation. His best-known argument is considered to be unconvincing because it seems to depend upon introducing into our consciousness a 'clear and distinct idea', and so in consequence a conviction, that God must be a perfect being, and so must exist (for existence is a perfection), before there has been and can be an opportunity to introduce God as a guarantor that any such 'clear and distinct ideas', and subsequent convictions, are not illusory. God as guarantor can only come after God has been shown to exist but, embarrassingly, here God seems to be needed to show that He Himself exists. This point was made in Descartes's own time by his contemporary Antoine Arnauld as part of his set of objections to the *Meditations*.

Descartes himself believed, however, that the upshot of this intricate series of arguments was the firm conclusion that we can be assured that we do have knowledge of the existence of an external material world and of our own bodies, and that the essence (or essential characteristics) of matter is to be extended and to be at rest or in motion.

I have spent some time explaining Descartes's quite complex progress in arriving at what he believed was a firm and indubitable foundation for our scientific observations because it is also the source of what later critics of the Cartesian system have dubbed the 'two worlds' view in regard to humans. Descartes's sharp division, between our immediately certain knowledge of the facts of self-consciousness and our more shaky and roundabout knowledge of the physical world, mirrors his sharp distinction between the natures of our mind and of our body. Descartes's account of human nature is called the 'two worlds' view because it described humans as composed of two sharply distinct substances, mind (or soul) and body, which in turn forces them to live or have existence in two distinct worlds. The essence of what we refer to as 'our body', like all material substances and physical things, is to be extended, which in turn means that our bodies are three dimensional (have some height, breadth and length), are divisible (for example, by a surgeon's knife), and have a location in space (that is, they are over here by the window or out there in the street, or somewhere). The essence of what we refer to as 'our mind' (or, in Descartes's day, as 'our soul') is to be a thinking thing, that is, to be conscious (to be conscious of objects and events in the world, or of imaginary objects and events, and to be self-conscious).

Because, according to Descartes, humans were composed of two such different and divergent substances or 'stuffs', consciousness and matter, they were forced to inhabit two parallel worlds and so to live two parallel lives. They lived their conscious life, for example, when they were thinking about the film they saw last night or were wondering whether to get up out of bed now that the alarm has rung. They lived their bodily life, for example, when they ran for the bus or drank a cup of coffee. Sometimes the two lives interconnected, such as occurred when they became conscious of a damaged toe or consciously decided to move the cup into their left hand. Sometimes the two were sharply disconnected, such as when they were asleep or when they were put under an anaesthetic or when they suffered that final disconnection, death. However, in general, it had to be said that a single human being lived two harmonious and parallel, though by and large mutually uncomprehending, lives. They delivered speeches unaware of the exertions of their heart or lungs that enabled them to do so, or they pondered upon Pythagoras's Theorem in total ignorance of what their brain was up to. In the twentieth century, the Oxford philosopher Gilbert Ryle depicted this Cartesian 'two worlds' view with characteristic pungency in his famous 'hatchet job' on Cartesian dualism, *The Concept of Mind*:

> The official doctrine, which hails chiefly from Descartes, is something like this. With the doubtful exceptions of idiots and infants in arms every human being has both a body and a mind. Some would prefer to say that every human being is both a body and a mind. His body and his mind are ordinarily harnessed together, but after the death of the body his mind may continue to exist and function.
>
> Human bodies are in space and are subject to the mechanical laws which govern all other bodies in space. Bodily processes and states can be inspected by external observers. So a man's bodily life is as much a public affair as are the lives of animals and reptiles and even as the careers of trees, crystals and planets.
>
> But minds are not in space, nor are their operations subject to mechanical laws. The workings of one mind are not witnessable by other observers; its career is private. Only I can take direct cognisance of the states and processes of my own mind. A person therefore lives through two collateral histories, one consisting of what happens in and to his body, the other consisting of what happens in and to his mind. The first is public, the second private. The events in the first history are events in the physical world, those in the second are events in the mental world.[5]

This view, that humans are bodies inhabited and governed in some intimate if mysterious way by minds (or souls), seemed and still seems to be nothing more than good common sense. That is just the way we are. We can see and touch and taste and smell bodies, but we cannot see or touch or taste or smell minds. Seen in a purely negative way, minds seem to be the negation of everything that characterises bodies. Minds have no dimensions, no sensory qualities (qualities associated with the senses of taste, touch and so on), no mass or solidity and only the vaguest of locations, namely in someone's body and, especially, in and around a person's brain. When the neurosurgeon operates, he operates on the brain not on the mind. When the mad axeman attacks the lonely hiker, he dismembers the body not the mind. On the other hand, even if our body be rendered more or less totally inactive, say by some paralysing damage to the central nervous system, the mind might remain healthy and active, thinking, imagining, regretting, hoping, planning, dreaming and day-dreaming. When the psychoanalyst treats his or her patients, eschewing the psychiatrist's application of surgery or chemicals to the body, he or she seeks a cure by contacting the mind directly. In short, we do seem to live two parallel lives such that it comes naturally to speak of ourselves and others as having both mental powers and physical skills, as having *a* mind and *a* body. We come readily to recognise that some people are more successful in their mental life than in their physical one. These are the computer 'whizz kids' or chess champions or mathematical prodigies. Others are more successful in their physical life. These are the champion sprinters or tennis stars or the ones who hold records for weight-lifting.

Common sense also endorses the view that nevertheless there must be an intimate confluence between these two kinds of life lived in these two parallel worlds. A blow to the head may affect our consciousness by rendering us unconscious and then, later, leaving us with the legacy of a fearsome headache. Ingrown toenails may make us change our minds about wearing fashionable narrowly pointed Italian shoes. Contrariwise morbid anxiety over the coming final-year examinations may cause us to break out in spots, grow thin and haggard, and suffer insomnia and halitosis. Or thinking about a good CD of the Brandenburg Concertos may direct our steps to the nearest music store.

Cartesian 'substance dualism', and its allied 'two worlds' account, also makes good religious sense. Christianity, the dominant religion of western culture, in all its major branches, and Islam, the dominant religion of eastern culture, both have as a central doctrine that our souls are immortal and that, in consequence, there is a life after death. Christian theologians, for example, have developed a complex eschatology or 'theology of the last things', namely of death, judgement, hell and heaven. One of the strongest Christian motives for living a morally good life is the threat of being found guilty on the Day of Judgement of not having lived a good life and, in consequence, of being condemned to that purest of retributive punishments, the ever-lasting pains of hell. Some Christians say that the possibility of life after death, and of being punished eternally for wrongdoing in that afterlife, is ultimately the only motive strong enough to make us even attempt to live a morally good life. In 1911, in his book *Body and Mind*, William McDougall, a committed psychological Cartesian and Christian, wrote that,

> Apart from any hope of rewards or fear of punishment after death, the belief [in a soul and so in a life after death] must have, it seems to me, a moralizing influence upon our thought and conduct that we can ill afford to dispense with . . . [and] I gravely doubt whether whole nations could rise to the level of an austere morality, or even maintain a decent working standard of conduct, after losing those beliefs.[6]

Without such a belief in a soul and a life after death, the McDougalls of this world are inclined to conclude that the more confident among us would be tempted to adopt the view, as had Thrasymachus in Plato's dialogue *The Republic* and Nietzsche's Superman in *Thus Spake Zarathustra* or *The Anti-Christ*,[7] that morality is dispensable, as it is just the protection that the weak seek against the strong, and the product of jealousy and sour grapes on the part of the world's failures. They would be tempted to conclude that the strong, those with superior skills of mind and body, would be able to stand outside moral systems and reap the rewards of those who dare. Who dares, wins.

However Cartesian dualism and its 'two worlds' account are not merely compatible with a belief in life after death. It is probably true to say that only the Cartesian view of mind and body makes life after death a plausible doctrine to hold. Unless the mind is of such a nature that it is separable from the body in death, it cannot even be a candidate for life after the death of the body. But the mind must be more than merely separable, it must be immortal, otherwise it would be just another more enduring form of matter. Bodies are mortal because they are bodies. Being material and so extended in space, they are divisible into parts and so can distintegrate into those parts. Descartes himself thought of the body as little more than a sophisticated machine, a physiological automaton, which was made human by the presence of the soul with its powers of thought and possession of free will. Death was the distintegration of the body, which in turn caused the soul to abandon ship because it was no longer able to sail the stricken vessel.

By contrast, the soul is immortal because it is not at all like a body. It is simple in the sense that it is non-extended and non-dimensional and so indivisible. Being indivisible it cannot disintegrate into parts. Being immune to disintegration, it is immune to death. Strictly speaking, with the hindsight of modern physics, Descartes would have had to add that, being immaterial, the soul also cannot be destroyed by its matter being transformed into energy. Descartes, being in love with science, would readily have embraced this modern gloss.

In the 'life after death' stakes, the only serious rival to Descartes's immortal, free-floating soul, whether it be reunited with a body or not, is the possibility of life after death via merely the resurrection of the dead person's body at some time after the death of that person. How this could come about, however, seems to defy convincing explanation. The best attempts at explanation involve God putting the body-pieces back together again, as well as, presumably, his mending the 'breakdown' that originally caused death and the subsequent disintegration in the grave and, also, finally, his reanimating or revivifying the body. This would certainly make the concept of a soul redundant. However, since this explanation needs to draw deeply upon direct, divine intervention, it amounts to an 'explanation' with a much higher quotient of the supernatural, and so of the mysterious, than does the Cartesian one.

Figure 1.3 A somewhat anachronistic and ironic twentieth-century view of life after death: Stanley Spencer's *The Resurrection, Cookham*

The Cartesian legacy

Between the seventeenth and twentieth centuries there were other views about the nature of mind and body besides that of Cartesian substance dualism. For example, the Englishman Thomas Hobbes (1588–1679), a contemporary of Descartes, was an out and out materialist who held that there was only one substance, material substance. Another contemporary, the Dutchman Baruch de Spinoza (1632–77), held the curious view that, while mind and body were distinct, they were not distinct substances but merely distinct attributes or modes of just one and only one substance which was infinite and divine. In the eighteenth century the Irish philosopher George Berkeley (1685–1753) simply denied that there was any material substance at all. In the nineteenth century the English philosopher John Stuart Mill (1806–73), while not claiming the complete non-existence of matter, seemed to view mind (consciousness) as much more real than bodies or any other form of matter. For Mill, external objects, such as this desk at which I am working, are nothing more than the formation in my mind of a continuing expectation or conviction that, when I next come into my office, I will again have a sensory (conscious) experience, for example a visual one, that there is a desk over there by the window. Almost every imaginable position about the nature of mind and body was explored by some philosopher somewhere between the time of Descartes and our own time. Yet, throughout those years from Descartes to the twentieth century, despite the exploration of different views and challenges to Cartesianism from almost all directions, certain aspects of the Cartesian account of mind and of the Cartesian account of how one should study the mind remained when the rivals had retreated from the arena. Why should this be so?

One can only speculate. The most plausible reason would seem to be that, to most people, whether they be academics or not, the most obvious feature of minds, and the most obvious way of studying them, is that to which Descartes drew our attention with such clarity and style. The most obvious feature of minds is the focus of our attention whenever, in our waking moments, we turn away from the world and engage in contemplation, namely that inner, private world we call 'consciousness'. The obvious starting point, therefore, for anyone's serious enquiry into the nature of mind, would seem to be a subject's first-person, direct, knowledge-by-acquaintance with his or her very own stream of consciousness. The most obvious product of such an enquiry would seem to be that the essence of mind is consciousness.

When, in the second half of the nineteenth century, psychology finally broke away from philosophy, philosophy's allegiance to the Cartesian approach to mind was more stable than it had been in the previous century and arguably it was more explicit and undiluted than was the allegiance in the new science of psychology. One reason for this may be that philosophers have always been more interested in producing explicit theories of mind, grand or otherwise, than have psychologists. Such speculations are their business. As we shall see, however, there is no doubt at all that, by the last decades of the nineteenth century and during the first decades of the twentieth century, the new scientific psychologist's view of the correct way of finding out about minds, and implicitly of the nature of minds, was deeply Cartesian.

The position in philosophy, during that same period, can be illustrated by quoting from John Laird's book, *Our Minds and Their Bodies*, written in 1925. At that time John Laird (1887–1946) was the Regius Professor of Moral Philosophy in the University of Aberdeen, and his little book was part of 'The World's Manuals' series published by Oxford University Press. Each book in this series was intended to give students 'some idea of the landmarks which will guide him' in the subject area being presented, as well as being an 'authoritative and scholarly work' to inform the general reader. In the last section of the last chapter of that book, Laird wrote that

> The conclusion of our previous chapters has been that mind and body, regarded as going concerns, are characteristically different from one another, however closely they may be allied; and that, in all probability, these partners are capable of mutual influence or interaction. This implies a dualism of some sort between a thinking mind and its living body...
>
> In our view, the order of mental regulation is truly *sui generis* [unique], because, in a wide sense of the term, it is either spiritual or capable of becoming so...
>
> The most probable theory would appear to be that spirits in their partnership with living bodies exhibit the mutual influence of two orders which are themselves members within a wider metaphysical pluralism.[8]

With the exception of the last clause of the last paragraph, referring to 'metaphysical pluralism', by which phrase Laird seemed to imply that he held for more than two 'orders' (which term he used elsewhere as a synonym for 'substances') in nature, Descartes himself would have been quite happy with all of the above.

Leaving aside a slight dilution of its Cartesianism, the situation in turn-of-the-century psychology was not that much different. The founding fathers of the new experimental psychology, which broke away from philosophy of mind around 1870, were all Cartesian in orientation. Sometimes they professed to be rejecting Cartesian 'substance dualism' while retaining the Cartesian 'two worlds' account of human nature. But this usually turned out to mean that they had misunderstood Descartes's account of mind by fathering upon him a view of mental substance as some shadowy substrate underlying a human's conscious life rather than as being that conscious life itself. Thus Wilhelm Wundt, Professor of Philosophy at Leipzig University, and sometimes accorded the title of *the* Father of the Science of Psychology, concluded the 1896 edition of his *Lectures on Human and Animal Psychology*,[9] as follows:

> What now is the nature of mind? The real answer to this question is contained in all that has been said before. Our mind is nothing else than the sum of our inner experiences, than our ideation [thinking], feeling, and willing collected together to a unity in consciousness, and rising in a series of developmental stages to culminate in self-conscious thought and a will that is morally free . . .
>
> If you answer, as is sometimes done, that it is these very operations of mind that go to make up its nature, and that therefore mind cannot be thought or conceived without them, why, then the position is granted: the real nature of mind consists in nothing else than our mental [conscious] life itself.[10]

Between the two paragraphs above Wundt inveighed against conceiving of mind as a 'mental substrate' existing independently of and behind our stream of consciousness itself, and against such 'metaphysical' (unjustifiably speculative) ways of thinking in general.[11] But there seems little doubt that, in a somewhat furtive and reluctant manner, he was putting foward an account of mind which is remarkably close to that put forward by Descartes himself.

Figure 1.4 Wilhelm Wundt, the founder of modern experimental psychology.

Later psychologists, producing their popular student textbooks in the first, second and even third decades of the twentieth century, generally concurred with Wundt's version of Cartesianism, by openly endorsing a 'two worlds' account while furtively giving allegiance to some form of 'substance dualism'. William McDougall (1871–1938) was a Fellow of the Royal Society and later, as successor to William James, Professor of Psychology at Harvard. In his book *Body and Mind* (1911), while he shies away from the word 'substance' itself, McDougall gives a 'substance account' of the soul (the latter being a word he does not shy away from). In the final concluding chapter, he writes that

> [W]e may describe a soul as a sum of enduring capacities for thoughts, feelings, and efforts of determinate kinds. Since the word substance retains the flavour of so many controversial doctrines, we shall do well to avoid it as the name for any such sum of enduring capacities, and to use instead the word thing or being.[12]

However, one important alteration to the doctrines of Descartes himself can be discerned in these later Cartesian texts, whether

Figure 1.5 William McDougall, an important Anglo-American psychologist who had deep convictions about life after death.

philosophical or psychological, namely that the differences between the two worlds, the mental and the physical, and their incompatibility, came to be emphasised. Thus, in 1924, in the tenth impression of the third edition of his immensely popular and authoritative *Manual of Psychology*, the philosopher-psychologist G. F. Stout (1860–1944), a Fellow of the British Academy and Professor of Logic and Metaphysics at the University of St Andrews, wrote that

> It thus appears that even if the being which is a mind is also supposed to be a body, yet the mental aspect of its nature is so distinct from its bodily aspect that each requires separate and independent investigation. Knowledge concerning the mind does not of itself include or conduct to knowledge concerning the body as such. Knowledge concerning the body does not of itself involve or conduct to knowledge concerning the mind as such. Hence Physiology and Psychology are radically distinct sciences, each dealing with its own subject matter.[13]

This stark separation of the 'two worlds' of mind and body was to have important ramifications for both the ethos and the practice of the new science of psychology itself. In the first place, as Stout emphasised, it gave real autonomy to psychology. It enabled psychologists to claim that they had a science of their own and one which could not be taken over gradually by physiologists or, in particular, by the brain scientists. More importantly, it also provided psychologists with their very own experimental methods which were unique to their new experimental science. Ironically, as we shall see in due course, it was this emphasis on the autonomy of psychology and the uniqueness of its methods that led not merely to the downfall of Cartesianism in psychology but more or less to the complete neglect, for a very long time, of consciousness as even a serious topic in psychology.

That a Cartesian view of mind should present psychologists with an *autonomous science*, is easier enough to see. Geology is the scientific study of the earth's crust. Chemistry is the scientific study of chemical substances. Zoology is the scientific study of animals. As we can see from the above examples, the usual way to distinguish one science from another is in terms of its subject matter. If mind is something completely distinct from body, and from material things in general, and so from everything else in the universe, then psychology is clearly a distinct science. Its subject matter is something unique to itself, namely mind. So Cartesian psychology came to be defined as 'the science of mind'.

That a Cartesian view of mind should present psychologists with a *unique method* of scientific investigation needs more careful explanation. The practitioners of the new science of psychology accepted, as part of the traditional Cartesian package, that a human's mental life was more or less coextensive with a human's *conscious* life,[14] that is, with their 'stream of consciousness' (or interior conscious life which seems to 'flow by' like a stream).[15] In addition, they accepted that the methods employed by any respectable science had to be *empirical* (a word derived from the Greek word for 'experiencing by means of the senses'),[16] and so based, at least ultimately, upon sensory observation. Finally they accepted that the methods employed by any modern science had to be *experimental*. In short, what was needed was an experimentally supported, empirical means of access to a subject's own stream of consciousness.

At this point they drew less upon Descartes's own view than upon subsequent debates, which they revived and added to, about the nature of our empirical access to our own conscious states. These debates produced the crucial distinction between our passive *capacity for self-consciousness* and our more active, and from the point of view of the new science of psychology, more important *ability to introspect*.[17] Self-consciousness was explained as an unavoidable noticing, from time to time, of what was going on in our own streams of consciousness. From time to time something in our low-key conscious life forced itself upon our notice, upon our full consciousness, rather than our having deliberately set out consciously to scrutinise it. A person, for example, might catch herself day-dreaming. Day-dreaming is a conscious episode, but it is a sort of low-key one. However, in '*catching* oneself day-dreaming', one finds that the process of day-dreaming has suddenly been pulled into the full glare of consciousness. Or, to take another example, a man might catch himself staring at a woman's legs in a bus and, in becoming fully conscious of what he is doing, become acutely embarrassed. By analogy with sight, self-consciousness was like someone initially seeing something out of the corner of his eye rather than attentively looking at it, but then involuntarily coming to notice more fully what he has first seen in a peripheral inattentive way.

By contrast, introspection was like deliberately and attentively setting out to observe something, excepting one was doing it with one's 'inner mental eye' (to employ the much-used but arguably misleading metaphor). The term 'introspection' became a technical term of early experimental psychology and was explained by analogy with the ordinary deliberate, attentive and careful scrutiny, with our ordinary eyes, of objects and events in the natural world. Introspection was 'inner observation' by means of an inner, non-sensory capacity for observation. Introspection was scrutinising one part of consciousness, say an episode of thinking about the tennis match last night between Martina Hingis and Venus Williams, by means of another part of consciousness. It was using one portion of consciousness to observe another portion. So it amounted to becoming conscious in a *second-level* monitoring way of what was going on at the *ground-floor level* of our conscious life. Because this way of gaining knowledge of objects and events in our stream of consciousness was active and deliberate and controllable, it was the one that was deemed useful, indeed essential, as *the* method for obtaining useful data about the mind in the new science of psychology.

These more theoretical considerations about the nature of our introspective access to our stream of consciousness had quite elaborate, indeed baroque, implications for the experimental methods employed in the new laboratories set up by the first practitioners of the new science of psychology. Put in a very general way, the method for investigating our inner mental processes of thinking, imagining, willing and so on was to train self-experimenters or 'subjects' in the art of introspecting and then of reporting on what discoveries they made by this method.[18] The training consisted of getting them, by dint of much practice, first to concentrate with complete attention on what was going on in their own streams of consciousness, then to disregard any distractions or preconceptions or prejudices, and finally to report in a clear and concise and relevant way on what they were inwardly observing. Sometimes the experiment might also involve a second person who observed the behaviour of the introspector, and noted such things as the involuntary movements of her limbs and any variations in her heart beat or rate of breathing.[19]

Most often the introspection laboratories would be bristling with experimental apparatus, just like a respectable physics or chemistry laboratory. For example, the experiment might involve a subject looking at something and, once the 'target' or object of visual perception was removed, then concentrating on the 'after-image' (that is, on the conscious visual experience that remains in your stream of consciousness for some seconds after the 'target' has been removed), and finally reporting on aspects of that 'afterimage'.[20] Such an experiment might make use of a tachisto-scope or shutter-like system, as might be found in a camera, for presenting the 'target' visual stimulus for only a very brief and accurately timed period. Other experimental apparatus, that were used in various experiments, were the prism, plethysmograph, chronometer, chronograph, pendulum, metronome, lever and tambour.

Figure 1.6a An early instrument of psychological research, a plethysmo-graph was an instrument for recording changes in the volume of some part of the body, such as, here, an arm, usually due to variations in blood supply.

The only unfamiliar pieces of equipment here are likely to be the plethysmograph, the chronograph and the tambour. A plethysmograph is an instrument for recording changes in the volume of some part of the body, usually due to a swelling or shrinking caused by a variation in blood supply. A chronograph is just a very accurate clock (or chronometer), capable of measuring and then recording 'split seconds'. A tambour is a drum covered with a membrane sensitive even to the slightest vibration or movement. The tambour was usually used in conjunction with a lever so that any movement arising in the membrane was magnified by the lever attached to it. In turn, the lever might be mechanically hooked up to a pen which then inscribed variations in the movements of the membrane on to moving graph paper.

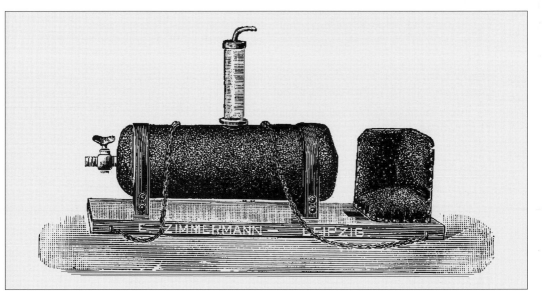

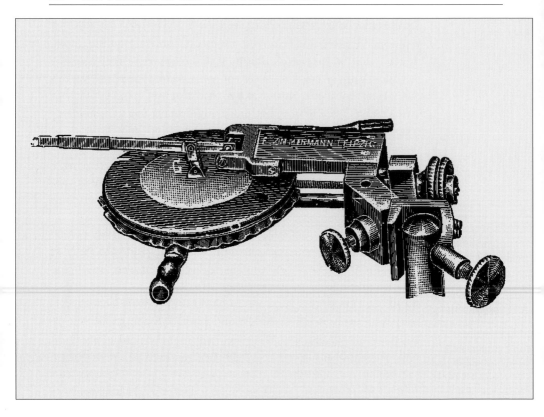

The training of a subject for introspection experiments also included very lengthy and involved guidelines as to how to introspect in a scientific way and how the introspection reports were to be made. It took a while for a 'subject' to master the relevant details and to apply them correctly. This was one reason why these experiments needed to be done over and over again. One extract from an article discussing these guidelines might suffice to illustrate these points. I have included only the core segments of the instructions from an account which went on for several pages. I have added, in square brackets, some of my own comments, to make clear what the instructions really mean:

Figure 6.1b Another early instrument, a tambour and lever was an instrument with a sensitive membrane, for recording and, via a lever, magnifying changes in, for example, heart beat. The lever was usually attached to a pen and moving graph paper.

> Our first rule, therefore, is: *As far as possible, describe the constituent features of the experience in terms that resist further analysis. Describe in terms of part-processes which cannot be thought of as being themselves made up of smaller or simpler part-processes, or of part-processes found in other contexts.* [In short, make sure that you have penetrated to the basic elements or atoms of consciousness.] . . .

A second rule: *In addition to analytic description, experiences which are rapidly changing should be characterized or communicated by descriptive appellations, laying stress upon the sequences and order of the part-processes.* [It is also important to map the sequence or correct order in which these atoms occur.] . . .

Rule 3: . . . *Include interpretation sparingly and always label it carefully as such* . . . [Where 'interpretation' meant anything that went beyond pure description.]

Rule 4: *Avoid the 'stimulus error', make no attempt to estimate the stimulus; confine your report to your consciousness, to your experiences. Nothing else is introspection; it is merely physical observation under difficulties.* [Concentrate on internal conscious states and avoid all reference to what external event or internal physiological occurrence you think may have caused the conscious state.]

Rule 5: *Ordinarily describe experiences in their temporal order. But sacrifice this if necessary to catch some fleeting and elusive experience* . . .

Rule 6: *The experience or part of an experience selected for observation should not be too long, only a few seconds at the most.* [Otherwise one will forget the details of the experience and so be unable to report on it.] . . .

Rule 7: Avoid *'putative recollection'.* [Confine oneself strictly to what in fact you introspected and avoid any inference to what you think you must or should have introspected.][21]

It is interesting to note that, in the above list, there are no rules setting down how soon after the occurrence of the internal conscious experience the report on it by the subject should be made. Nor any rules about how long the report should take. In practice it was not unknown for a report to go on for as long as twenty minutes, even though the target stimulus, such as a two-dimensional coloured object projected upon a screen, may have been visible only for a second or so.

Finally, these introspection experiments, with their experimental apparatus and labyrinthine rules of engagement, were to be repeated many times. This ensured both that the 'subject' gained the necessary experience and that the experiments were properly scientific. One of the marks of scientific experiments and scientific observations is that they be replicable time after time, for the final report should be a sort of 'averaging' of a long series of individual reports. This last requirement prompted William James (1842–1910), himself one of the founding fathers of modern American psychology, to write, with his characteristic wit and style, that,

> Within a few years what one may call a microscopic psychology has arisen in Germany, carried on by experimental methods, asking of course every moment for introspective data, but eliminating their uncertainty by operating on a large scale and taking statistical means. This method taxes patience to the utmost, and could hardly have arisen in a country whose natives could be *bored* . . . There is little of the grand style about these new prism, pendulum and chronograph-philosophers. They mean business not chivalry.[22]

It will come as no surprise that while William James saw to the setting up of the first psychological laboratory at Harvard University, he himself did not find experimenting very congenial. So he hired Hugo Münsterberg, from Wundt's laboratory in Leipzig, to run the new laboratory at Harvard.

Gaps in the theory

As one might expect, philosophers were more interested in Cartesianism as a theory of mind than as an inspiration for a new science of psychology, and what began to trouble them about the Cartesian legacy in philosophy of mind was, above all, the intractable nature of what had come to be known as 'the interaction problem'. Put briefly, 'the interaction problem' is the problem of making sense, at the theoretical level, of how a Cartesian mind, that is, a mind defined in Cartesian terms, could have any effect at all upon a body as characterised in Cartesian theory, and vice versa. While Descartes presumed that our mental acts, such as 'acts of will' (or 'volitions', as they were called in the academic literature) could cause happenings in our bodies, such as movements of our arms or legs, he seemed so to define mind (or soul) and body that any such causal interaction between the two was impossible. If a mind is a substance which has no material properties, including no dimensions and no solidity of any sort, and which has only the vaguest of locations in space, how could it even come into contact with a body which is material? And, in addition, how could such an elusive and ethereal thing as a Cartesian mind, given that it could make contact with something physical, give even the slightest push to a body, let alone engage it in more complex ways? When we see one billard ball in motion and see it come in contact with another, and then see that the latter ball is put in motion through its contact with the former, we think of the first billiard ball as having caused motion in the second. We think of that causal process in terms of the first billiard ball transferring its momentum, or part of it, to the second billiard ball. But it does not seem plausible to say that a ghost-like substance could take part in such causal interactions. Such a substance seems to lack the ability both to have momentum and even to make contact with things. As even Hollywood acknowledges, ghosts tend to walk through walls and tables and chairs, and for that matter billiard balls, rather than bump into them or stumble over them or move them about.

This 'interaction problem' arose in Descartes's own day, most famously in the course of a correspondence between Descartes himself and one of his patrons, Princess Elizabeth of Bohemia (1618–80), daughter of 'the Great Elector' of Brandenburg in Germany. At the time of the correspondence, she was exiled in the Hague in Holland, where Descartes himself had gone to live in 1628.[23] In October 1642, Descartes heard that Princess Elizabeth had been reading his *Meditations* with enthusiasm. In what nowadays might be considered a patronising manner, he offered to explain any difficulties she might encounter in his work. In response he received not so much an enquiry as a philosophical interrogation. In a letter to Descartes, of 6 May 1643, Princess Elizabeth responded by putting to him the following question:

> How can the soul of man, being only a thinking substance [i.e. pure consciousness], determine [i.e. causally interact with] his bodily spirits [in modern terms, the neurotransmitters of his nervous system][24] to perform voluntary actions?[25]

Descartes's reply was notoriously unsatisfactory. First he suggested that the soul's causal influence upon the body was somewhat like the effect of gravity upon some body causing it to fall. This reply does not help to explain matters, because, as was known even in Descartes's own time, gravity was itself a *physical* force. What Princess Elizabeth was asking was how a non-physical, wholly spiritual something (thing or force) could bring about any effect in a physical thing. It has been suggested that, perhaps, all Descartes was trying to say was that it was as mysterious how a mind or soul could causally interact with a body as it was

Figure 1.7
One of
Descartes's
earliest critics,
Princess
Elizabeth of
Bohemia.

mysterious how gravity in fact operated upon bodies. We know, he might have put it, that gravity does so operate, and we know that minds or souls do so operate, but we do not really know how they do so in either case. We just have to accept, in each case, that it is a mystery.

Nor did it help Descartes's case to suggest, as he did, that the pineal gland was the most likely point at which the soul actually made contact with the brain and so with the body. This too seemed, ultimately, to be an overreliance upon the unknown or mysterious. The pineal gland was free to serve in this august role of link between soul and body, because little was known about the role of the pineal gland at that time. In fact, not much has been known about the pineal gland until comparatively recently.[26] Another reason for his choice, Descartes's explicit reason, was that the pineal gland was the most inward part of the brain, located at its very centre. It was also a singleton, while nearly everything else in the brain came, like the animals into the Ark, in twos, one for the left hemisphere and one for the right. So perhaps, Descartes seemed to have surmised, the pineal gland was a central 'point of union' for the nervous system and so, perhaps, also the point of interaction between mind and body.

Princess Elizabeth's reply to this 'mystery mongering' was to say that 'I must admit that it would be easier for me to attribute matter and extension to the soul, than to attribute to an immaterial being the capacity to move and be moved by a body.'[27] In short, Princess Elizabeth is suggesting, a better hypothesis might be to say that the mind is material, just like or somewhat like the body. If so, then there would be no 'interaction problem'. This, as we shall see in subsequent chapters, has been a favoured outlook for most philosophers of mind in the modern era. However, as we have seen, by the time of the first, second and perhaps even the third decades of the twentieth century, the majority of philosophers of mind, and psychologists with more theoretical interests, still more or less endorsed Descartes's response. While acknowledging that there was an 'interaction problem', they felt that this did not impugn the overall attraction of Cartesian dualism in regard to mind and body. What does a mystery or two matter if the rest of the theory is fine, they seemed to be saying. What does a mystery or two matter if the Cartesian theory coheres better with our common sense and with our yearnings for immortality, than does any competing theory?

While 'the interaction problem' was indubitably the major theoretical concern for those seeking to defend Cartesian dualism, it was by no means the only theoretical problem to cause concern. With the publication of Freud's work on the unconscious, and with mainstream psychologists themselves beginning to admit that there must be subconscious mental events (or mental events which are not present to our consciousness), it soon became impossible to retain the classical Cartesian view that the mind is nothing but our consciousness. As is well known, Sigmund Freud (1856–1939) gave birth to psychoanalysis after going to Paris in 1885 to further his studies. Prior to that period, he had been a medical student at the University of Vienna, receiving his MD (or

Doctor of Medicine degree) in 1881. In 1885, Freud received a small postgraduate grant to study clinical neurology at the Salpêtrière, a hospital for insane women in Paris. He studied under Jean Martin Charcot (1825–93), who made great use of hypnosis both as a method of studying and as a way of curing hysterias. So it is not surprising that, in many of his works, Freud used hypnosis as a compelling example of the unconscious mind at work. It is appropriate to take a passage illustrating this use from Freud's *Five Lectures on Psycho-Analysis*. It is appropriate because it is arguable that it was the invitation from the eminent American psychologist G.(Granville) Stanley Hall (1844–1924) to deliver these lectures at Clark University in Massachusetts, in 1909, that finally brought international recognition to Freud's work. This recognition (which included the award of an honorary doctorate in psychology from Clark University) was also aided by the fact that Hall generously ensured that these lectures were published the following year in English, under the title 'The Origin and Development of Psychoanalysis', in the *American Journal of Psychology*, which was the first ever journal of psychology in the United States and founded by Hall himself. In the first of these lectures, Freud makes his point about the unconscious succinctly:

Figure 1.8 Sigmund Freud, the founder of psychoanalysis. His revolutionary ideas on the unconscious are still controversial today.

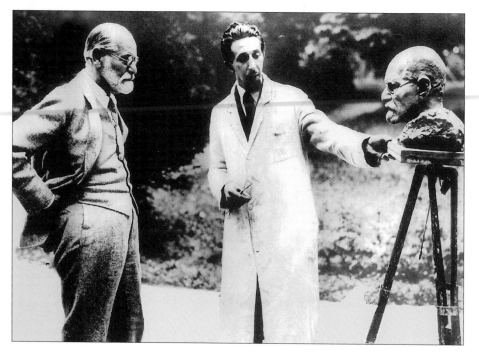

In the familiar condition known as 'post-hypnotic suggestion', a command given under hypnosis is slavishly carried out subsequently in the normal state. This phenomenon affords an admirable example of the influences which the unconscious state can exercise over the conscious one.[28]

What Freud is drawing attention to is, first, the fact that putting someone under hypnosis is like putting them into a trance. Second, although no longer fully awake, the hypnotised person can act upon verbal suggestions made by the hypnotist. Third, even when properly awake, the no longer hypnotised person's actions can still be affected by the suggestions made earlier under hypnosis (the 'post-hypnotic suggestions'). Thus hypnotism is a very dramatic and easily observed demonstration of the power that the unconscious part of the mind can have over a person's behaviour.

Being very interested in the phenomenon of subliminal perception, contemporary psychology is also committed to a 'secular' version of the unconscious. The word 'subliminal' is derived from two Latin words, *sub* meaning 'under', and *limen* meaning 'threshold' or 'limit'. Thus 'subliminal perception' refers to the fact that a person can receive via his or her eyes (or via other sense organs) information of which he or she is not consciously aware, and the implication is that such a person can be influenced by that subliminal perceptual information. For example, my attention might be wholly taken up by orchestrating a discussion class on political liberalism but, nevertheless, during that period I might be taking in information subliminally. Without calling the roll and while not consciously realising it, I might have noted subliminally that Mary Lou Watkins was not present at the class, so that, when I next run across Mary Lou in Front Square, I might say to her with a tone of voice that indicates that I think she definitely was not present, 'Were you at my seminar on political liberalism on Friday?'

A more exact, because laboratory-controlled, demonstration of the subliminal workings of our mind is the following sort of experiment. A number of subjects are seated and headphones placed on their head. They are not told exactly what the experiments are about.[29] Unknown to them, the headphones are special laboratory ones such that different messages, at different levels of loudness, can be relayed to each ear. In their right ears, they receive the message, 'The man walked by the bank.' In their left ears, but at a level of loudness and for such a short period of time that it is at a level below the threshold where one can consciously hear something,[30] they receive the single-word message, 'River'. Then, afterwards, they are asked to say whether the sentence they heard, namely 'The man walked by the bank,' means that 'The man walked by a bank where money was kept' or 'The man walked by the river.' The majority of the answers, with a majority well beyond what could be accounted for by random guessing, will favour the second interpretation, namely that which was fed to their left ear subliminally.[31]

More dramatically, the potential power of our unconscious mind is underlined by the recent sale in America of 'self-help' tapes with subliminal messages. While the audible content of these tapes might be soothing music, the subliminal message, overlaid (or 'underlaid') on the same tape, might be one about losing weight or giving up smoking cigarettes. So far, there is little evidence that they work.[32] It also occurs to me that, since the message on these self-help tapes is avowedly subliminal, the buyer must take it on trust that there is such a hidden message and that it is the one they bargained for. If the technology should improve, the possibility of the misuse of such tapes, or any tapes, hardly bears thinking about.

Practical problems

Historically it was an inescapable practical problem, or series of problems of a practical sort, which brought about the demise of the Cartesian view of mind, first in psychology and then in philosophy of mind. Despite growing doubts about its adequacy as a theory of mind, Cartesian dualism would almost certainly have limped along for a lot longer than it did, if psychologists had not pulled away its walking stick. It was psychology's growing dissatisfaction with Cartesian experimental methods in psychology which finally brought Cartesianism to its knees in both philosophy and psychology.

For many decades, some of the psychologists themselves who employed introspection as a method for investigating conscious mental events, events such as feelings or imaginings or episodes of thought,[33] felt that it was not entirely convincing as a method and started to 'twiddle its nobs' this way and that. William James, for example, held the view that whatever else one was doing when introspecting, it could not be splitting attention (consciously attending to something) into two parts, one for attentively

Subliminal rats now gnawing at credibility of Bush's campaign

Irish Times 13.9.2000

Figure 1.9 In September 2000, the American Republican political party was accused of using subliminal messages to discredit the Democratic candidate for the presidency. A TV ad attacking Democrat healthcare policies, paid for by the Republicans, was discovered to contain the image 'Rats' which appeared on the screen for just one thirtieth of a second.

observing the activity of attending to something and one for the ground-level activity itself of attending to something. Humans, he believed, just could not split consciousness in two and at the same time preserve the integrity of both parts. If you did split your attention (focus of consciousness) in two, say by doing two tasks at once – such as arguing about political liberalism with the visiting speaker to the departmental colloquium and at the same time driving her to the airport – then the best you could do was to oscillate your attention from one thing to the other, or else put one task, such as the driving, on 'automatic pilot' as best you can, and then give your attention for a while to the other. Though there is still the danger that you will run into the car in front if the argument gets heated enough to upset the 'automatic pilot'.[34]

A clear illustration of William James's point is to recall the move you make when the children's party has got so out of hand that little Johnny is throwing jelly at his sister while wee Mary from across the street is smearing chocolate cake on the wall. If you are an unusually self-controlled, liberal-minded, modernist reader of *The Guardian*, you clap your hands and call the children together. Then you announce that there will be a prize for the first person who is able, using the index or 'pointing' finger of their right hand, to trace a circle clockwise around their head and, at the same time, using the 'pointing finger' of their left hand, trace in an anti-clockwise direction a square around their stomach. It is extremely difficult to do so, and you will inevitably fail if you try to concentrate your full attention on both tasks at the same time. The trick is to get the easiest of the two tasks, the right-hand index finger's tracing of the clockwise circle around the head, on 'automatic pilot', while, as best you can, with the index finder of your left hand, you trace out in jerky fashion an anti-clockwise square on your stomach.

Believing that you could not split attention, and in so doing also preserve full attention for two tasks at one and the same time, William James took up a suggestion made previously by the nineteenth-century English philosopher John Stuart Mill. James suggested that one could consciously introspect mental events by converting introspection into 'retrospection'. By this term 'retrospection', James seems to have meant that we could only study the mental events in our stream of consciousness, with full attention, in the following way. First a subject should record the target events in his stream of consciousness in memory. The next step was to recall those events carefully in correct order in a conscious episode of remembering them. The split was thereby avoided. In 'retrospection', there is just one conscious episode, namely that of remembering. The first drawback, as James himself realised, was that it relied on that notoriously unreliable witness, ordinary human memory. Hardly the best basis for a scientific psychology. Second, it struck most people as not very much like what introspection was supposed to be.[35]

Putting aside his doubts about the very possibility of intro-specting in the way introspectionists claimed one could, William James questioned whether any sort of introspection could deliver anything very useful about the nature of mind. Surely, James felt, introspection just focuses on individual episodes in indi-vidual streams of consciousness. You focus on your earache or he focuses on his worrying about the mortgage or she focuses on her puzzling over how to factorise some complex algebraic equation. Reports from such personal introspections cannot give us insights into the nature of mental acts, such as feeling, imagining or thinking, and *a fortiori* they cannot discover truths about the very nature of the mind itself. But if that is so, introspection begins to look less than useful as a basic method of enquiry for the 'Science of Mental Life'.[36]

These signs of a growing loss of faith on the part of at least some introspectionists was but the last act before the curtain finally came down on, or more accurately fell on top of, the whole Cartesian approach to psychology. This descent of the curtain is usually associated with a certain notorious academic deadlock or 'stand off' between two schools of introspectionist psychology that arose in the first decade of the twentieth century.[37] E. B. Titchener (1867–1927), a former student of Wilhelm Wundt, and his colleagues at Cornell University in the United States of America believed that their scientific introspections had demonstrated that 'non-sensory conscious thought' was impossible. Put positively, they believed that all conscious thinking (all here-and-now episodes of thinking that occurred in one's stream of consciousness) must involve sensory material, such as images or sounds or feelings, in order to be conscious. All episodes of thinking must be either in terms of heard speech, or of visualised written or printed sentences or, say, in the case of an infant, in the form of mental pictures or images of some sort. It was held as axiomatic that the activation of consciousness *ipso facto* resulted from the activation of one of the senses or from the active reassembly, in remembering or imagining or dreaming or day-dreaming, of bits and pieces culled from such sensory experiences. Opposed to this claim was the Würzburg school, that is, the introspection laboratory and research group attached to it, at the University of Würzburg in Bavaria. The leader of this school, Oswald Külpe (1862–1915), another former student of Wundt, and his colleagues believed that their introspection experiments showed that you could have pure conscious thought that needed no sensory medium. Each group, the one at Cornell and the one at Würzburg, claimed the backing of exhaustive and exhausting, replicated, laboratory-controlled, introspection experiments with properly trained subjects.

Somewhat surprisingly, while there was such clear lack of accord between the two groups or laboratories, there was a wholly unexpected and highly suspicious agreement within a single group or laboratory. Every series of experiments conducted by Titchener's research group, no matter how many subjects there were, produced the result that thought was only possible when using a sensory medium. The same was true, as regards the contrary claim, from the series of rigorous experiments conducted by Külpe's research group.

There seemed to be no way that this deadlock could be resolved. For what was needed was some way of deciding when results from any single introspection experiment were to be believed. But how could one person verify or check in any way the report by another person on a wholly private introspection of the latter's own stream of consciousness? You cannot get inside another person's head to introspect along with him and so corroborate his claims about the results of his introspections. Besides what I internally 'spect' in my own completely private and personal stream of consciousness, even if reported accurately, may be different from what you do, even though the items in your stream of consciousness were caused by exactly the same things which caused mine. For the simple reason that I am different from you, and our streams of consciousness may be just the very place where our individuality is most flamboyant. Further experiments would not help, for the problem is in verifying the data from each individual subject's reports. To produce yet more unverifiable data is no help in verifying previously unverifiable data.

This debate about the possibility of 'non-sensory conscious thought' was, of course, just one example of the confidence-sapping controversies that beset introspectionist psychology. In his 'manifesto article' of 1913, J. B. Watson, the vociferously anti-Cartesian behaviourist, was only too glad to list others:

> I firmly believe that two hundred years from now, unless the introspective method is discarded, psychology will still be divided on the question as to whether auditory sensations have the quality of 'extension', whether intensity is an attribute which can be applied to color, whether there is a difference in 'texture' between image and sensation and upon many hundreds of others of like character.[38]

What was becoming increasingly clear, and increasingly at variance with what was believed in the foundation years of Cartesian psychology, was that introspection was not a scientific, at least in the sense of objective, method of enquiry. It was not objective in the sense of being a method which avoided being purely personal and private, and it was not objective in the sense of being amenable to experiments which could be checked for accuracy by others. J. B. Watson (1878–1958), the founder of behaviourism, that is, the approach to psychology which suc-ceeded introspectionism and which by and large dictated the methods in psychology for the rest of the twentieth century, used to refer to introspective psychology as 'subjective psychology' and used to refer to the Cartesian concept of mind as something belonging to 'the ancient days of superstition and magic'.[39] In his very influential textbook, *Behaviorism*, in a passage recapitulating the recent history of psychology, Watson wrote:

> In 1912 the objective psychologists or behaviorists reached the conclusion that they could no longer be content to work with Wundt's formulations. They felt that the 30 odd barren years since the establishment of Wundt's laboratory had proved conclusively that the so-called introspective psychology of Germany was founded upon wrong hypotheses – that no psychology which included the religious mind–body problem could ever arrive at verifiable conclusions. They decided either to give up psychology or else to make it a natural science.[40]

Watson, in the same book, went on to suggest the complete 'elimination of states of consciousness as proper objects of investigation in themselves' and, in their place, the substitution of human behaviour. In psychology Watson had his way for the next thirty or forty years and, arguably, he and his immediate disciples set the experimental tone in psychology for the rest of the twentieth century. His great influence was acknowledged, in 1957, by the American Psychological Association, at a meeting in New York. The Association presented a citation 'to John B. Watson, whose work has been one of the vital determinants of the form and substance of modern psychology'.

In philosophy, while behaviourism itself had a comparatively short reign, its critique of Cartesian substance dualism produced a profound and permanent change of climate in the philosophy of mind. Future theories of mind were to reject substance dualism in such trenchant terms that it now seems impossible that this sort of fundamental dualism will ever be rehabilitated. Descartes and his ghost have been laid permanently to rest. With this rejection came a rejection of the religious view of mind as soul, and a rejection of the consequences that were attached to that doctrine, namely that there is an afterlife where human souls or spirits, if they are good, will dwell in heaven with God, the angels and the saints, and, if they are bad, will be consigned along with the devil and his minions to the everlasting pains of hell.

In place of Cartesian substance dualism and its 'two worlds' view of human life, psychologists and especially philosophers substituted a 'single world' of an uncompromising materialist nature (and in so doing could be said to have reverted to a very ancient model first put forward by the Greek Atomist Democritus and by Epicurus).[41] First of all came the behaviourist analysis of our mental concepts in terms of human behaviour. Then came a comparatively crude if ground-breaking version of mind as being nothing but the brain, though, for decades after, this 'one (material) world' view was to be refined in increasingly clever and subtle ways. For this new materialism of the twentieth century found common cause with and drew inspiration from the new and exciting sciences of evolutionary biology, neurophysiology, computing and artificial intelligence. However, these far-reaching, and indeed for many people, astonishing and alarming views about the nature of the mind are the matter of subsequent chapters. In this chapter I have been intent on explaining what sort of answer to the question 'What is the mind?' philosophers and psychologists gave in the last decades of the nineteenth and in the first decades of the twentieth century, and the reasons they had for giving that answer. In subsequent chapters we shall see that the remainder of the twentieth century was a philosophical and psychological reactor whose internal processes have produced great turbulence. However, out of this turbulence, there came theoretical insights of the greatest importance.

CHAPTER TWO

Observing the Human Animal

The behaviourist manifesto

In 1913 J. B. (John Broadus) Watson radically altered the methods and scope of the still comparatively new science of psychology when he published his article, 'Psychology as the Behaviorist Views It', in the American journal *Psychological Review*. In this bracing and combative article, Watson laid out his new model for psychology:

> Psychology as the behaviorist views it is a purely objective experimental branch of natural science. Its theoretical goal is the prediction and control of behavior. Introspection forms no essential part of its methods, nor is the scientific value of its data dependent upon the readiness with which they lend themselves to interpretation in terms of consciousness. The behaviorist, in his efforts to get a unitary scheme of animal response, recognizes no dividing line between man and brute. The behavior of man, with all of its refinement and complexity, forms only a part of the behaviorist's total scheme of investigation.[1]

Justifiably this article has been called the manifesto for the new school of psychology which Watson labelled 'behaviorism', and ever afterwards the year 1913 has been considered its birthdate. For Watson not merely jettisoned Cartesianism in psychology, he confidently sketched in a new methodology and a new programme whereby psychology would indisputably take its place among the natural sciences. The new psychologists were to study human psychology in exactly the same way as ethologists and zoologists, or for that matter animal psychologists, had already been studying animal psychology. That is to say, they were to study it from the outside, and by observing in a wholly objective manner how the human animal acted or reacted in carefully observed environments. Introspection was neither possible nor needed in the project of studying animal psychology, so why should we employ such a dubious and subjective method in human psychology when we had perfectly good objective methods to hand? Along with this abandonment of introspection as a method went a refusal to consider consciousness, and the 'interior life', even as suitable subject matter for investigation in a scientific psychology. However, let me backtrack a little, for an account of how Watson himself arrived at such a view of the method and scope of psychology is, in effect, an account of the conception and birth of behaviourism itself as well as, arguably, of psychology as we now know it.

Watson was born on a farm in Greenville, South Carolina, in 1878.[2] His mother was a deeply religious Baptist; his father an irreligious, violent, womanising alcoholic. When his father ran off with another woman, the thirteen-year-old Watson and his mother were reduced to poverty. Despite a record of rebelliousness at school, Watson made sufficient academic progress so as to be admitted, in 1893, into Furman University, a Baptist institution then located in Greenville. His BA included a number of courses in philosophy and philosophical psychology.[3] After studying for his postgraduate MA at Furman, and then being employed briefly as a school teacher, Watson was admitted in 1900 into the graduate school of philosophy at the University of Chicago. John Dewey, the only American philosopher ever to appear on an American postage stamp,[4] and now remembered mainly for his views on education, was the Professor of Philosophy there at that time.

At Chicago Watson found philosophy in general, and Dewey in particular, abstract and uncongenial. As Watson himself put it, 'I passed my exams but the spark was not there.' However, among the philosophy faculty was the patrician figure of James Angell, who had been a student of William James at Harvard. It was on Angell's advice that Watson decided to do his doctoral dissertation on 'animal education'. The supervision of his research was to be undertaken, jointly, by Angell and a neurologist, H. H. Donaldson. His method involved studying how rats could be trained to accomplish various tasks – such as finding their way through a maze to food – and investigating the rat's brain at each stage of growth in age and abilities. Though it was a very odd project for a student in a philosophy department, it was not so strange for Chicago, where philosophy was the dominant segment of a large hybrid department of philosophy, psychology and education. It was also not so strange when seen in a larger context. In the last two decades of the nineteenth century there

Figure 2.1
John B. Watson,
the founder of
behaviourism
in psychology.

had been a number of renowned experimenters in animal behaviour, such as the Russian Pavlov, the Englishman Lloyd Morgan, the American Thorndike, and the Frenchman Jacques Loeb. The last named was at the University of Chicago during Watson's time there. These experimenters, being almost always physiologists, but with a strong interest in psychology, came to their work on animal behaviour via their work on the connection between animal behaviour and animal physiology. Watson's behaviourism, as we shall see, was also often strongly physiological in orientation.

Watson's doctoral work on his rats enabled him to be granted his Ph.D. 'magna cum laude' and his thesis was published by the University of Chicago Press, in 1903, under the title *Animal Education*. Up to that time he was the youngest student ever to gain his Ph.D. at Chicago, and he was appointed immediately to teach psychology there. After taking up this post, he continued to work on animal behaviour and animal physiology, extending his interest now to first birds and then monkeys. From 1904 to 1908 there followed a series of papers resulting from this work on animals, such as 'The Effect of the Bearing of Young upon the Body-Weight and the Weight of the Central Nervous System of the Female White Rat' (Watson, 1905), 'The Need of an Experimental Station for the Study of Certain Problems in Animal Behavior' (Watson, 1906), 'Condition of Noddy and Sooty Tern Colony, Bird Key, Tortugas, Fla.' (Watson, 1907), and 'Imitation in Monkeys' (Watson, 1908).[5]

Watson's views on human psychology – on its scope and methods – seem to have been germinated between 1908 and the publication of his behaviourist manifesto in 1913. In 1908 Watson accepted the offer of a Professorship of Experimental and Comparative Psychology at the Johns Hopkins University in Baltimore, Maryland, when he was still just twenty-nine years of age, and around the same time became the youngest person ever to have appeared in *Who's Who in America*. These achievements gave him both the confidence and freedom to speak out. Towards the end of 1908, in his first few months at Johns Hopkins, Watson aired a tentative and embryonic version of his view, that the methods and aims of human psychology should be more or less the same as the methods and aims of animal psychology, first in a lecture at Yale University and then in a paper at the annual meeting of the Southern Society for Philosophy and Psychology in Baltimore. The immediate response was chilly. In fact, at this time, his only intellectual allies were probably his colleagues at Johns Hopkins: the psychologist Knight Dunlap and the young neurologist Karl Lashley.

For the next five years, besides his work on animals, Watson continued to work on the fundamental problem of the nature of psychology itself but still without publishing anything on that topic. However, at the beginning of 1913, in a series of invited public lectures at Columbia University in New York, Watson gave a very clear and uncompromising account of what he took to be the methods, aims and scope of a psychology that wished to be considered a genuinely natural science. This time his views generated enormous interest and controversy. The final revised text of his first lecture became his famous manifesto article, published in the *Psychological Review* later that same year. The fact that Watson was himself editor of the *Psychological Review* at that time may explain its being published so speedily and, given its adversarial style and controversial content, so readily.

In that article, he introduced the now famous, or notorious, phrase 'stimulus and response'. In describing a human's psychology, he tells us that we should make no mention of 'the terms consciousness, mental states, mind, content, introspectively verifiable, imagery, and the like'. All we need to refer to are the environmental conditions, which act as the stimulus that elicits some behaviour from the human we are observing, and the ensuing behavioural response. That is all we need to refer to because the goal of a scientific psychology is 'the control of human behavior'. Experiments in psychology consist in so controlling the environmental conditions, that the study of which conditions elicit which behavioural responses becomes a manageable enterprise.[6]

While Watson, and many later psychological behaviourists, such as B. F. Skinner, would sometimes say that they were only interested in revising the scope, methods and goals of psychology, and had no interest in 'metaphysical' questions, such as 'What is mind?', such a claim was always rather disingenuous. For behaviourists themselves, as well as their critics, realised that they were confronted by a dilemma:[7] either a behaviourist psychology studied at least the fundamental aspects of the human 'psyche' (or mental life)[8] or it did not. If it did study the fundamentals of the human 'psyche', then it meant that, implicit in the behaviourists' methodological proposals, was at least one important doctrine about the nature of mind, namely that its fundamental aspects could be studied properly by behaviourist methods. If a behaviourist psychology did not study the fundamentals of the human 'psyche', then it could hardly claim to be introducing a new way of doing psychology. Perforce, then, the behaviourists embraced the first alternative. They admitted that, implicit in behaviourism, was a thesis about the nature of the human mind.

Watson was certainly quite explicit, indeed quite combative, about certain key aspects of the behaviourist view of mind, namely about the behaviourist view on consciousness and introspection. Introspection, he suggested, was not a way of knowing, even subjectively and qualitatively, about anything, because there were no such things as mental states, including consciousness, in the Cartesian sense of the term. Consciousness and introspection were illusions engendered in psychologists and ordinary people by the employment of obsolete Cartesian concepts:

> It is a serious misunderstanding of the behaviouristic position to say, as Mr Thomson does[9] – 'And of course a behaviourist does not deny that mental states exist. He merely prefers to ignore them.' He 'ignores' them in the same sense that chemistry ignores alchemy, astronomy horoscopy, and psychology telepathy and psychic manifestations. The behaviourist does not concern himself with them because as the stream of his science broadens and deepens such older concepts are sucked under, never to reappear.[10]

In other words, Watson's position was that one ignored introspection and consciousness not merely because consciousness was not amenable to scientific investigation but because the very concepts of consciousness and introspection were groundless and unscientific. One of Watson's teachers, when he was a student at the University of Chicago, was the pragmatist or social behaviourist G. H. Mead. Mead said that Watson's attitude to consciousness and introspection 'was that of the Queen in *Alice in Wonderland* – "Off with their heads!" – there were no such things'.[11]

By 1930, when he had published the revised edition of his book, *Behaviorism*, first published in 1924, Watson explicitly considered the question, 'Does this behaviouristic approach leave anything out of psychology?' His reply was that it does not leave anything out, because all the old questions – about consciousness or about mental acts, such as those of imagining or thinking or hoping or desiring – can be translated into a scientific, that is, a behaviouristic form and so given a scientific answer.[12]

In fact this revised edition of *Behaviorism* appeared long after Watson, owing to a scandal, had been forced to leave not merely his chair at the Johns Hopkins University but academic life. In the autumn of 1919 Watson had become the supervisor of a very intelligent and very beautiful MA student, Rosalie Rayner, who had been an undergraduate student at Vassar, the exclusive women's college in New York. Watson fell deeply in love with Rosalie. At that time, if it became public knowledge, such an adulterous affair was considered scandalous. After coming across a number of his torrid love letters to Rosalie, Watson's wife instituted divorce proceedings. Those proceedings became a public sensation when a number of his love letters to Rosalie found their way into the pages of the *Baltimore Sun*. The President of Johns Hopkins, Frank Johnson Goodnow, demanded Watson's immediate resignation. Watson felt that there was no alternative but to resign. He married Rosalie soon afterwards. Though not long before Watson had been President of the American Psychological Association and a number of universities, including Harvard, had tried to lure him to their psychology department, he was never able afterwards to obtain any academic post of even the most humble kind. After a period of unemployment he ended up working for the J. Walter Thompson advertising agency at a salary about four times his previous academic one. Through his work at the agency, he became instrumental in introducing some of the psychological ploys still used by supermarkets to sell their goods.

Behaviourism did not disappear with the expulsion of Watson from the academic scene. By the time of his dismissal in 1920, behaviourism had a firm foothold. By the time B. F. (Burrhus Frederick) Skinner (1904–90), the best-known psychological behaviourist since Watson, had published his first paper in psychology in 1930, the behaviourist view of mind was the dominant one in psychology. In a book written in the last quarter of his life, *About Behaviourism* (1974), which he described as a book about 'the philosophy' of the science of behaviour, Skinner was engagingly explicit about what view of mind was implied by behaviorism:

> A much simpler solution [simpler than equating the mind with the brain] is to identify the mind with the [physical] person. Human thought is human behaviour. The history of human thought is what people have said and done.[13]

Skinner's view of the nature of mind was that what we, in our unreformed way, think of as mind and mental acts are quite simply just an artificially selected grouping of certain types of human behaviour. For a scientific behaviourist to report that Mary had been engaged in a mental act of thinking might mean, for example, nothing more than to report that Mary had been observed making marks on a piece of paper, so that when she showed the psychologist the piece of paper, and the psychologist

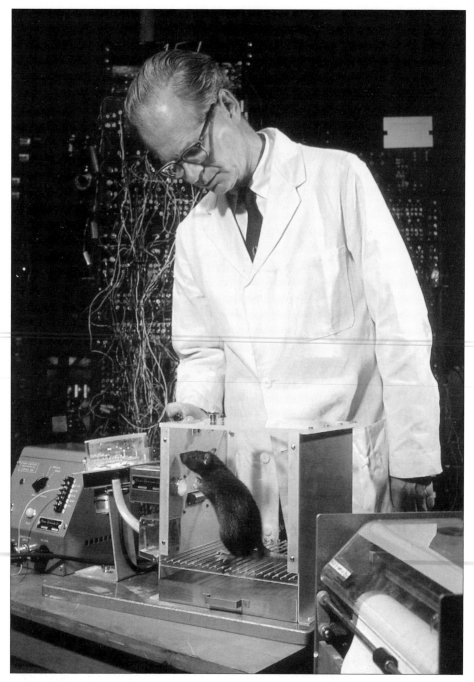

Figure 2.2
The American behaviourist
psychologist, B. F. Skinner,
training a rat in his laboratory.

saw that she had on it '2189 + 4275 = 6464', he was able to say that Mary had solved the simple arithmetical problem of adding '2189' to '4275'. To take another example, Fred's solving by trial and error the problem of how to stack four objects of different shapes, one on top of the other, so that they do not fall down immediately, is an example of Fred thinking. For a behaviourist, to observe Fred doing that public task is to observe Fred thinking. More generally, for a behaviourist, having a mind is nothing more than being capable of doing those observable behavioural tasks which we think of as exhibiting intellectual or other mental skills.

Logical positivism and the 'logico-linguistic turn'

Behaviourism in psychology, as we have just seen, arose as a theory about the proper or truly scientific way to investigate the psychology of humans and other animals. Implicitly it involved an underlying monistic, physicalist view of the human *person* as being nothing but an evolved physical organism which behaved in certain ways in certain specifiable circumstances. Implicitly it also involved an underlying monistic, physicalist view of the human *mind* as being nothing but the grouping together of certain sorts of behaviour of this evolved physical organism, the human person. While psychologists, then, became behaviourists for methodological reasons, philosophers of mind became so for logico-linguistic reasons. But, as it stands, that contrast is misleading and anyway needs explaining. The philosophy of mind took a 'logico-linguistic turn' because philosophy in general had first done so, as the outcome of an immensely important background debate in philosophy itself over its own methods, aims and scope. To make sense of this claim, I need to describe the advent of that most important of twentieth-century move-ments in philosophy, logical positivism; for it was the protagonist in that great debate. As we shall see, logical positivism had an enormous influence on that part of modern philosophy which gradually acquired the tag 'analytic philosophy'.

Analytic philosophy is that style of philosophy which is most common in the English-speaking world. It is usually described by way of contrast with the other main contemporary philosophical tradition, Continental philosophy, which, as the name indicates, is associated with Continental Europe. Analytic philosophy sees itself as a philosophical ally of science and looks upon logic (including the formalities of mathematical or symbolic logic) as its chief tool in much the same way as mathematics might be considered to be the chief tool of the physical sciences. Analytic philosophy also puts a premium upon clarity of expression and formal rigour of argumentation in its defence of any claim or critique of any theory. In comparison, Continental philosophy sees itself as allied to literature, such that its claims and critical forays are better expressed in the figurative, rhetorical and more allusive language of poets, playwrights and novelists. Continental philosophers, such as, for example, the French philosophers Jean-Paul Sartre (1905–80) and Albert Camus (1913–60), have often been noted for their literary works, such as their novels and plays. Camus was awarded the Nobel Prize for Literature in 1957. Sartre was nominated for the Nobel Prize for Literature in 1964 (as earlier he had also been offered the Legion of Honour and a Chair at the Collège de France) but felt that a true existentialist philosopher ought not to accept such honours.[14]

On the other hand, to refer to one of the main currents of contemporary philosophy as 'analytic' is not to imply that a great part of the philosophical world, or even of the Anglophone philosophical world, is now peopled by logical positivists. For the contrary is true, namely that logical positivists are an extinct species. It is, rather, that a great deal of the style, values and subject matter of modern analytical philosophy has been shaped, for better or worse, by its attempts to meet various challenges laid down by the logical positivists. This is certainly true in the case of philosophy of mind. So it is important, therefore, that I say something about logical positivism.

Logical positivism is the name given to the doctrines promulgated by that extraordinarily gifted group of Austro-German scientists, mathematicians, social scientists and philosophers who gave themselves the name 'Vienna Circle' (*Wiener Kreis*). The Vienna Circle emerged from discussions in Vienna, beginning in 1907, between the sociologist Otto Neurath, the mathematician Hans Hahn and the physicist Philip Frank. However the name became associated especially with the enlarged group that became more organised under the leadership of the German physicist-philosopher Moritz Schlick (1882–1936), when he succeeded Ernst Mach to the Chair of the Philosophy of the Inductive Sciences at the University of Vienna in 1922. This larger group included Friedrich Waismann, Rudolf Carnap, Herbert Feigl, Victor Kraft, Karl Menger and Kurt Gödel, and as 'Berlin

Figure 2.3
The leader of
the Vienna
Circle, Moritz
Schlick, who
was killed by
a demented
philosophy
student.

associate members' Carl Hempel, Hans Reichenbach, Richard von Mises and Kurt Grelling. The Circle could be said to have become a movement with the publication, in 1929, of its manifesto, 'The Vienna Circle; Its Scientific Outlook',[15] and its organisation of an international congress in Prague that same year in order to promulgate its views. In the following year, the Circle took over the journal *Annalen der Philosophie* (Annals of Philosophy), renamed it *Erkenntnis* (Perception)[16] and made it, under the editorship of Carnap and Reichenbach, the principal organ of the positivist movement. While the movement gathered more and more adherents, the Vienna Circle itself began to fall apart. First Hahn died in 1934. Then Schlick himself was murdered in 1936, shot on the steps of the university by a demented student whose thesis on ethics he had refused to pass. A sign of what was to come was displayed by the hostile tone of the obituaries in the governmental press. As the English philosopher A. J. Ayer, who had himself visited the Vienna Circle as a student in 1933, put it, the obituaries almost implied 'that logical positivists deserved to be murdered by their pupils'.[17] As many of the members of the Circle were either Jewish or Marxist or both, the rise of Hitler and National Socialism inevitably spelt the end of the Circle. Those that left Germany (Grelling did not and died at the hands of the Nazis) went mainly to America (for example, Carnap, Reichenbach, Gödel, Menger, Hempel and Feigl) and gave philosophy in that country an unexpected maturity and vigour for many decades, and a style that persists in some quarters to this day.

The group's doctrines attracted the label 'logical positivism' because they seemed to be a logico-linguistic version of nineteenth-century positivism, a doctrine which was first enunciated in the 'positive philosophy' of the French philosopher and sociologist Auguste Comte (1798–1857), who in turn derived at least the germ of many of his ideas from his mentor, the socialist writer and reformer, Saint-Simon (1760–1825).[18] Nineteenth-century positivism was a hymn to scientific progress and depicted the evolution of human thought about the nature of the world and human societies as comprising a definite, inevitable and irreversible progress towards a scientific outlook. Our views of the natural world and human societies, said Comte, were first dominated by religious thought, then they advanced to a viewpoint that was infused with metaphysical ideas where explanations were given in terms of abstractions which had no real scientific basis. Finally, at the terminus of this evolution of thought, humans would arrive at the most advanced view, namely one which would be guided by the explanations of positive science, which in turn would shape the societies in which they lived into scientific, industrialised ones.

This adoration of science became the basis of the positivists' view of knowledge in general. In earlier periods, knowledge (or *scientia* in Latin) included any disciplined form of enquiry which led to knowledge, and so would have included, say, history or biblical studies or philosophy as well as physics or chemistry or astronomy. Now, for the positivists, science (a word derived directly from *scientia*) included only the natural experimental sciences. In addition the nineteenth-century positivists came to believe that the only genuine method of gaining knowledge was the scientific method. In turn, by scientific method, they meant the method of producing causal hypotheses (or theories about what is the cause of what) and then testing them by reference to observation (ultimately by human senses) and experiment (by which our observations might be controlled, aided and refined).

What the twentieth-century positivists, the logical positivists, added to nineteenth-century positivism was, first of all, a rigorous logico-linguistic framework for expressing these core doctrines of positivism. They claimed to derive this framework from, or at least that it was consonant with, the doctrines of Frege, Russell and especially Wittgenstein, about the nature of meaning, language and logic. Though the Austrian philosopher Ludwig Wittgenstein (1889–1951) was never a member of the Vienna Circle, Schlick in particular greatly admired Wittgenstein's *Tractatus Logico-Philosophicus* (1921), the only book of his that was published in his lifetime, and would wholeheartedly have endorsed such uncompromising proclamations of the centrality of scientific knowledge as this Tractarian proposition:

> 4.11 The totality of true propositions is the whole of natural science (or the whole corpus of the natural sciences).[19]

The number, that prefixes the quotation above, needs some explanation. In the *Tractatus* (as the mouthful *Tractatus Logico-Philosophicus* soon became known), Wittgenstein used a curious style of composition. The text was an assembly of, usually quite short, sections, each with its own decimal number. The very first section, just one sentence ('The world is all that is the case'), was numbered 1. The second, a comment or gloss on the first, was numbered 1.1. A comment upon this comment, was numbered 1.11, a second comment 1.12, and so on. In addition, as Wittgenstein himself explained, 'The decimal numbers assigned to the individual propositions indicate the logical importance of the propositions, the stress laid on them in my exposition.' The decimal numbering has certainly added to the subsequent mystique of the text.[20]

In typical fashion, these latter-day positivists of the Vienna

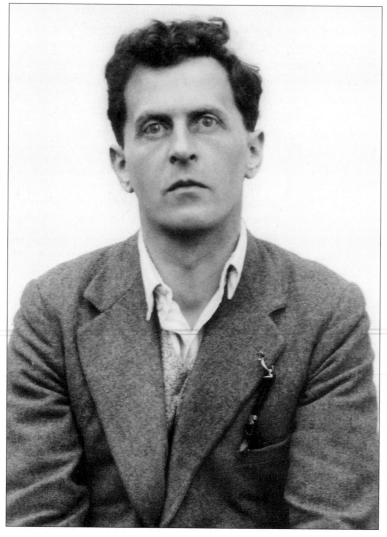

Figure 2.4
The Austrian
philosopher,
Wittgenstein,
who, though
not a member
of the
Vienna Circle,
exercised
considerable
influence
upon it.

Circle sometimes expressed their pro-scientific and anti-meta-physical stance in terms of an uncompromisingly clear and austere logico-linguistic principle called a 'verification principle'. A simplified version of a verification principle might be expressed as follows: *a statement (or sentence or proposition) is literally meaningful (or significant) if and only if it is either empirically verifiable (or falsifiable) or it can be seen, or shown, to be true (or self-contradictory) simply by analysing the conventional meanings of the signs or symbols used in the statement.* The implication is that if something cannot be shown to be either true or false, then it cannot really be saying anything at all. It is vacuous, a favourite word of the logical positivists, and so must be without real meaning.

Examples of the first sort of meaningful statement would be ones such as 'It is now raining' or 'At 1500 hours the thermometer in the room was showing 330°C' or 'At standard temperature and pressure, water boils at 100°C.' These are empirically verifiable, and so meaningful, because they can be shown to be true (or false) by immediate observation, that is, by the employment of the human senses of sight or touch (as in the case of 'It is now raining', when I go outside and see or feel the rain coming down) or by instrument-aided observation (as in the other two examples, when I carefully observe a thermometer and barometer).

Examples of the second sort of meaningful statement would be the dictionary definition, 'A bachelor is an unmarried man', or this simple arithmetic statement, '3 + 3 = 6', or this simple logical definition, '(p⊃q) = (~p v q) [i.e. "p implies q" is logically equivalent to "either not-p is true or else q is true"]'. These examples of the second sort of statement can be shown to be true (or false) simply by knowing about the rules for the correct use of the words, signs or symbols of the relevant language, code or calculus. If you know the meaning of the English word 'bachelor', of the phrase 'unmarried man', and of the words 'is', 'an' and 'a', then, with this 'dictionary and grammatical knowledge' alone, you can be certain that the sentence 'A bachelor is an unmarried man' is true. You can know it to be true independently of any empirical concern about whether or not there are any bachelors still in existence. In like manner, the statements in simple arithmetic and in propositional logic can be declared true (or false) solely in terms of someone's knowledge and valid application of 'the rules of the game' of arithmetic and logic.

According to such a verification principle, then, the meaning of all terms or phrases, and so sentences, is therefore to be anchored to checkable facts either about the world or about language and quasi-linguistic systems. Thus, argued the logical positivists, with our principle we have shown how scientific statements can be shown to be true or false (verified or falsified), and so meaningful, and we have also shown how the statements of logic and mathematics, the essential tools of all scientific enterprises, can be shown to be true or false, and so meaningful. So these, they declared, are the two paradigms or models of meaningful statements in general. Any statements that do not approximate to these two models of meaningful statements will turn out to be meaningless, or nonsense, when looked at closely.

Sometimes some logical positivists went on to claim that the meanings of empirical statements were to be *identified* with the methods employed to verify them. Their catchcry became, 'The meaning of a sentence is its method of verification.' Thus the sentence 'It is now raining' *means* 'If I go outside at this moment, then I will feel drops of water on my head which, if I look up, will be seen to be pouring down from the sky and . . .' or some such rigmarole. If this account of meaning involves a confusion, as many think it does, then, as we shall see in due course, it is a confusion that the logical positivists fell into very readily and very happily in the context of philosophy of mind.

The logical positivists' adoration of science and its chief tool mathematics did not stop at making science the model of real knowledge and real meaningfulness. They went further and singled out physics as the basic science, and so canonised its statements and its methods of verification as the most perfect forms of both knowledge and the means for arriving at it. For physics, they believed, explained the world and everything in it at its most fundamental level. It described things and events as they really are, not as they might appear. So it is not difficult to see their final step, their doctrine of 'unifying science', as the culmination of all their previous doctrines. For, in terms of the doctrine of 'unifying science', the logical positivists put forward their claim that, at least in some 'future perfect' time, all other sciences would be shown to be reducible to the basic science, physics. By the term 'reducible' they meant, ultimately, a linguistic thesis. For the hoped-for reduction of all sciences to physics was to be achieved by a gradual translation of, say, the vocabulary of biology into the vocabulary of the more basic sciences, biochemistry and neurophysiology. Then, in turn, the vocabulary of biochemistry and neurophysiology would be translated into the vocabulary of the most basic science, physics, if necessary via a detour through basic chemistry.

On the other hand, sometimes this reductionist thesis took a different form, particularly when applied to the social sciences. There the 'downward thrust' of the translation process was not so much a literal translation of the terms of a social science into the terms a physicist would use, as the translation of the methods of a social science into the methods of physics. For this methodological translation would ensure that all statements in the reformed social science would now be couched in publicly observable and so 'physicalist' terms.

This doctrine of 'unified science' is one of the main sources, though by no means the only one, of the constant desire in much modern philosophy of mind to seek to reduce the vocabulary of psychology or philosophy of mind to 'something more fundamental', such as the vocabulary of neurophysiology. However, to do that, as we shall see, is to go beyond where, in practice, even the positivists were prepared to go.

Where did all this leave philosophy itself? Philosophy was clearly not a science. It did no experiments and engaged in no specialised forms of observation. Nor did its practitioners want to say it was just the practice of logic. For logic, like mathematics, tells us nothing about the universe, including about the humans or other animals in it. Like mathematics, logic is a formal system where neat and undeniable conclusions can be drawn by the application of approved rules of inference from agreed axioms. Its symbols are symbols for such things as propositions or predicates, which, like the numbers of mathematics, are not to be found in the world. However, if the statements of philosophy itself were neither scientific nor quasi-mathematical, how could they be meaningful? There did not seem to be any space left over for them on the shelf indelibly marked 'meaningful statements'.

When formulating their answer, the Vienna Circle once again found support in the aphoristic sentences of Wittgenstein's *Tractatus*. There they read:

4.111   Philosophy is not one of the natural sciences.
(The word 'philosophy' must mean something whose place is above or below the natural sciences, not beside them.)

4.112   Philosophy aims at the logical clarification of thoughts.
Philosophy is not a body of doctrine but an activity.
A philosophical work consists essentially of elucidations.
Philosophy does not result in 'philosophical propositions', but rather in the clarification of propositions.
Without philosophy thoughts are, as it were, cloudy and indistinct: its task is to make them clear and to give them sharp boundaries.[21]

In other words, the task of philosophy was to be not the hand-maiden of theology, as it had been in the Middle Ages, but the handmaiden of science, the new 'religion of humanity', if I might borrow and somewhat alter the direction of Comte's famous phrase.[22] Philosophy had no subject matter, no propositions, of its own. Its work was to be that of a logico-linguistic accountant auditing the propositions of the sciences. Logic and conceptual analysis were the chief tools of philosophy and its major task was to help in the long-term process of 'unifying science'. In a sense, science, the great god whom the logical positivists tended with such loving care, had grown so large and hungry that it had ended up devouring their own subject, philosophy. Or so it seemed at that time. Mercifully logical positivism has died out, and philosophy has assumed something like its old, more elevated role of producing theses and theories about those fundamental things which other disciplines put to one side or assume, such as the nature of cause or mind or justice or moral values.

Nevertheless it is undeniable that positivism left behind a very strong legacy in philosophy, and not least in philosophy of mind. Some of this legacy has been beneficial; some has not. A part of this legacy, which lasted for the next two or three decades, if not longer, was that the philosophy of logic and language became the core areas of philosophy, and 'linguistic analysis' became the dominant style for philosophical investigations including those in philosophy of mind.

Philosophical or logical behaviourism

As we have seen, one of the members of the Vienna Circle was the German philosopher Rudolf Carnap (1891–1970), who moved to the the United States in 1935. One of his most famous papers was 'Psychology in the Language of Physics', first published in *Erkenntnis* in 1931. In that paper, Carnap proclaimed:

> Now psychology, which has hitherto enjoyed a certain elevated position as the theory of psychic or mental processes, is to be degraded into a part of physics.[23]

Now, by such a reduction of psychology or any other social science to physics, it turned out in practice that Carnap and the logical positivists did not mean that, eventually, we should be able to substitute talk about electrons and protons for talk about, say, being excited or wishing for success in the bridge tournament or hoping to win the tennis match. What Carnap and the logical positivists meant was that we should construct a scientific psychology *in the way* physics is constructed. That is to say, first, we should move from the observation of particular cases to the eventual formation of generalisations. Second, and more importantly, we should confine the reports of our observations solely to what is objective and checkable, that is, to physical objects and events. Thus, in the same paper, Carnap also wrote:

> All sentences of psychology are about physical processes, namely about the physical behaviour of humans and other animals.[24]

These 'sentences' that Carnap was referring to are not the sentences practising psychologists themselves might employ, for they might still be unredeemed Cartesian introspectionists who refer to 'psychic or mental processes'. These 'sentences' are the sentences *into which*, Carnap believed, any meaningful sentences employed by psychologists could and should be translated. For example, this means that one should translate a sentence, such as 'He is excited', not into something about inner, private 'psychical' feelings, but into something like 'His body is characterised by a high pulse rate, by the occurrence of agitated movements, by vehement and factually unsatisfactiory answers to questions, etc.' For pulse rates, agitated movements, unusually loud tones of voice, and failures to give right answers, are all observable, checkable, physical and so public events.

To put this another way, in physics it is agreed that a physicist should only refer to a physical thing, such as an electron, after he has observed those events which he takes to be the grounds for his being able legitimately to assert, 'Here we have an electron.' That is to say, in the case of an electron, the physicist must observe a certain sort of mark on his oscilloscope screen or look at a laboratory photograph of a particular type of track in a Wilson Cloud Chamber or some such. An *oscilloscope* is a cathode ray oscilloscope, which in turn is a cathode ray tube used as the 'picture tube' (it is the same sort of tube as is found in our television sets) for displaying on its screen the presence of electrons (produced, say, by an electron gun). For the screen luminesces when struck by an electron. A *Wilson Cloud Chamber*, named after the British physicist C. T. R. Wilson (1869–1961), is an apparatus for making the tracks of charged particles, such as an electron, visible. For the chamber contains a cloud of supersaturated vapour which forms droplets of water around any such particle travelling through it.

In similar fashion, a truly physicalist psychologist should only refer to a psychological 'thing', such as a state of excitement, after he has observed those events which he takes to be the grounds for his being able legitimately to assert, 'Here we have a state of excitement.' That is, in the case of excitement, the physicalist psychologist must observe a high pulse rate, an agitation of movement, a vehement tone of voice, and a failure to respond adequately to certain questions.

When I first came across it, I was surprised to learn that Carnap took an avid interest in graphology or the alleged science of predicting a person's personality from a scrutiny of his or her handwriting. It was like discovering that an eminent astronomer took an interest in astrology or that a professional chemist dabbled in alchemy. But when I thought about it a little more, it seemed perfectly in keeping with Carnap's positivism. For if one could discover definite correlations between, on the one hand, observable characteristics of a person's handwriting, such as certain flourishes at the end of a word or thickness of upstrokes or ways of dotting 'i's or of crossing 't's, and, on the other hand, that same person's psychological characteristics, such as introversion or extroversion, then such a science would be truly positivistic. For, as regards psychological evidence, handwriting would be at the opposite end of the spectrum from the inner, private and subjective evidence of introspection. Indeed handwriting is so non-subjective that the writer of the handwriting under scrutiny might now be dead. Unfortunately, graphology has never lived up to these high expectations.[25]

Strictly speaking, Rudolf Carnap was not particularly interested in philosophy of mind. His work in that area was presented more as a practical demonstration of some reductive theses of logical positivism (particularly, as we have seen, those to do with 'unifying science'). The Oxford philosopher Gilbert Ryle (1900–76), on the other hand, who shared much of the outlook of the positivists, made philosophy of mind the main arena for his philosophical work. Ryle certainly knew the work of the Vienna Circle very well. He had met Schlick at a conference in Oxford in 1930 and was greatly impressed by him. He had also read the official journal of logical positivism, *Erkenntnis*. When

Figure 2.5
The English
philosopher,
Gilbert Ryle,
who is often
regarded as
the most
famous
philosophical
behaviourist.

his student, A. J. Ayer (1910–89), visited the Vienna Circle in
1933, it was on the advice of his teacher, Ryle, and armed with
a letter of introduction from Ryle to Schlick.

There is also no doubt that Ryle shared the anti-Cartesian and
anti-metaphysical views of the logical positivists, and held a view
about the role of philosophy which was similar to their own.
However he did not share the logical positivists' penchant for
peppering their articles with symbolic logic or their love affair

with science, nor did he see much value in their programme of 'unifying science'. Unlike the Viennese logical positivists, but like many British philosophers of that period, Ryle came to philosophy from classics (the study of ancient Greek and Latin language and literature), not from physics or mathematics.

Nevertheless, while definitely not a card-carrying member of logical positivism, nor an acknowledged subscriber to its verification principle, he was very sympathetic to their movement. So it should come as no surprise that he was quite prepared to make the welcoming speech to the Fourth International Congress for Unified Science at Cambridge, in 1938, and to have his Inaugural Address, on his appointment in 1945 to the Waynflete Professorship of Metaphysical Philosophy at Oxford (such a splendidly ironic title for someone with such positivist leanings), reprinted in a volume entitled *Logical Positivism*.[26]

The clearest and most uncompromising account of Ryle's view of the nature and role of philosophy is in his article, 'Systematically Misleading Expressions', published in 1932. Its most famous passage is the following:

> I conclude, then, that there is, after all, a sense in which we can properly enquire and even say 'what it really means to say so and so'. For we can ask what is the real form of the fact recorded when this is concealed or disguised and not duly exhibited by the expression in question. And we can often succeed in stating this fact in a new form of words which does exhibit what the other failed to exhibit. And I am for the present inclined to believe that this is what philosophical analysis is and that this is the sole and whole function of philosophy.[27]

In short, there is here a remarkable similarity to the logical positivist view of philosophy. Ryle gives philosophy no more than a clarificatory role, though this is now expressed as the task of revealing the true facts underlying some purported description or report, when these have been disguised in some way. This task was to be accomplished by recasting the misleading way in which some description or report is expressed, so that the recast version makes clear the underlying facts of the matter. What is missing, when compared to the positivists' version of philosophy's role, is any mention by Ryle of this task applying especially to the statements of science, or to furthering the goal of unifying the sciences, or to the function of saying when something is truly scientific or not. Ryle saw philosophy's subject matter, the statements needing to be recast, as those of philosophy itself when they are expressed in ordinary language and about a wide variety of things.

Because of his occupation of the senior chair of philosophy in Britain, and his editorship of the leading British philosophy journal, *Mind*, for some twenty-five years, Ryle came to exercise enormous influence over philosophy in Britain. His article on the role of philosophy became known as the manifesto of Linguistic Analysis and Ryle as the leading Linguistic Analyst. Eventually the tag 'linguistic analysis' (sometimes 'conceptual analysis' or, less accurately, 'ordinary language philosophy')[28] became attached, somewhat loosely, to philosophy as a whole as practised in Britain in the middle years of the twentieth century.

Just as the logical positivists' view of philosophy led them to embrace a behaviourist view of mind, so did Ryle's 'linguistic analysis' view of philosophy. His *magnum opus*, *The Concept of Mind*, published in 1949, was Ryle's self-proclaimed 'sustained piece of analytical hatchet-work' on the Cartesian dogma of mind and body as 'the ghost in the machine'. True to his principles, Ryle systematically restated the Cartesian account of mind in terms which better displayed the underlying facts. These facts turned out to be, in his view, facts about human behaviour and so his 'systematic restatement' came to be an unusually comprehensive, meticulous and linguistic version of a behaviourist view of mind. By reason of its wit and style and lucidity, *The Concept of Mind* is also unusual in being a very readable work of analytic philosophy and written in a very distinctive, deliberately unacademic, style. As one distinguished reviewer put it, '*Le style, c'est Ryle.*'[29]

In *The Concept of Mind* Ryle began his logico-linguistic attack on Cartesian dualism by introducing the term 'category mistake'. By the term 'category mistake', Ryle meant the mistake of incorrectly assigning some term to one logico-linguistic category or type when in fact it should be assigned to another. Ryle defined a category as 'the set of ways in which it is logically legitimate to operate with [some term]'.[30] Thus it followed on this account that one made a category mistake if one said, for example, 'My pain is green.' For a pain is not the sort of thing which can be green. Feelings, such as pain, are not visible and so cannot be correctly assigned colours. Or, to use Ryle's own well-known example, a foreigner visits Oxford or Cambridge for the first time and is shown around the university. After having seen the colleges, libraries, offices, laboratories and playing fields, the visitor then asks 'But where is the university?' Ryle used a variant of this example in lectures, where another foreigner, having been taken to see a game of cricket at Lords, says, 'I see the pitch, stumps, bat, ball, players, umpires, sight screens and pavilion, but where is the sportsmanship which I hear is so essential to cricket?'[31]

Ryle believed that Cartesian dualism was one large category mistake because it wrongly assigned the terms of our common-sense psychological vocabulary to one logico-linguistic category when they should be assigned to another. For, after careful philosophical analysis, it would be discovered that our mental terms, such as 'mind' or 'thought' or 'belief', are not words which refer to or describe an inner private mental world of faculties with their proprietary activities but, for the most part, are to be analysed as dispositional terms whose meaning depends upon the ordinary observation of ordinary behaviour. For dispositions, according to Ryle, are not inner, or even outer, states of affairs. One does not have a disposition in the way one has an arm or a leg. A disposition is a behaviour pattern. One does not possess a behaviour pattern, one displays it through a number of episodes of behaviour on a number of occasions. Being brittle, for example, is a non-psychological disposition. A piece of Venetian glass is brittle in so far as it, or pieces just like it (with the same chemical composition), breaks very easily, say, when let fall from even a moderate height or when tapped even lightly with a hard object. Being vain is a psychological disposition. One is not vain in so far as, in one's inner private Cartesian mental world, one harbours something called 'a belief that I am the most beautiful person in the world'. Rather a person is said to be vain if she is given to turning every conversation around to the topic of her own beauty compared with that of others or if, whenever the opportunity arises, she always preens herself in front of a mirror. To give another example of a psychological disposition, Ryle's own well-known example, a hypocrite is not someone who believes one thing secretly in the inner sanctum of his Cartesian mind but speaks and behaves in a manner which gives the lie to that belief. A hypocrite must be defined entirely in terms of publicly observable behaviour. A hypocrite is, as Ryle put it, the avowed atheist who secretly goes to church in another village.

To even the most 'inner' and 'private', and so the most

Cartesian of mental activities, Ryle gave an unblinking behaviourist analysis. Thus imagining is not to be explained as the production of mental images or pictures in one's head. Imagining is typically an outward performance, such as when a boxer, by shuffling his feet and plying his fists in this afternoon's shadowboxing, imagines how the fight will go this evening. To take another example, to introspect is not to observe inwardly, in some non-sensuous manner with our inner 'mind's eyes', some item in our own streams of consciousness. Rather, it is to 'retrospect' in an act of remembering some behaviour of our own, covert or public, which we have perceived in the past with our ordinary 'outer' senses, and then to make some overall dispositional claims about what we have been able to recall. Indeed, notoriously, Ryle asserted in *The Concept of Mind* that 'the sorts of things that I can find out about myself are the same as the sorts of things that I can find out about other people, and the methods of finding them out are much the same.'[32]

Ryle's view of mind, then, was that there was no mind, if by 'mind' you meant some inner, private, Cartesian world of consciousness where special 'faculties', such as those of the intellect and will, were activated from time to time and influenced the body in which they dwelt. Nor was there any mind, if by 'mind' you meant any sort of non-material entity that exists and performs actions and has experiences and a history of its own, in the way that a body exists and performs actions and has experiences and a history of its own. A mind is not a special sort of thing. That account of mind, he said, was a myth but, nevertheless,

> A myth is, of course, not a fairy story. It is the presentation of facts belonging to one category in the idioms appropriate to another. To explode a myth is accordingly not to deny the facts but to re-allocate them. And this is what I am trying to do.[33]

'Mind', in Ryle's explosion of the myth, is a generic or 'umbrella' term which we apply to a whole bunch of psychological dispositions, which in turn are nothing but ordinary observable pronenesses to behave or react or be inactive in certain ways in certain specifiable circumstances. It is similar in its use to the term 'university'. For the term 'university' is an 'umbrella' term which we apply to a group of buildings, usually on one particular site, their staff and students, and the practices of teaching and learning that go on in them.[34] However, this is not to deny the reality of minds. Minds, just like universities, really exist. It is to deny that minds are anything like what most people, influenced by the Cartesian legacy, think they are like.

'The problem of diffuseness'

Behaviourism, then, in both philosophy and psychology, changed theorising about the mind in a very radical way. In the first place, in effect, it said, look to the objective scientific point of view if you want to produce an objective scientific account of mind. Contrariwise, abandon the subjective unscientific approach which has dominated both philosophy and psychology for so long. The result has been that this 'from the outside looking on' or objective approach has pushed aside the 'from the inside looking in' or subjective approach almost entirely in both contemporary psychology and philosophy of mind.

Behaviourism also made both philosophy and psychology much less anthropocentric. In making the move from animal psychology to human psychology, while at the same time keeping the same methods and the same goals as were deemed appropriate for animal psychology, Watson presented humans as continuous with the other animals. Behaviourists emphasised that we should not let the fact that we humans happen to be the scientific investigators interrupt or spoil the austere, cool, scientific study of the psychology of the human animal. As objects or targets of our own investigations, we humans must be accorded no special status. This still remains one of the norms of modern thought in both psychology and philosophy of mind.

Another major change of stance was behaviourism's abandonment of any concept of mind as an entity residing in or even especially associated with the human head. Unfortunately this went along with a wild swing of the pendulum in the opposite direction. In their explanations and analyses behaviourists refused to make reference to anything, of any sort, that went on inside the human head. References to consciousness and the interior life were simply taboo. At the turn of the nineteenth century, psychology was still the science of the mind, and so the science of what went on in a mind. In that sense it was 'centralist' or 'head-centred'. Behaviourism made both psychology and philosophy of mind 'externalist' or 'behaviour fixated'.

It was this 'externalism', with its close relative, virulent 'anticentralism', that began to reveal the flaws in the behaviourist model of mind. The emphasis of behaviourist explanations and analyses had come down so inflexibly, and more or less exclusively, upon behaviour that both the critics of behaviourism and many behaviourists themselves began to feel that there were just insufficient tools in the behaviourist tool box to repair the flaws. Behaviourists had simply not allowed themselves sufficient explanatory items with which to give adequate explanations of all aspects of our mental life.

One area where this inadequacy caused problems for the psychological behaviourists' account of mind was their account of emotion. At first glance it might be thought that behaviourism could cope more than adequately with emotion. Just as it seems, even now, that many of our psychological characteristics are indeed dispositional in character, so it seemed then that emotions were as well. After all, it does make sense to analyse very many character traits, like shyness or extroversion, in terms of dispositions. A shy person is the one you find sticking to the wall at parties, with face averted, clinging to a half-filled and rarely sipped glass of wine, and leaving early. The extrovert, on the other hand, is the one who is prone to get up and suggest a bout of karaoke singing, who introduces himself to you at even the merest pause in your conversation with someone else, and who is the last to leave unless he has another party to go to. Likewise, when we speak of someone as irascible or affectionate or melancholic or phlegmatic, we seem to be commenting on their emotional life as a disposition to be or do certain things. An irascible person is one disposed to anger; an affectionate person is one disposed to displays of affection; and so on.

The answer is, of course, that some aspects of our emotional life can be given the usual behaviourist treatment in terms of dispositions. An irascible person is indeed someone who is disposed or prone to be angry at the drop of a peanut on the carpet. An affectionate person is someone who is disposed to frequent displays of loving behaviour such as hugs and kisses and compliments. Where the problem comes in, for behaviourism, is in giving an adequate account of how we come to associate this sort of behaviour with anger, and that sort of behaviour with being in love and, more generally, in giving an adequate account of what anger or love or any emotion really is. To quote from the behaviourist college textbook, *The Analysis of Behavior*, by B. F. Skinner and J. G. Holland,

Under different emotional conditions, different events serve as reinforcers [stimuli], and different groups of operants [actions] increase in probability of emission [the likelihood of their appearance].

By these *predispositions* we can (do) define a specific emotion.[35]

Thus

> An *angry* man may pound the table, slam the door, or pick a fight. The angry man is predisposed (more likely) to emit certain operants [to perform certain actions] rather than others.[36]

Unfortunately what a person is predisposed to do when angry will depend on a lot of things. His or her race, gender, age, education, social status and cultural background, to name just a few. So, to define an emotion *x* in terms of the behaviour likely to be displayed by a person in the grip of emotion *x* is going to be a frustrating if not impossible task. For an angry person may not 'pound the table, slam the door, or pick a fight', she may 'very quietly and slowly stand up and move away from the table, close the door with exaggerated care and decline any form of confrontation'. Or the angry person may 'shout a lot, wave his arms about and stumble over his own feet as he tries to get up from the table'. Or the angry person may 'remain seated at the table, make her mouth look like a piece of string and stare with an unblinking gaze at the person who said that women should stay at home'. Or the angry person may display more or less any permutation or combination from the cumulative list of the foregoing possibilities, plus another hundred or more possibilities added.

I presume it is clear by now that any account of anger, or love or hate or envy or jealousy, or any other emotion, merely in terms of some supposedly predictable behaviour pattern is doomed to failure. Matters are just too diffuse. There are just too many possibilities. Besides there is a large amount of 'begging the question', or presuming as part of your argument what you are supposed to be arguing for, lurking in the behaviourist account. For how can a behaviourist even attempt to reduce any list of possibilities by packaging this lot together as, say, angry behaviour, and that lot together as, say, loving behaviour, and that lot together as, say, envious behaviour, without some reason for grouping some bits of behaviour together and not others, and for excluding some behaviour altogether as non-emotional? How does a behaviourist group together 'pounding tables, slamming doors and picking fights' as angry behaviour rather than jealous behaviour or a display of hate? Or, for that matter, how can a behaviourist rule in 'pounding tables, slamming doors and picking fights' as emotional behaviour, but rule out, as not, pounding dough, slamming volleys and picking roses?

The behaviourist cannot say, 'Because I have studied angry people and pounding tables and slamming doors, but not picking roses, is the sort of thing they do.' For that still begs the question. For how could he, the behaviourist, first pick out the group labelled 'angry people'? He could not have done so behaviouristically, because that method was not yet available. For that is the very method he is now trying to put in place. He could not have referred to the context, because that is only associated with any particular emotion in so far as it is liable (or disposed) to stimulate the batch of behaviour associated with that emotion. Finally, he could not have done it in any other way because, as a card-carrying behaviourist, he has sworn to refrain from including in his explanatory kit anything else besides behaviour (the response) and the context (the stimulus, with its effect of being either positive or negative reinforcement).

I do not think that there is any way out here for the behaviourist. The behaviourist cannot solve this problem of the diffuseness of the behaviour we associate with particular emotions. Though this is another story, it is now accepted that, without 'begging any questions', you cannot differentiate one emotion from another, or emotions from non-emotions, without reference to 'cognitions', that is, to what the subject of the emotion (the person undergoing the emotion) is believing and also how he (or she) is evaluating the situation in which he finds himself in relation to himself (his own goals and needs, etc.).[37]

Curiously, the founder of behaviourism, Watson, had a much stronger hand, than did later behaviourists who followed Skinner, when attempting to give an explanation of emotions behaviouristically. For Watson allowed, as a legitimate sort of explanation, reference to such 'centralist' goings-on as patterns of physiological changes, especially those of an aroused sort which occurred in the viscera (or abdominal organs). Thus Watson followed William James's account of emotion to a certain extent.[38] For William James had said that an emotion was the feeling or sensation, in the subject's stream of consciousness, of the visceral or other physiological changes associated with emotional states. We feel sad because we weep (in certain specifiable circumstances). We

[Digital reconstruction © Phillip Prodger and Daniel Hillman.]

Figure 2.6
An illustration from Darwin's *The
Expression of the Emotions in Man and Animals*
showing some of the variety and intricacy of
human expressions of emotions.

do not weep because we feel sad. For sadness is the recording, in consciousness, of the preceding physiological states, namely the flow of tears from the tear ducts, the diminution of the pulse rate, and so on. To take another example, according to James we feel excited because the adrenaline (one of the body's hormones which stimulates the nervous system) is flowing, and in consequence our pulse rate and respiration rate have increased. The feeling of excitement is nothing but the reflection or record in our stream of consciousness of the bodily perturbations (the increase in pulse rate and respiration rate) that the increase in adrenaline gave rise to.

Watson, in effect, took this latter explanation as the model for emotion and then simply ruled out of court, as he was bound to by his own principles, any reference to consciousness. Thus an emotion like excitement became, for Watson, just the pattern of physiological changes, not its reflection in consciousness. This made emotional states scientifically observable, if not by students of behaviour, then at least by physiologists. It was this allowance of so much room to physiology that made later behaviourists nervous and made them try to give purely behaviouristic accounts. If they did not, they felt, the precious autonomy of psychology, as a science on its own, was at risk.

In the final analysis this early version of a behaviourist account fared no better than did the later more purely behaviouristic accounts. For the Watsonian account was open to investigation by physiologists and was found wanting. It was simply not possible to find sufficient differences in the visceral and other physiological patterns present during emotional states such that one could then go on and distinguish emotions physiologically. Besides, as with the more purely behaviouristic accounts, a 'begging of the question' was soon apparent. How does one decide, without 'begging the question' and without being simply arbitrary, which physiological patterns are to be grouped together as emotion x and which as emotion y?[39]

'The problem of privacy'

'The problem of diffuseness' illustrated the problems that arose through behaviourism's fixation on behaviour. For it was the problem of how to select and confine and neatly package what was intractably diffuse. Its obverse is 'the problem of privacy', for this illustrates the problems that arose through behaviourism's refusal to make any mention of inner, private, non-behavioural, mental events. 'The problem of privacy' is the problem any baptised behaviourist has in giving an account of, or even acknowledging the existence of, wholly 'centralised' and wholly non-behavioural mental events such as thinking to oneself, doing mental arithmetic, imagining, composing a tune in one's head, and so on. To their credit both psychological and philosophical behaviourists were well aware of this problem and confronted it openly and honestly. However, as we shall see in due course, neither was able to provide a convincing solution and, without much qualification, it can be said that it was above all this 'problem of privacy' which forced both philosophers, generally speaking fairly rapidly, and psychologists, on the whole very reluctantly, to move on to a new account of mind.

As far back as 1914, in his well-known response to Watson's behaviourist manifesto, entitled 'On "Psychology as the Behaviourist Views It"', the introspectionist psychologist and former pupil of Wundt, E. B. Titchener hinted at this problem when he wrote that

> Behaviorism would be . . . within its logical rights in assuming that all central processes [such as consciously imagining, thinking or remembering] may be transformed into peripheral [external behavioural ones]: given Watson's premises, they must be so transformed.[40]

Titchener then went on to hint that this programme of transforming all 'centralist processes' into 'peripheral processes' was unlikely to be successful. For how, for example, can a behaviourist give a convincing peripheral, behavioural account of so wholly centralised a mental process as thinking to oneself? For when a person is thinking to himself, he may not be engaging in any sort of behaviour at all. He may be immobile. Moreover he may be completely indifferent to or even unaware of his surroundings. Thinking to oneself or doing mental arithmetic or composing a tune in one's head seems to be as completely non-behavioural and purely cerebral an act as you can get. So how could it be 'transformed' into behaviour of any sort?

In his paper, 'Is Thinking merely the Action of Language Mechanisms?', of 1920,[41] Watson confronted this problem in a typically ingenious way. He created a halfway house which was 'sort of centralist' but was also 'sort of behavioural'. Watson argued that there was a form of 'centralist behaviour' which must be what was involved in such acts as thinking to oneself. Thinking, he suggested, was paradigmatically 'internal truncated speech'. Just as, say, when you are now conversing, you move your lips and tongue and vocal chords and larynx, and voice your thoughts to someone else, so, when you are thinking but keeping your thoughts to yourself, you must be, as it were, conversing with yourself subvocally. As the talking is subvocal, it will involve movements in the main organs of speech, such as the tongue and larynx, most probably, but will not engage the lips, vocal chords or other bits and pieces needed for vocalisation. In that sense it is 'truncated' or 'implicit' speech. Of course, if you are a sign-language 'speaker', thinking would have to be analysed as a truncated or cut-down version of the arm- and finger-movements associated with using sign-language. Or, if there are people who are given overmuch to writing, they may think to themselves in the 'movements involved in writing'. As Watson himself put it:

> Thinking would comprise then the subvocal use of any language or related material whatever, such as the implicit repetition of poetry, day dreaming, rephrasing word processes in logical terms, running over the day's events verbally, as well as implicit planning for the morrow and the verbal working out of difficult life situations. The term 'verbal' here must be made broad enough to cover processes substitutable for verbal activity, such as the shrug of the shoulder and the lifting of the brows. It must embrace the implicit movements involved in written words or the implicit movements demanded in the use of the deaf-and-dumb sign manual, which are, in essence, word activity. Thinking then might become our general term to cover all subvocal activity.[42]

Unfortunately for Watson, such an hypothesis was easily tested experimentally, and the results proved disappointing. In their monumental compendium, *Experimental Psychology*, the American psychologists Robert Woodworth and Harold Schlosberg described the experiments designed to test the 'thinking is movements in the muscles of speech' part of Watson's theory, which was after all its central part. They described first the early experiments involving the attachment of the thinker's tongue to a mechanical tambour and lever system. They then described the later, more sophisticated, experiments involving the amplification and recording, by a rapid galvanometer (an instrument for detecting, comparing or measuring small electric currents), of the electrical currents given off by the movements of the muscles associated with speech. Then they described the results of both sorts of experiments in the following sentence, 'As to speech *movements*, the evidence for their always being present during thinking is not convincing.'[43]

In *Science and Human Behaviour*, first published in 1953,[44] B. F. Skinner began his account of 'inner private mental events' by, somewhat half-heartedly, repeating Watson's 'classical solution' to 'the problem of privacy' in terms of movements in the muscles of speech (or in the equivalent muscles for sign-language and writing). He repeated Watson's 'solution' because he felt that, in the future, better experimental equipment might produce new results which supported it. His only other addition seemed to be his suggestion that subjects come to have direct knowledge of the movements of their muscles of speech, and so have direct knowledge of their own thoughts, by means of their proprioceptive feelings of them, that is, by means of their having sensations of these muscular movements. If anything, this seems to add a Cartesian tinge to Watson's account, for it makes crucial reference to internal conscious episodes, namely to sensations.

Realising that Watson's account had not worn well, and in keeping with his own radical 'ultra-peripheral [externalist]' behaviourism, Skinner offered a novel account of his own which referred only to ordinary 'outer' behaviour. Skinner suggested that in many cases an alleged inner mental event, such as, say, someone's planning or deciding or intending to do something, is really just a case of that person summing up a number of behavioural clues about himself and then predicting his own immediate action on the basis of that summary. For example, according to Skinner, when someone is planning or intending to go home from his office at five past six in the evening, then all that has really occurred is captured by a behaviourist's 'describing a history of variables which would enable an independent observer to describe the behaviour in the same way if a knowledge of the variables were available to him'.[45] Without the jargon, this means that for a person to say, for example, that he is planning or intending to go home is not to report on some inner conscious mental event but *to make a self-prediction* about his immediate future actions based on a comparison between his present and his past behaviour. The self-prediction is that he himself will go home soon because he has just caught himself looking at the clock, then putting his working papers neatly in a folder, putting his pen in its holder, and then getting up and fetching his jacket from the coat hanger. For he has coupled these observations with his memory that, on previous occasions when he looked at the clock, put away his pen and papers, and fetched his jacket, he went home more or less immediately afterwards.

There are a number of implausible consequences for such an account of inner mental events. For a start, it means that, even to talk knowledgeably about our own intentions, plans and decisions, we have to be fairly alert and sophisticated detectives. We have to hunt out behavioural clues about ourselves, put them together in a relevant way, and then, with the help of our memories, discover exactly what it was we did when we last exhibited just such behaviour, or perhaps something relevantly similar to it, in just such circumstances, or circumstances relevantly similar to it. Given that we can often tell someone more or less immediately, and before we have even thought of putting away our papers and pens, what we are intending to do in the next half hour, this Byzantine account seems quite implausible.

Another difficulty for this Skinnerian analysis is that, quite simply, it could not supply any account at all of anyone's quite novel plan or intention. If I suddenly decide, at five o'clock today, to tell the boss that I am quitting my job, after forty years in the department, and having never previously been involved in resigning from this or any other job, then there could be no past clues as to what I am now about to do. So, on Skinner's account, I myself could not know what I myself intended to do. Indeed, when I went to tell the boss I was resigning, I would be as surprised as my boss.

Finally this self-inspecting and self-predicting Inspector Morse analysis does not really come to grips with 'the problem of privacy'. For Skinner's self-predictions are only possible on the basis of clues garnered from a scrutiny of current behaviour. But 'the problem of privacy' is precisely the problem, for behaviourists, of giving an account of thinking when *no behaviour* is currently going on.

When the objections I have been outlining above, or variants of them, were put to Skinner in 1984, in a special Skinner retrospective issue of *The Behavioral and Brain Sciences*, Skinner admitted that his 'solution' to 'the problem of privacy' was 'far from adequate'.[46]

Gilbert Ryle was also greatly exercised by 'the problem of

Figure 2.7
The French
sculptor,
Auguste
Rodin's *Le
Penseur*.
Gilbert Ryle
famously
asked, 'What
is he doing?'

privacy'. He called it 'the problem of what *Le Penseur* is doing'.
For *Le Penseur* was Rodin's famous bronze statue of 'The
Thinker', which depicts the thinker, seated in something like a
crouched position, with his chin on his hand, pondering deeply
while quite oblivious to his surroundings. So oblivious that he has
forgotten to put his clothes on. Ryle granted that this problem

was one that he had dealt with quite inadequately in *The Concept of Mind*, and so he spent a great deal of the last two decades of his life trying to solve it.

Before seeing Ryle's attempt at solving this problem, it is important to see his 'regular' account of thinking. In a classical behaviourist manner, Ryle took, as the paradigm case of thinking, certain public episodes, such as talking the class through a philosophical problem in a seminar or doing mathematics with pen and paper or composing a tune by humming it out loud. His contribution was to say that thinking was not an additional, inner, secret activity, standing behind or above or below some public activity, such as speaking or writing or humming. Thinking was that public activity done in a certain careful, attentive, controlled and self-correcting way. Thinking was not a secret inner episode of problem-solving, which one did first and then, if suitable circumstances arose, published in speech or in bouts of humming or via the making of marks on paper. It was simply the modification of some quite ordinary public activity. It was merely the manner in which the public activity was done. To think was to do something thinkingly.

He then extended this adverbial account of thinking to activities which we would not normally associate with thought. Thus the driver who is carefully threading her way through the traffic, and the tennis player who, realising that his top-spin second serve is getting hammered by the receiver, tries a flat second serve, and the shadow boxer practising new combinations in front of the mirror would all be examples of thinking according to Ryle's analysis.

He also cautioned anyone attempting to give an account of a mental act, such as thinking, that it was strewn with linguistic traps. Sometimes, because of the idioms we use, we confuse our ability deliberately to refrain from or to inhibit outer activity, with the presence of inner Cartesian episodes. To take just one example, one person on a walking tour talks all the time, saying such things as, 'Look at that mountain! Isn't it beautiful! It reminds me of the week we spent in Switzerland when we . . .' Though his companion also notices the mountain, and hears his comments, she keeps quiet or just nods her head. In referring to this second person, quite naturally we might say something like, 'She's keeping her thoughts to herself.' But, Ryle suggested, if taken literally, this description is very misleading. For she has not been engaged in inner mental processing, she has merely refrained from voicing her opinions.

However Ryle realised that neither of these moves provides any obvious solution to the problem of what *Le Penseur* is doing. For, on the one hand, *Le Penseur* is not engaging in public activity, so his thinking cannot be a modification of that sort of activity. On the other hand, *Le Penseur* cannot readily be described as merely inhibiting or deliberately refraining from some activity that a bystander might have expected in the circumstances, for he is totally disengaged from his surroundings or circumstances. Yet *Le Penseur* is clearly up to something because, some twenty minutes later, he may produce, say, a new geometrical theorem or a new sonnet or a new partita for solo flute.

If he was to analyse *Le Penseur*'s thinking as adverbial, as he was committed to doing, it seemed as if Ryle had to nominate some inner activity which was done thinkingly. Ryle resisted the 'muscular' movement suggestion of Watson's, and would not even have given the time of day to any suggestion that inside *Le Penseur*'s head were conscious activities. For to make that move would have appeared to Ryle like backsliding into Cartesianism. So what Ryle eventually came up with was a failure of nerve, a failure to be explicit about what exactly *Le Penseur* was doing when he was said to be thinking.

In a conversation with the philosopher, broadcaster and one-time Labour politician in Britain, Brian Magee, on BBC radio during the winter of 1970–1, Ryle suddenly found himself facing a 'finals' *viva voce* examination in philosophical behaviourism, focusing on the question of what exactly *Le Penseur* was doing. Following an earlier exchange in the dialogue, a contemplative Pythagoras had been substituted for *Le Penseur*. The dialogue went as follows:

MAGEE: . . . So Mr Pythagoras carries on with solving his problem but without doing any more muttering. It's perfectly conceivable that he might stop muttering without stopping thinking.

RYLE: Certainly, certainly. But what he's going on doing 'in his head', if anything, will be, so to speak, some '*As if*' muttering, or something like it . . .

MAGEE: But aren't you making the mistake you've spent so much of your life combatting? You're now suggesting

> that even if he's [Pythagoras's] not doing any
> actual muttering he's bound to go on doing some
> ghostly [Cartesian] muttering.

RYLE: Ah, but even if, what may not be the case, he does
do some 'As-if' muttering in his head, I don't think
this is ghostly. Whatever the right account may be
of seeing things in the mind's eye, or of 'As-if'
muttering things, so to speak, on the mind's tongue,
I don't think it produces an any more ghostly story
than, as I think I hinted in the book [*The Concept
of Mind*], does the difference between one person
who is asleep, and another person who is pretending
to be asleep. . . . Roughly he [the person pretending
to be asleep] just deliberately *doesn't*, for the
duration of the pretence, act, look or sound like
waking people act, look and sound. . . . Well, I think
the same sort of story, though it won't quite do as it
stands, is that Pythagoras, if he's, so to speak,
muttering on the tip of his mind's tongue, is rather
like the person who isn't asleep, but is pretending to
be asleep; the same *sort* of story will do, I hope, and
it doesn't involve any ghostly '*something else as
well*'.[47]

This hesitant and hedging 'explanation' of what *Le Penseur* or
Pythagoras was doing, in terms of 'As-if' and 'so to speak'
mutterings with the 'tips of mind's tongues', and as a form of
pretence which merely involves carefully abstaining from ordinary expected behaviour, did not satisfy even Ryle himself. How
could it be satisfying, for no one is going to accept that *Le
Penseur*'s or Pythagoras's private but laborious production of a
new theorem or sonnet or partita was just a pretence of some
sort or just an abstention from behaviour.

The 'big book', about what *Le Penseur* was doing, never
emerged. As Ryle himself put it, 'the big thing I haven't got is the
peg on which to hang them [the philosophical clothing of this
account]'.[48] His missing peg was, of course, some non-ghostly
but also non-public activity on which to hang *Le Penseur*'s or
Pythagoras's adverbial mode of thinking. What became clear was
that behaviourism had sat its examinations and had failed in a
number of areas. In particular it had failed to solve 'the problem
of privacy'. As a result, as we shall see in the next chapter, the

pendulum swung firmly back to a 'centralist' position but this time to an uncompromisingly non-Cartesian account of 'centralist' activities, such as thinking.

There were, of course, other problems besetting behaviourism besides 'the problem of diffuseness' and 'the problem of privacy'. I selected those two for discussion because they were the most salient in regard to the mind–body debate in the twentieth century. Another well-known problem was that which the American philosopher and linguist Noam Chomsky (1928–) drew attention to, in 1959, in his now justly famous review of B. F. Skinner's book *Verbal Behavior*. A classical behaviourist account of why a particular speaker said what he said must always be in terms of stimulus and response. The *stimulus* is the context, including its influence, on previous occasions, as either positively or negatively reinforcing in regard to a particular response. The *response* is the word or words spoken or, as Skinner preferred to say, emitted.

In a dialectical move, similar to the one that was outlined when discussing 'the problem of diffuseness', Chomsky demonstrates the problems a Skinnerian behaviourist account has in framing any general law, and so in predicting, what someone will say. He takes the example of someone viewing a Dutch painting. Chomsky points out that if a person stood in front of a Dutch painting and looked at it, he might say 'Dutch'. On the other hand, he might not, as Chomsky gleefully pointed out:

> Suppose instead of saying *Dutch* we had said *Clashes with the wallpaper, I thought you liked abstract work, Never saw it before, Tilted, Hanging too low, Beautiful, Hideous, Remember our camping trip last summer?*, or whatever else might come into our minds when looking at a picture . . .[49]

Chomsky's point is that neither Skinner nor anyone else will get very far in framing general laws about, or in trying to predict, what a person standing in front of a painting will say, without taking into account such things as the observer's interests, beliefs and present intentions. But, of course, references to interests, beliefs and intentions are forbidden to a behaviourist.

In that same review, Chomsky went on to make a more general and more fundamental point. The crux of this point is that speaking a language is a very creative task. When even a child of, say, five or six years old speaks his or her native language, that child will produce sentences in a very creative way. He or she will put together words in a way that he or she has never put them together before, and in ways that he or she has never heard anyone else put them together before. On the other hand, behaviourist accounts of language acquisition and competence are based on such concepts as stimulus, response, control, habit, disposition, conditioning and reinforcement; concepts that leave no room for creativity.

It would be wrong to finish this discussion of behaviourism on a completely negative note. A lot had been gained during the reign of behaviourism. The objective, scientific standpoint was to become the norm for almost all future accounts of mind in both philosophy and psychology. Seeing human psychology against the background of the evolution of animal life was also to become a permanent part of the background for future discussions about the nature of the human mind. In keeping with the aims of the logical positivists, future psychology and philosophy of mind were to make an ever more intimate alliance with science, in particular with the brain sciences. The 'linguistic turn', so central to philosophical behaviourism, also maintained a strong grip on almost all future philosophical work on the mind. For example, the logic of the dispositional accounts of philosophical behaviourism were, with modifications, to become an integral part of the logic of many future philosophical accounts of mind, such as those of the identity theorists, and of psychology's accounts of personality and of some mental illnesses. And, to take another example, the status of our ordinary commonsense psychological descriptions, our 'folk psychology' as it came to be called, was to become a central topic in philosophy of mind.

So, while behaviourism was about to be left behind, it left more than bad memories in those that came after. Wittingly or unwittingly, almost all future psychology and philosophy of mind drew upon the legacy of behaviourism and its positivist precursors.

CHAPTER THREE

Nothing but the Brain

New knowledge about the brain

Figure 3.1
Galvani's
experiments
on frogs
suggested that
electrical
impulses
played a role
in initiating
muscular
motion.

I dissected and prepared a frog, and placed it on a table, on
which was an electrical machine [a machine for producing
electricity] widely removed from its conductor and separated
by no brief interval. When by chance one of those who were
assisting me gently touched the point of a scalpel to the medial
crural [mid-thigh] nerves of this frog, immediately all the muscles of the limbs seemed to be so contracted that they appeared
to have fallen into violent tonic convulsions. But another of the
assistants, who was on hand when I did electrical experiments,
seemed to observe that the same thing occurred whenever a
spark was discharged from the conductor of the machine.[1]

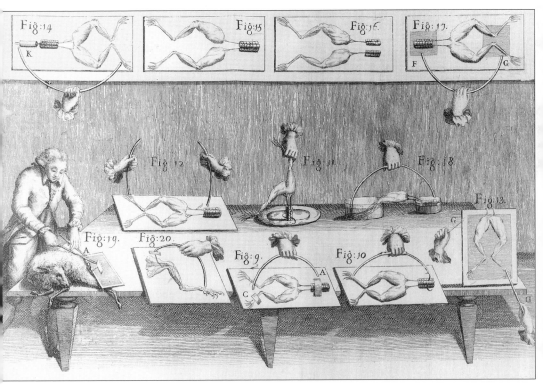

This morning in our Hospital of Saint Ursula, in which the Professor of Surgery is the learned and my most distinguished colleague Doctor Gaspar Gentili, excellent master of surgery, I tested, with my customary devices, an amputated leg and arm, immediately after the operation, in the presence of the aforesaid professor and other physicians and men of learning, and the flexor muscles of the thumb and of the adjacent digits [fingers] were seen to contract, both of the hand and of the foot, and in consequence the aforesaid digits to move . . . Therefore the existence of animal electricity seems proved, and its law in man also proposed.[2]

The experimental work described in the above two extracts could be said to mark the foundation of modern neurophysiology, as it is the very first experimental demonstration of the electrical nature of our neural system. The work was undertaken by the Italian Luigi Galvani (1737–98), who was Professor of Anatomy at the University of Bologna from 1762 to almost the end of the eighteenth century, and was made known to the world in 1791 in his *Commentary on the Effect of Electricity on Muscular Motion*. In that work Galvani described in great detail his discovery of what he called 'animal electricity', namely the fact that the movements of muscles (in his initial experiments, in frogs) are in an important respect electrical in nature. He found not merely that he could measure this electrical current with an instrument, which he himself invented and to which his name was eventually given, the galvanometer, but that he could also induce movements in muscles by introducing, via a thin conducting wire or electrode, an electric current of roughly the same magnitude as the frog's nervous system itself produced.

Throughout the nineteenth century the human brain and the central nervous system were a major object of research for physiologists. France, in particular, became a major centre of research into the functions of the various parts of the brain (usually, via experiments on the brains of animals). In 1811, for example, Julien Legallois, a French surgeon, found that an injury to a part of the brain stem, the *medulla oblongata* (literally 'the oblong-shaped, innermost part'), interfered with breathing. In experiments around 1822, François Magendie, Professor of Anatomy in the Collège de France, discovered the distinction between afferent nerves (or nerves that transmitted electrical impulses from the periphery of the central nervous system to the brain)

Figure 3.2
The eighteenth-century Italian scientist, Luigi Galvani, who discovered the electrical nature of human neurophysiology.

and efferent ones (which operated in the opposite direction). Around 1824, Pierre Flourens discovered that an important function of the *cerebellum* (meaning literally 'little brain' and situated below and to the back of the main bulk of the brain) was to enable a person, or animal, to keep his balance and control his movements.

More intriguing, from the point of view of those interested in the nature of the 'higher' brain functions, associated especially

Figure 3.3
The nineteenth-century French surgeon, Pierre-Paul Broca, who made important discoveries in regard to the areas of the brain associated with the production of speech.

with a human's mental life, was the work of the French surgeon Pierre-Paul Broca (1824–80). He engaged in a study of patients who suffered from *aphasia* (or *aphemia*, as Broca himself called it), that is, the inability either to speak or to understand speech or both. One result of his work was that, in 1861, he was able to pinpoint the lower frontal lobe area of the left hemisphere of the human brain as the area associated with the organisation and control of the muscles of speech. That is to say, he found the area of the brain that had overall control over the movements of, in particular, the lips, tongue and larynx during speech. This area is still known today as 'Broca's brain' and *motor aphasia*, or the speech impairment associated with a breakdown in the control of the movements in the muscles of speech, is still associated with this area. Broca's most famous patient was nicknamed 'Tan', because, owing to brain damage, 'tan-tan' were the only syllables he was able to utter.

It may be useful, at this juncture, to point out that brains are divided into two parts or 'hemispheres'. In humans, certain areas of the left hemisphere alone are, almost always and almost entirely, associated with the production and understanding of language and quasi-linguistic systems. The right hemisphere (in right-handed people) is capable of some simple (say, single-word) language comprehension but otherwise it has little or no part to play in the production or understanding of speech or writing or quasi-linguistic systems. The only other animals with such a specialised left hemisphere are birds, where the left hemisphere is associated with the production and understanding of bird song.

Figure 3.4
The brain's
hemispheres,
as seen from
above.

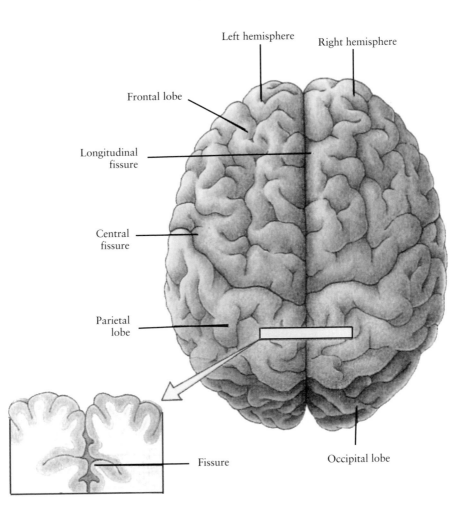

The twin of Broca's discovery was that made by Karl Wernicke (1848–1905), the German neurologist and psychiatrist, who became Professor of Neurology at the University of Breslau in Germany, in the 1870s. He found that an area in the rear portion of the temporal lobe of the left hemisphere was associated with the function of understanding speech, either one's own or someone else's. This area is still known today as 'Wernicke's area' and is still associated with what has become known (somewhat misleadingly) as *sensory aphasia* or the speech impairment associated with the inability to choose the correct words or to put words in their correct order when speaking or the inability to understand the speech of others. In severe cases of damage to Wernicke's area, say because of a 'stroke' (or damage to the brain caused, say, by rupture or clotting of blood vessels), a patient's speech might become an imcomprehensible jumble of words.

As the nineteenth century became the twentieth, new instrumentation accelerated the process of mapping the brain's structures and functions. These in turn produced yet more knowledge about the brain. For example, galvanometers became so sophisticated that they formed the basis for the new comprehensive 'electrical maps' of the brain or electroencephalograms. The electroencephalograph,[3] which produces the electroencephalogram or EEG, registers the difference in 'electric potential' (that is, the electromotive force or voltage) at various points on the scalp, which differences arise as a result of the small currents produced by a working brain. The resulting map is thus an 'electrical map' of the brain. Subsequently, such mapping ability has enabled neuroscientists to identify the particular 'brain waves' associated with various states of the whole person, such as, for example, those associated with sleep or with some group of emotions.

Then came the discovery of techniques for 'fixing' (preserving in a stable condition) and 'staining' (highlighting by colour) very thin slices of brain tissue, prepared by the newly invented microtomes (or refined brain 'meat slicers'). The pioneers in this work of 'staining' were the Italian Camillo Golgi (1843–1926), and the Spaniard Santiago Ramòn y Cajal (1852–1934), who both, initially, used the method of selectively 'black staining', with silver nitrate, individual nerve cells.[4]

Once 'fixed' and 'stained', the fine slices of brain tissue were ready for scrutiny by using the newly invented achromatic microscopes, and, eventually, the electron microscope. The pioneers in the invention of the achromatic microscope were the German Carl Zeiss (1816–88) and the Englishman Joseph Jackson Lister (1786–1869). An achromatic microscope is one that employs an achromatic lens. An achromatic lens is, strictly, a pair of lenses whereby a flint-glass lens corrects the light dispersion arising from an optical-glass lens (that is, a lens made from 'crown glass' or glass with potassium or barium substituted for sodium). Such a lens system, being free from the 'coloured fringes' associated with the prism-like dispersion (or *diffraction*) of light, gives a very clear outline. An electron microscope was the first microscope that did not operate via the reflection of light waves from the object of inspection, via lenses, to the eye. Instead an electron microscope operates via the 'scattering' or deflection of electrons accelerated through the object held in a vacuum, and focused, not by lenses, but by magnets. The result of this process only becomes visible to the observing scientist when the scattered electrons hit a screen and fluoresce. The 'resolving' (or magnifying) power of an electron microscope is about two hundred times better than anything achieved by light microscopy. 'Staining' also occurs in electron microscopy, but this time, not in order to achieve greater visibility, but to achieve more determinate electron scattering. Thus the 'stains' are usually the salts of heavy metals.

Cajal himself was the first to map the detailed structure of an individual nerve cell or 'neurone', and so make clear that it comprised a branch-like tracery or series of 'dendrites' at one end (the receiving end), a central cell nucleus, and a cable-like tail or 'axon' at the other end (the transmitter end). Strictly speaking, nerve cells come in different shapes and sizes – sometimes, for example, with a very short axon, sometimes with a very long one, sometimes with an average size one. The size and shape of the neurone depends on its location and function.

Cajal also discovered that nerve-currents travel in only one direction, from dendrites via nuclei (usually but not always) to axons. Then, usually, this axon connects with other neurones via their dendrites, so that the electrical impulse or signal is carried forward, selectively, through certain neuronal pathways of the nervous system.

The English physiologist Sir Charles Sherrington (1857–1952), was one of those who greatly admired Cajal's work, and was instrumental in inviting Cajal to deliver the prestigious Croonian

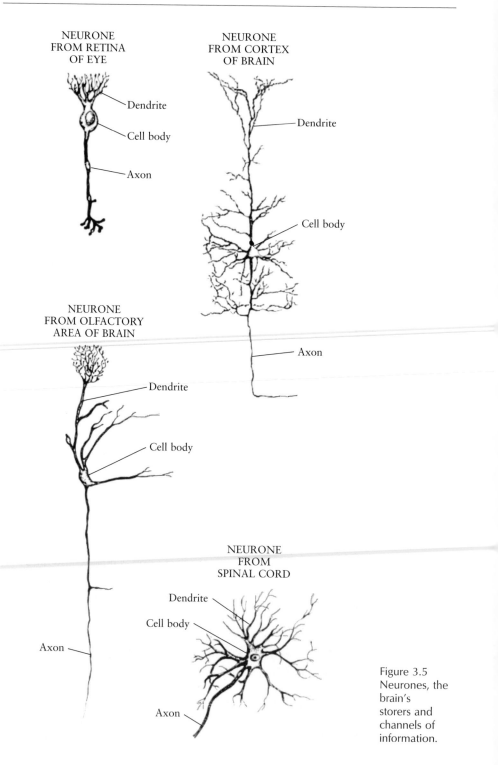

NEURONE
FROM RETINA
OF EYE

Dendrite

Cell body

Axon

NEURONE
FROM CORTEX
OF BRAIN

Dendrite

Cell body

Axon

NEURONE
FROM OLFACTORY
AREA OF BRAIN

Dendrite

Cell body

Axon

NEURONE
FROM
SPINAL CORD

Dendrite

Cell body

Axon

Figure 3.5
Neurones, the
brain's
storers and
channels of
information.

Lecture of the Royal Society in 1894. His own work can be seen as building upon Cajal's pioneering investigations. Sherrington was especially interested in mapping 'the larger picture' or aspects of the whole nervous system. In particular he investigated the 'reflex arcs' or the automatic periphery-to-centre-and-back-again loops. When such an arc or loop is activated, the afferent

Figure 3.6 The English physiologist, Sir Charles Sherrington, who made important discoveries about the integrative action of the nervous system.

nerves of some sensory system (such as, say, that of touch) carry an electrical signal from the body's periphery to the centre, say from the foot to the brain, and then, immediately, automatically and swiftly, the brain, via the spinal cord, sends back a 'summated' electrical signal (or summarised signal from a bundle of them) to the appropriate muscles of the body so that a foot movement ensues. Thus, for example, a cat that stands on a sharp stone or spike will immediately, automatically and swiftly, that is, reflexly, withdraw its paw.[5]

The next major series of advances in neuroscience might be described as chemical rather than electrical. For example, in the 1920s and 1930s, the English physiologist and pharmacologist Sir Henry Dale (1875–1968) and the German pharmacologist Otto Loewi (1873–1961) led research teams that discovered the importance of the brain's 'chemical transmitters'. In 1936 Dale and Loewi jointly shared a Nobel Prize for that research. In particular, they discovered that a chemical transmitter (such as, say, *noradrenaline* or *acetylcholine*) was always an essential part of the bridging mechanism that enables one neurone to transmit its electrical impulse to another and so form the basis of that immensely large and complex information network which is the brain. When an electrical impulse arrives at the end-point of an *axon*, it is transmitted (either as an inhibitor or stimulant of further impulses) to the next neurone, usually (but not always) at its *dendrite*, via a chemically-operated junction system or *synapse*. These various 'chemical operators' are the brain's *neurotransmitters*. These discoveries, along with others, such as the importance of the chemicals sodium and potassium in generating the neurone's electrical impulses, emphasised that the brain was not so much an 'electrical engine' as an 'electro-chemical system'.

From the point of view of psychology and philosophy of mind, two of the most astonishing series of experiments of more recent times arose out of the treatment of patients with epilepsy. The first series is associated with the neurologist Wilder Penfield (1891–1976), a onetime student of Sherrington's at Oxford. In 1934 he founded the now world-famous Montreal Neurological Institute at McGill University. The Institute was remarkable in integrating its activities as a neurological hospital with multidisciplinary research into the brain. While at the Institute in Montreal, Penfield spent some twenty-five years treating epileptic patients by means of the surgical excision of those parts of the brain that had been rendered prone to cause epileptic seizures

Figure 3.7
The American
neurosurgeon,
Wilder Penfield,
who made
important
advances in
the surgical
treatment of
epilepsy.

through prior damage by disease. An epileptic seizure, at least in the case of major ones (or *grand mal*), takes the form of a severe convulsion (with the limbs going into spasm), which then usually renders the patient comatose for some time afterwards. The attack is almost always also followed by amnesia in regard to the seizure. The seizure itself is thought to be caused by a cerebral 'electrical storm' or severe electrical discharge which then damages further the part of the brain in and around where it occurs. Such an 'electrical storm' seems to arise out of the ordinary electrical activity of the brain when it enters areas previously weakened by some disease.

Part of Penfield's treatment involved an ingenious way of finding out which areas of a patient's brain were those that were prone to cause epileptic seizures. To do this he used the fact that, shortly before a seizure occurred, the person suffering from epilepsy would often report suffering hallucinations, or experiencing a disgusting smell, or being overcome by a strange feeling (called the epileptic 'aura'). He believed that he could isolate the disease-damaged areas, and so those areas which were the likely cause of future epileptic seizures, by introducing into those areas an electrical current that mimicked to a certain extent the brain's own electrical activity. If the result was an 'aura', he knew that he had located the right areas.

Of course, to achieve that result, he needed the patient to be awake during this period of electrical probing, so that he or she could report if and when the hallucinations or strange smells or feelings occurred. As the brain can be probed with electrodes, or for that matter cut in certain ways, without a patient suffering any pain, most patients readily agreed to this probing.

Penfield reported that some of the results of his electrical probings, especially in the area of the temporal lobes, astonished even himself. He mentioned some of these results in his Sherrington Lectures delivered at the University of Liverpool in January 1957, and subsequently published as *The Excitable Cortex in Conscious Man* in 1958.

One of the early cases in 1938 was that of M.G., a young French Canadian woman of 16, who complained of seizures that were ushered in by hearing a song, a lullaby her mother had often sung to her, 'Hush a bye, my baby –'. There was often what she called a 'dream' in this stage of her attacks, during which she would be in church or in the convent. But always she heard the song.

At operation, when the posterior portion of the superior convolution of the right temporal lobe was stimulated, she gave a little exclamation. Then after the electrode had been withdrawn she said, 'I had a dream. I wasn't here'. After talking with her for a little while, the electrode was reapplied at the same point without her knowledge. She broke off suddenly and said, 'I hear people coming in'. Then she added, 'I hear music now, a funny little piece'. The electrode was kept in place and she became more talkative, saying that the music she was hearing was something she had heard on the radio.

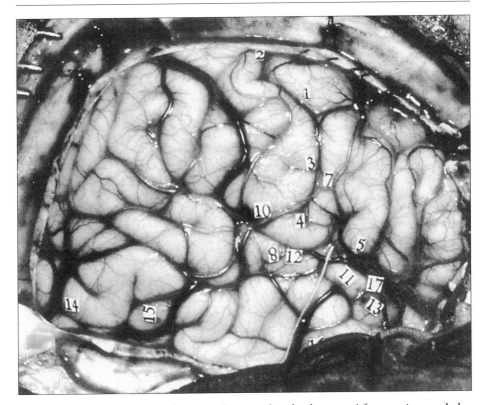

Figure 3.8
One of
Penfield's
experiments
involving
electrical
stimulation of
the brain.

It was the song her mother had sung. After an interval the same point was stimulated, again without warning her. She said, 'Another dream. People coming in –'. In this case we had succeeded in electrical reproduction of the hallucination drawn from her past experience which had, for years, introduced her epileptic seizures.[6]

The important phrase here is 'drawn from her past experiences'. For Penfield remarked that time and time again he found that the 'hallucinations' were made up of elements from the individual's past experiences. In effect, the subjects, while conscious of themselves as in the present, and in the clinic, were not so much recalling, as actually reliving, in a very vivid, if also somewhat fractured, way, certain past experiences. That is why they seemed invariably to think of them as dreams. What is more, these past experiences were not ones that the patient would have been able to relive in this way in normal circumstances. Penfield, it seemed, had tapped directly into the hidden world of lived past experiences. One could even say that a type of time travel, into the past, had been achieved.

The next series of experiments are even more remarkable. To understand them it is necessary, first, to point out that the two hemispheres or halves of the brain are able to work as a unity only because they are conjoined by means of the brain stem and a number of other links, especially, the link called the *corpus callosum* (which means literally 'body with a hard skin') or *central commissure* (which means literally 'central junction'), which joins the two hemispheres at the cortical level. This latter link might be thought of as a large coaxial cable (made up of, on a very rough estimate, about 800 million nerve fibres) that relays the bulk of the messages from one half of the brain to the other. The second point to remember is that there is a 'cross-over' in regard to which parts of the body and their functions are controlled by which hemisphere of the brain. By and large everything on the left-hand side of the body is controlled by the right hemisphere, and everything on the right-hand side is controlled by the left hemisphere. This 'cross-over' even extends to the eyes, where everything in the 'left visual field' (that is, anything seen as on the left-hand side) is transferred to the right hemisphere and vice versa. Thus, when someone who is right-handed suffers a 'stroke' or perhaps a series of severe epileptic fits that results in damage to their left hemisphere, they will often be incapacitated as regards the movements of their right leg or arm or the muscles on the right-hand side of their face, while at the same time, perhaps, incapacitated as regards their speech.

Certain very severe cases of epilepsy involve an increasingly severe series of convulsions which seem to widen in their scope on each successive occasion. These convulsions leave a trail of destruction in their wake. As a last resort, to stop the progress of this trail of damaged areas from one hemisphere to the other, the corpus callosum has to be surgically severed. This operation is called *commissurotomy* (that is, 'the cutting of the central commissure') or, more popularly, a 'split-brain' operation. These operations are associated especially with the work of the American psychoneurologist Roger Sperry (1913–94), who shared the Nobel Prize in Physiology or Medicine in 1981. In the 1960s Sperry had the opportunity to study the effects of such commissurotomy on epileptic patients treated by Philip Vogel and Joseph Bogen, neurosurgeons at the Institute of Nervous Diseases of Loma Linda University in Los Angeles, California.[7] Sperry and his team, at the California Institute of Technology, discovered that, for split-brain patients, consciousness is no

Figure 3.9
The American
neurologist,
Roger Sperry,
collecting his
Nobel Prize,
in 1981, for
his research
into the
specialised
functions of
each side of
the brain.

longer a single 'thing'. For example, a split-brain patient cannot
relate an object felt by the left hand (but out of sight) with an
object felt by the right hand (but out of sight). It is as if two
different 'consciousnesses' and so two distinct persons are present
in one and the same body. Under experimental conditions, similar
divisions in consciousness related to the other senses are experienced. The most astonishing finding was that if something were
presented, say, just to the left visual field, then the ensuing visual

experiences would be governed by the right cerebral hemisphere. But, since in humans, the power of speech is limited to the governance of the left hemisphere, the person undergoing these visual experiences could say nothing about them. In addition, the person in question would deny, in speech, having any such experiences. The 'left-hemisphere-speaking person' had become cut off from the 'right-hemisphere non-speaking person'. They did not know each other. They were, as Sperry himself put it, like 'two minds in one body'.[8]

In an invited address presented to the American Psychological Association in Washington, DC, in September 1967, Sperry provided a summary of the psychological state of split-brain patients:

> Instead of the normally unified single stream of consciousness, these patients behave in many ways as if they have two independent streams of conscious awareness, one in each hemisphere, each of which is cut off from and out of contact with the mental experiences of the other. In other words, each hemisphere seems to have its own separate and private sensations; its own perceptions; its own concepts; and its own impulses to act, with related volitional, cognitive and learning experiences. Following the surgery, each hemisphere also has thereafter its own separate chain of memories that are rendered inaccessible to the recall processes of the other.[9]

To put it in the headline manner of a tabloid newspaper, in the 'split-brain' operations, with god-like power, the neurosurgeon is able to create not merely two minds but two persons out of one.

The 'identity theory' of mind

By any standards, the advances in our knowledge of the brain and its functions from roughly 1800 to 1950 were quite extraordinary. At the end of each decade the brain sciences seemed to have revealed still more not merely about the human brain, but also about the human mind. By the middle of the twentieth century it seemed clear that even the most secret processes of our mental life, which lay hidden in the stream of consciousness, were related intimately to identifiable brain processes. It was increasingly tempting to think that, in the process of laying bare the workings of the brain and the central nervous system, one would learn all there was to know about a human's mental life

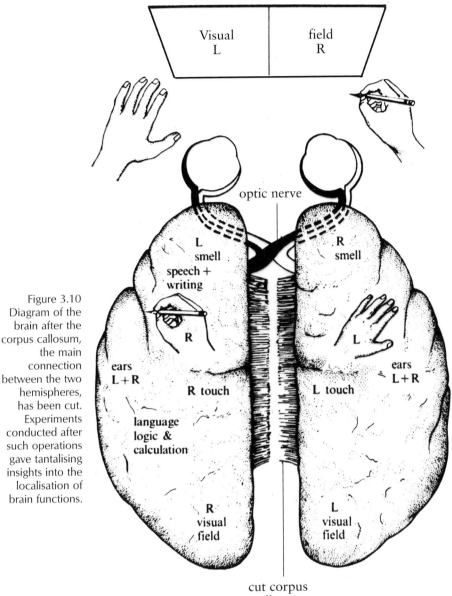

Figure 3.10
Diagram of the
brain after the
corpus callosum,
the main
connection
between the two
hemispheres,
has been cut.
Experiments
conducted after
such operations
gave tantalising
insights into the
localisation of
brain functions.

as well. While brain scientists themselves were often remarkably
conservative in their views about the nature of mind – for example,
Sherrington, Penfield and Sir John Eccles were all either classical
Cartesians or something very close to it – philosophers of mind
felt that these remarkable advances in our knowledge of the
brain and its functions pushed them towards a completely

materialist and 'centralist' (or 'everything that is mental is totally inside the head') view of the mind.

Psychologists remained comparatively indifferent to these advances in neuroscience because, being still either behaviourists or deeply influenced by its ethos, they had come to think of neurophysiology as more or less irrelevant to the science of behaviour. Advances in neuroscience, they believed, were just that, advances in neuroscience, and had little or no positive consequences for psychology, except, perhaps, to reinforce its implicit and rather general commitment to materialism. Even Watson's friend and early colleague in advancing the behaviourist cause, the neurologist Karl Lashley (1890–1958), made little connection between his neurological work on animal intelligence and vision, and his behaviourist psychology. Lashley's major research work, on studying the effects of brain lesions in monkeys and rats on their vision and ability to learn, culminated in his famous monograph, *Brain Mechanisms and Intelligence*, 1929. His most famous behaviourist paper is his two-part article, 'The Behavioristic Interpretation of Consciousness' (Lashley, 1923). In that latter article, he did not, as one might expect, identify consciousness with specific brain functions, but simply repeated Watson's view, saying that '"Conscious states" have outlived their usefulness to science and with Watson we may say that, "the behaviorist does not concern himself with them because as the stream of his science broadens and deepens such older concepts are sucked under, never to reappear".'[10]

More importantly it was very much in the interests of psychology, as a profession, to keep neurophysiology at a distance, otherwise it would be out of a job. Physiology, psychologists said, was the science that dealt with the 'central' aspects of human life, what went on inside humans' bodies, including inside their heads. Psychology, on the other hand, was the science that dealt with the 'peripheral' or external aspects of human life. Psychology was the science of human behaviour. So there was no obvious overlap between these two sciences. Each had its own territory clearly marked out.

Behaviourism had also come to be associated with an outright refusal to be in any way associated with the dubious practice of theory-building. Both Watson and Skinner always said that the goal of psychology was limited to the prediction and control of behaviour, and that they were not interested in hypotheses, theorems or theories, especially theories about the nature of

Figure 3.11
The American
neuro-
psychologist,
Karl Lashley,
who famously
asserted that
no activity
of the mind
is ever
conscious.

mind. In his address in Philadelphia, in April 1955, as President
of the Eastern Psychological Association, Skinner said that

> I never attacked a problem by constructing a Hypothesis. I
> never deduced Theorems or submitted them to Experimental
> Check. So far as I can see, I had no preconceived Model of
> behavior – certainly not a physiological or mentalistic one, and,
> I believe, not a conceptual one. . . . [My own one attempt at
> conceptual work] lived up to my opinion of theories in general
> by proving utterly worthless in suggesting further experiments.[11]

There was one notable exception to this reluctance, on the
part of psychologists of that time, to knit the new knowledge
obtained from the brain sciences into their psychology. This
was Edwin G. Boring (1886–1968).[12] In 1933 he published *The
Physical Dimensions of Consciousness*.[13] In the first chapter of
that book, Boring wrote:

While there is no possibility of disproving or proving dualism, the exposition of the present book is based on the assumption that it is scientifically more useful to consider that all psychological data are of the same kind and that consciousness is a physiological event.[14]

The bulk of the book was spent in attempting to show that all the aspects of consciousness which the introspectionists (such as his teacher, Titchener) had discerned could be given a physiological interpretation.

From our point of view, the most remarkable thing about Boring's book was that, for a very long time, it made little or no impact, either in psychology or philosophy. The more or less complete indifference which greeted this book, which Boring himself considered to be his major original contribution to psychology, led in part to his neurotic depression which developed around that time.[15] One can only speculate that it was the behaviourists' iron grip on psychology for most of the first half of the twentieth century, and their veto on theorising, that made psychologists neglect it. And one can only speculate that it was the, by that time, quite wide gap between psychology and philosophy that made most philosophers ignorant of the book.

It took almost twenty years for anyone to take any notice of Boring's *The Physical Dimensions of Consciousness*. Herbert Feigl, a member of the Vienna Circle who had migrated to America in the 1930s, introduced Boring's idea to the philosophical world in a paper entitled, 'The Mind–Body Problem in the Development of Logical Empiricism', which appeared first in the *Revue Internationale de Philosophie* in 1950.[16] However it was the English psychologist turned philosopher Ullin T. Place (1925–2000), who became the route to the full fruition of Boring's original idea. Having read *The Physical Dimensions of Consciousness* while still an undergraduate at Oxford in the 1940s reading psychology and philosophy, Place gradually became impressed by Boring's programme of giving a physiological interpretation of consciousness and, in so doing, of producing a 'physiological solution' to 'the problem of privacy'. Place's version of an 'identity theory', a 'brain-consciousness identity theory', was given its first clear formulation after his appointment as Lecturer in Psychology in the Philosophy Department at the University of Adelaide in 1951. It had been refined through a series of discussions with the philosophers J. J. C. Smart and, especially, C. B. Martin, in and around 1954. Ironically, it could be said that it was only when it fell among the philosophers that Boring's idea found fertile soil. For, as we shall see, it was the philosophers Smart and David Armstrong who fully exploited Boring's initial move, via Feigl's and Place's revival of it, by developing an identity theory not merely of consciousness but of the mind itself.

Philosophers, certainly, had no reason to ignore the remarkable advances in neuroscience that had taken place over the last hundred years. Since philosophy was not an empirical science of any sort, nor had any ambitions to be one, philosophers were able to view advances in neuroscience as neither threatening nor foreign to their interests. Besides, behaviourism never did have the hold over philosophy that it had over psychology, and was only in the ascendancy in philosophy for a very short period. In addition, there was never any explicit, nor even implicit, veto on theorising in philosophy as there was in psychology. Generally speaking, for most philosophers, at least after the influence of positivism began to wane, theorising was what philosophy was about, and theorising about the mind was what philosophy of mind was about.

Place's 'identity theory', or theory that consciousness is to be identified with certain brain processes, was published as 'Is Consciousness a Brain Process?', in the *British Journal of Psychology*, in 1956. Near the beginning of that article he gives the bald outline of his solution to the 'problem of privacy'.

> In the case of cognitive concepts like 'knowing', 'believing', 'understanding', 'remembering', and volitional concepts like 'wanting' and 'intending', there can be little doubt, I think, that an analysis in terms of dispositions to behave is fundamentally sound. [Here Place refers the reader to Wittgenstein's *Philosophical Investigations* and Ryle's *The Concept of Mind*.] On the other hand, there would seem to be an intractable residue of concepts clustering around the notions of consciousness, experience, sensation, and mental imagery [i.e. what *Le Penseur* is or might be doing], where some sort of inner process story is unavoidable. It is possible, of course, that a satisfactory behaviouristic account of this conceptual residuum will ultimately be found. For our present purposes, however, I shall assume that this cannot be done and that statements about pains and twinges, about how things look,

sound, and feel, about things dreamed of or pictured in the mind's eye, are statements referring to events and processes which are in some sense private or internal to the individual of whom they are predicated. . . . I shall argue that an acceptance of inner processes does not entail dualism and that the thesis that consciousness is a process in the brain cannot be dismissed on logical grounds.[17]

While Place made no secret of the fact that he remained a behaviourist in regard to the analysis of most mental concepts, the chief purpose of his article was to make progress on the task of making clear *the logic* of his claim that consciousness, that is, conscious experiences, is identical to brain processes.

Place began on this task by distinguishing between what he called 'The "Is" of Predication', 'The "Is" of Definition' and 'The "Is" of Composition'. 'The "Is" of Predication' occurs in such sentences as 'Helen is twelve years old', for 'is twelve years old', like 'has red hair', is a description of some property that is attributed to or predicated of the subject of the sentence, Helen. 'The "Is" of Definition' occurs in such sentences as 'A bachelor is an unmarried man.' Here the 'is so and so' phrase is not attributing a property to bachelors but telling us exactly what the term 'bachelor' means. It is defining 'bachelor' for us.

Now, according to Place, both of these senses of 'is' are to be contrasted with, and should not be confused with, 'The "Is" of Composition'. This latter use of 'is' occurs in such sentences as 'His table is an old packing case' or, when writing in the year 2000, 'The current president of the United States is Bill Clinton.' For a start, such sentences are talking about what is really the case, not about mere word definitions or linguistic predications. In such sentences, we are being informed that what is referred to by the phrase that comes before the 'is' *is, as a matter of fact,* identical with (and so composed of) what is referred to by the phrase that comes after the 'is'. To put this another way, the phrases either side of the 'is' are really just two different descriptions for one and the same thing. They are a way of *identifying* what someone is talking about in two different ways. His table *is in fact* just that old packing case. From the viewpoint of the year 2000, the current president of the United States *is* Bill Clinton from Arkansas.

In providing us with this taxonomy of our uses of the verb 'is' (or, in an old-fashioned grammarian's terminology, 'the copula'),

Place's aim was to say that the hypothesis that consciousness is a brain process was an example of the third sort of 'is', namely 'The "Is" of Composition'. In saying that consciousness is a brain process, Place is claiming (however superficially implausibly) that the term 'consciousness' and the term 'brain process' pick out (or refer to) one and the same thing. This one thing, Place adds, is the scientific, neurophysiological truth of the matter, namely some particular sort of brain process. Thus his thesis about the core of our mental life, our consciousness, is a strongly materialist thesis.

An important aspect of this hypothesis, Place emphasises, is that the claimed identity is a 'contingent' one. What this means is that the identity in question is just a result of the way things have 'panned out'. Things could have happened otherwise, but in fact they did not. In the year 2000 Bob Dole could have been the current president of the United States but, as it turned out, Bill Clinton was elected for a second term. Consciousness could have turned out to be a spiritual substance but, in fact, the evidence suggests that it is nothing but a certain sort of brain process. Just as there was nothing necessary about Bill Clinton's being elected to a second term, for it was not a Law of Nature nor a Law of Logic that he be so, so there is nothing necessary about the fact that consciousness turns out to be nothing but a sort of brain process. Humans could have evolved differently, or God could have made things differently. However, as a simple matter of fact, it is claimed, consciousness turns out to be a sort of brain process.

Since the 'The "Is" of Composition' operates by using two different sorts of description for one and the same thing, then there is a danger, Place points out, of failing to realise the distinctness of these distinct descriptions. Just because we can say 'Being president of the United States is the most prestigious political office in the world', we cannot then say, in the year 2000, 'Being Bill Clinton is the most prestigious political office in the world.' For a start, most Republicans might want to be president on account of its prestige, but none of them, most probably, would have wanted to be Bill Clinton. In similar fashion, while we might speak of some of our conscious experiences as vivid or frightening, we should not thereby think that we can say that any of our brain processes was vivid or frightening.

One of Place's 'sparring partners' in Adelaide had been the Professor of Philosophy there, J. J. C. (Jack) Smart (1920–).

Smart was born and went to school in Cambridge, England, but became an undergraduate at the University of Glasgow when his father moved from the Cambridge Observatory to take up the Regius Professorship of Astronomy at Glasgow. Either side of war service with the army in India, Jack Smart read mathematics and physics, with a 'minor' in philosophy, at Glasgow. However it was philosophy that came to interest him most, though he always thereafter imbued his work in philosophy with a strong scientific flavour. He believes with deep conviction that philosophers should be conversant with current science and that philosophical theories should always be constrained by the relevant scientific facts.

After Glasgow, Smart became a graduate student, reading for the newly invented B.Phil. in philosophy at Oxford. Here he fell under the spell of Rylean behaviourism, though, as he himself admits, he gave his logical behaviourism a much more openly materialist flavour than Ryle himself ever did. At Oxford he also imbibed some of the ethos of logical positivism and gained some acquaintance with Wittgenstein's views through his contact with Friedrich Waismann, who had been a member of the Vienna Circle, and George Paul, who had attended some of Wittgenstein's lectures at Cambridge.

After a brief period as a Junior Research Fellow at Corpus Christi College, Oxford, Smart was appointed in 1950 to the Hughes Chair of Philosophy at the University of Adelaide. Since then, he has lived in Australia, eventually taking out Australian citizenship. Soon after his appointment at Adelaide, Ullin Place joined his department as a junior colleague to teach the psychology segment of the curriculum. Smart saw the force of Place's grafting of a consciousness–brain identity theory on to regular behaviourism, and, together with his fellow Australian David Armstrong, and others, Smart eventually extended the theory into a comprehensive mind–brain identity theory. This theory became known as 'Australian materialism' or, to some of its Oxford critics, 'the Australian heresy'. For such a theory, besides flourishing on the Australian subcontinent, seemed to reflect the blunt no-nonsense realism of the Australian character itself.

Smart set himself the task of finding additional grounds for holding the identity theory. These grounds are to be found especially in his article 'Sensations and Brain Processes' (1959) and his major work *Philosophy and Scientific Realism* (1963). The first of these grounds, namely that we should not be

Figure 3.12
The Anglo-
Australian
philosopher,
J. J. C. Smart,
who became
the best
known figure
associated
with the
mind–brain
identity theory.

bewitched by our ordinary mental vocabulary, might be called Wittgensteinian. Smart argued that when we speak of beliefs and hopes, feelings and emotions, mental images and so on, this language is strictly speaking 'topic neutral' or 'reference neutral'. That is to say, it is neutral as regards what is being referred to by these mental vocabulary expressions, and so we cannot argue from these expressions to the existence of mental events or, indeed, to the existence of *any particular* sort of events. If someone says that she is imagining an orange, then, strictly speaking, this only commits the speaker to holding that something similar to *whatever it is that goes on* in her when she actually sees an orange, with normal vision and in good light, is now going on in her. This leaves it open that *whatever it is that is going on in her* could be just a brain process (though equally, as far as this argument is concerned, it leaves open the possibility that it could also be a Cartesian episode of some sort).

Smart was also keen to point out that the identity theory was supported by a very basic piece of well-grounded scientific advice called 'The Principle of Parsimony'. This principle, sometimes called 'Ockham's Razor' because of its association with the medieval English Franciscan logician William of Ockham (1285–1347), is about how to proceed when forming scientific or philosophical theories or hypotheses. It advocates the greatest possible simplicity or parsimony when constructing a theory, so that one should not multiply the basic axioms or the basic entities, or, in general, the basic 'bits' of one's theory, beyond absolute necessity. This being so, then, Smart argues,

> If it be agreed that there are no cogent philosophical arguments which force us into accepting dualism, and if the brain process theory [the mind–brain identity theory] and dualism are equally consistent with the facts, then the principles of parsimony and simplicity seem to me to decide overwhelmingly in favour of the brain-process theory.[18]

Smart usually added that, in fact, while there may not be cogent reasons of a purely philosophical sort, there are cogent reasons from evolutionary biology and the brain sciences that push us towards a materialist view of the mind.

> It seems to me that science in particular is increasingly giving us a viewpoint whereby organisms are able to be seen as physicochemical mechanisms: so it seems that even the behaviour of man himself will one day be explicable in mechanistic terms.[19]

Perhaps the most important addition to Place's initial statement of the identity theory came from another Australian philosopher, David Armstrong (1926–). He was born in Melbourne, though he received much of his early schooling in England. At the outbreak of the Second World War, his parents sent him back to Australia to finish his secondary schooling. After some war service in the Australian navy, he read philosophy as his major (or main subject) for his BA at the University of Sydney. There he came in contact with that remarkable teacher and iconoclast John Anderson (1893–1962). Like so many of his generation of philosophers, he then went to Oxford to obtain his B.Phil. After a brief period as an assistant lecturer at Birkbeck College, he returned to Australia on being appointed to a lectureship at Melbourne University. In 1964 he was appointed to the Challis Professorship of Philosophy at Sydney University, the chair which, during his undergraduate years, had been held by his esteemed teacher, John Anderson. His best-known work is the aptly, if bluntly, named, *A Materialist Theory of the Mind* (1968).[20] Armstrong could be said to have finally exorcised any trace of behaviourism from the identity theory. For, in a brilliant *coup de théâtre*, Armstrong took the behaviourists' own weapon, dispositions, which they had used with such devastating effect against the Cartesian view of mind, and turned it against the behaviourists themselves.

For what Armstrong did was to point out that a full account of dispositions involved making clear that a disposition always involved some inner physical 'something', which had a crucial causal role in producing the actions or reactions associated with the disposition in question. The behaviourists claimed that the correct account of, say, brittleness would go as follows: 'Brittleness is the disposition of, say, this glass to break very easily when let fall from even a moderate height or when tapped even lightly with a hard object.' Armstrong suggested that the correct account must go like this: 'Brittleness is *the physico-chemical crystalline structure* of the glass which causes it to break very easily when let fall from even a moderate height or when tapped even lightly with a hard object.' Indeed, Armstrong argued, that is the correct model for all dispositional analyses.

Dispositions, he said, strictly speaking *are* their inner physical structures which cause the behaviour (actions or reactions) typically associated with the dispositions. Behaviour only comes into dispositions, if at all, when this inner structure (sometimes called, in the academic papers, the 'structural basis' or 'categorical basis' of the disposition) interacts causally with the environment. This can be seen more clearly by taking another example, namely that of being a haemophiliac. A haemophiliac is some human (or animal) that lacks the usual clotting agent in the blood which makes it congeal when there is bleeding. Being a haemophiliac is a dispositional state definable as 'a person (or animal) having blood which lacks the usual clotting agent such that when that person (or animal) is cut or otherwise wounded, the blood flow is not staunched in the usual way'. The important thing to note is that a person can be a haemophiliac even if he has never been cut or wounded and so has never exhibited the unstoppable bleeding associated with haemophilia. A medical doctor or physiologist or veterinary doctor can attribute the disposition, being a haemophiliac, to someone or some animal, even though no haemophiliac behaviour has ever been exhibited. For the doctor or scientist or vet can spot the disposition simply by spotting that the person or animal's blood lacks the usual clotting agent. A scientific or true account of a disposition is all about *finding the inner cause* of the behaviour in question. In certain cases, such as medical conditions like haemophilia, it is important to find the inner cause before it actually causes anything to happen. So a doctor might tell a mother, soon after she has given birth, that her son is a haemophiliac, in order that appropriate measures can be taken.

It follows from this account of dispositions that if mental states are indeed dispositions (as Armstrong agrees with both Place, Smart and the behaviourists that most of them are), then mental states are to be identified with 'inner physical structures' of some sort. Thus Armstrong writes:

> According to this view, the concept of a mental state essentially involves, and is exhausted by, the concept of a state that is *apt to be the cause of certain effects or apt to be the effect of certain causes.*[21]

The obvious candidates in the case of mental dispositions, for being the relevant 'inner physical structures', are brain states or processes. So, Armstrong adds:

> But suppose that the physico-chemical view of the working of the brain is correct, as I take it to be. It will be very natural to conclude that mental states are not simply *determined* by corresponding states of the brain, but that they are actually *identical* with these brain-states, brain-states that involve nothing but physical properties.[22]

Thus Armstrong often went on to call his version of the identity theory, which had completely jettisoned any remnants of behaviourism, 'central state materialism'. The pendulum had swung back again from the 'peripheralism' or externalism of behaviourism to a hard-core non-Cartesian 'centralism'. Once more minds were things wholly inside heads, but this time they were also wholly physical and to be wholly identified with brains.

Identities prove elusive

Smart himself realised that the mind–brain identity theory was especially vulnerable to one particular sort of objection. He aired a version of this objection, in his own book *Philosophy and Scientific Realism*, in the following way:

> It will be remembered that I suggested that in reporting sensations we are in fact reporting likenesses and unlikenesses of brain processes. Now it may be objected (as has been done by K. E. M. Baier[23]): 'Suppose that you had some electro-encephalograph fixed to your brain, and you observed that, according to the electro-encephalograph, you did *not* have the sort of brain process that normally goes on when you have a yellow sense datum [an experience of seeing a patch of yellow]. Nevertheless, if you had a yellow sense datum you would not give up the proposition that you had such a sense datum, no matter *what* the encephalograph said.' This part of the objection can be easily answered. I simply reply that the brain-process theory [identity theory] was put forward as a factual identification, not as a logically necessary one. I can therefore agree that it is logically possible that the electro-encephalograph experiment should turn out as envisaged in the objection, but I can still believe *that this will never in fact happen.* If it did happen I should doubtless give up the brain-process theory (though later I might come to doubt the correctness of my memory of the experiment and thus reinstate the theory!).[24]

I know of no experiment whereby a person, who regularly has experiences of seeing yellow only when he or she is in brain state A, suddenly has an experience of seeing yellow when not in brain state A. However the crucial evidence, in regard to the claims of the identity theory, should be concerned with whether or not an experience of seeing yellow will be identifiable with the same brain process A *in all people.* The identity theory is an interpersonal theory. It is a theory that claims that any person whatsoever who merits *a particular type of mental description*, say, having a pang of anxiety or believing in God or seeing a patch of yellow, will be discovered to be in *exactly the same type of brain state* or undergoing exactly the same type of brain process as any other person who merits the same mental description. That is why the identity theory is called by philosophers a type–type identity theory.

To put this another way, a type–type identity claim is a very strong sort of identity claim. It is usually contrasted, in the philosophical literature, with a much weaker sort of identity claim, a token–token identity claim. In order to make this contrast clearer, let me introduce the terms 'type' and 'token'. A *type* is a class or sort of thing, for example, the class of Irish pound (or strictly *punt*) coins. A *token* is an actual example or specimen of that class. For example, the pound coin in my pocket today, which is slightly defaced on the side with the intaglio depiction of the Irish elk, is a token of the class or type called Irish pound coins. So is the pound coin in your purse, which, say, is not defaced but has damage to its rim.

To claim that there is a type–type identity between mental states and brain processes is to make the very strong claim that the true referent of (what is really referred to by), say, the mental description 'a thought that I will have a sausage for lunch' (that is, a type of thought) will be discovered, *on all occasions*, to be, say, the brain process described by the neurophysiologist's description 'brain process $_{289c}$ on the International Society of Neurophysiologists chart of brain processes' (a type of brain process). On the other hand, if one were to make merely a token–token identity claim about mental states being identical with brain processes, then the referent of the mental description 'a thought that I will have a sausage for lunch' will be discovered, on Monday, when thought by Fred (a token, in Fred, of the thinking-I-will-have-a-sausage-for-lunch type of thought), to be 'brain process $_{289c}$' (a token of the type of brain process called 'brain process $_{289c}$'). However, on Tuesday, when Fred again thinks that he will have a sausage for lunch (another token of the same type of thought), it will, say, turn out to be 'brain process $_{342a}$' (a token of a different type of brain process). And, on the same day, when the same thought is entertained by Mary (another token of the same type of thought), it will, say, turn out to be 'brain process $_{456d}$' (a token of yet another different type of brain process).[25]

Nowadays, many neurophysiologists would suggest that there are good grounds for saying that the mind–brain identity theory should be abandoned precisely because the predicted interpersonal, type–type identities have failed to appear. In turn, speaking more generally, this would suggest that our mental vocabulary 'does not carve the brain at its neurophysiological joints'. That is to say, it does not make neurophysiological sense even to expect that the appropriate use of a particular mental description would be an indicator of the presence of a quite particular sort or type of brain process on each and every occasion.

In more detail, there are no good reasons of a neurophysiological sort for supposing that every time someone has a particular type of belief (say, for example, a belief that it is not now raining), then, on each occasion that such a belief is attributable to any person, his or her brain will be discovered to be undergoing a particular type of process (say, brain process $_{296b}$ on the completed map of brain processing). Or, to take another example, there are no good reasons of a neurophysiological sort for supposing that each time a person is experiencing momentarily a particular type of conscious state (say, a visual image of a red hat), then that person or any other person meriting the same psychological description will be discovered on each such occasion, at just that moment, to be undergoing a particular type of brain process (say, brain process $_{782c}$).

By the 1950s and 1960s what was most remarkable was the lack of headway that had been made by neurophysiologists in identifying mental events with brain states or processes. In 1952, for example, in a synoptic article entitled 'Neurology and the Mind–Brain Problem', Roger Sperry was pointing out that

> Neurological science thus far has been quite unable to furnish an adequate description of the neural processes involved in even the very simplest forms of mental activity.[26]

Such a conclusion probably did not worry Jack Smart or any other mind–brain identity theorist. For an identity theorist could simply reply that failure to find something does not imply its non-existence. You cannot argue from the failure to find any neural counterparts for our mental states to the non-existence of those counterparts. At this point, the identity theorist would usually invoke that most famous of all allies of the identity theory, 'future science'. Future science, with its greater sophistication and superior instrumentation, he would suggest, will supply what cannot at present be supplied, namely the awaited type–type identities between types of our mental states as described by our ordinary commonsense psychology and types of brain processes picked out by latter-day neurophysiologists.

However, in that same 1952 article, Sperry recorded a long history of failure on the part of would-be identifiers. For, in that same article, Sperry gave details of the various attempts that had been made over the years to identify mental states with various aspects of brain processing. Scientists had tried to identify mental states (usually, specific sorts of conscious experiences) with *levels* of electrical activity in the brain, with the *distribution* of patterns of electrical activity in the brain, and through treating the electrical impulses of the brain as if they amounted to a *code* or system of representations. All these attempts failed dismally. His conclusion was to reiterate a comment of Sherrington's, namely that, 'We have to regard the relation of mind to brain as still not merely unsolved, but still devoid of a basis for its very beginning.'[27] By this he meant not only that science has not got very far in the experimental investigation of the possibility of identifying mental states with brain processes, but that it had made exhaustive investigations and failed to obtain any positive result. In recent years, neurophysiological knowledge has advanced. But this advance has not helped the cause of the mind–brain identity theorists. It has merely reinforced Sperry's pessimistic conclusion that, from the point of view of neurophysiology, a type–type identity between mental states and brain processes is most unlikely.

By the 1970s and 1980s the case against type–type identities between mind and brain had been strengthened. Gerald Edelman is a contemporary brain scientist who has been Vincent Astor Distinguished Professor at the Rockefeller University since 1974, and Director and Scientific Chairman of the Neurosciences Research Program at the same university since 1981. He received the Nobel Prize in Physiology or Medicine in 1972 for his research in the biochemistry of the human immune system. Edelman has argued that a type–type identity between mind and brain is most unlikely for the simple reason that brain processing, in even a single brain, is very labile (unstable) and variable in regard to its incarnation of one and the same mental state. In 'Neural Darwinism: Population Thinking and Higher Brain Function', a paper delivered at the twentieth Nobel Conference at Gustavus Adolphus College in Minnesota, Edelman suggested that we should look upon the formation of each individual human brain as the product of two levels of evolution. First, there is the evolution of humans, and so the evolution of their brains, from such prior species as *Homo Erectus*, *Homo Habilis* and, in the far distance, *Australopithecus*. Second, there is an evolution of each individual's brain, an evolution that is part of individual development and takes place from the foetal stage to childhood. It is this second sort of evolution, Edelman argues, that makes any type–type identity between mind and brain so unlikely. Edelman puts it thus:

> The network of the brain is made during development by cellular movements, extensions, and connections of increasing numbers of neurons. It is an example of a self-organizing system. An examination of such a system during its development and at its most microscopic ramifications after development indicates that precise point-to-point wiring cannot occur. Therefore, uniquely specific connections cannot, in general, exist. If one numbered the branches of a neuron and correspondingly numbered the neurons it touched, the numbers would not correspond in any two individuals of a species (even in identical twins or in genetically identical animals).[28]

In effect, each human is an individual species as regards the formation of his or her brain. This is so because major factors in the development of human brains are the formation of individual neurones into groups, the selection of certain neuronal connections rather than others within a group, and finally the selection of one group rather than another for particular tasks. Each of these processes is evolutionary in nature. In each, there is selection, of neurone or of neuronal pathway or of a whole group of neurones, according to the immediate pressure of the immediate environment and so in an *ad hoc* way. The upshot is that the 'wiring diagram' for any particular human is therefore unique. The clear implication is that this 'constitutes a crisis for those who believe that the nervous system is precise and "hard-wired" (like a computer)'.[29] He might have added that it also presents a crisis for anyone who thinks that the brains of humans are sufficiently uniform and precise in their wiring such that the electro-chemical activity that constitutes brain processing is the same in any two individuals, even when we might describe those same two individuals as being in the same mental state.[30]

This objection, that the identity of mental events with brain processing has proved not merely elusive but dubious, is unlikely to convince the 24-carat identity theorist. Smart himself, in the quotation with which I began this section, admitted as much. He indicated that, even after clear experimental proof, he would probably be moved to reinstate the identity theory at a later date. The usual moves to reinstate the theory are of two main sorts. The first is simply to doubt that the evidence from contemporary brain science is clear enough or sophisticated enough or sufficiently damning as to overthrow the identity theory. But this can look to those who do not support the identity theory as just a case of putting off the evil day when the theory has to be set aside.

The second move, a more interesting and important one, is to dilute the requirements for the identity in question. It is to move away from the strong type–type identity claim in the direction of a token–token identity claim, but without going all the way. All that we need to show, argue these more liberal identity theorists, is that some mental event, such as a sensation or an experience of some afterimage or a conscious thought, can be identified on any particular occasion with some brain process drawn from a list of possible brain processes which could be said to be 'of the same type' in a looser or more accommodating sense. Thus my current experience of toothache may be identical with brain process$_{234a}$, but last week the same sort of pain might have been identical with brain process$_{248b}$, and the week before the same sort of pain might have been identical with brain process$_{291c}$. However, as long as these brain processes all share some (but not all) properties, say, they share some similarities of structure or function or both, then we could still say that these brain processes are all 'of the same type'. Perhaps that is why they are all to be marked, on our future comprehensive map of human brain processes, with a similar subscript number, say, some subscript number between 200 and 299.

After all, by parity of reasoning, say the identity theorists, we can and do say that all these trees over there are cypresses, even though some are small, some tall, some broad, some thin, some dried up, some healthy, some dark green in colour, and some light green. They are all cypresses because they are all of the same arboreal type even though they do not share all their properties in common. Indeed they differ quite a lot among themselves. What makes these trees over there 'all of the same type' is their being all botanically the same. They share certain botanical properties. They can all be said to be botanically sufficiently the same because they have the same shape of leaves, the same angle at which their branches grow out from their trunk, and, say, the same taste and scent to their sap.

However, at this point, we need to look more closely at the analogy. For the analogy seems to highlight the deeper, underlying problem for the identity theory. The term 'cypress' can be analysed as a term which is shorthand for 'tree with x shape of leaf, y type of branches, and z type of sap'. We learn to use the word 'cypress' by having our primary school teacher or mother or uncle show us the continuity of the particular shape of leaf, and the particular type of branch and trunk formation, and the peculiar smell and taste of the sap, over a number of specimens of cypress tree. Or else we try and teach ourselves about the characteristics of cypress trees from the text and illustrations of *The So-and-So Book of Trees*. In other words, the order is first the noticing of botanical similarities in a number of trees (similarities of leaf, of branch configuration, and of colour and odour of sap), then the bestowing of a generic or 'type' label, namely the name 'cypress'.

In regard to how our mental terms were generated, the ordering must have been completely different. Our mental terms or descriptions, such as 'the thought that I'll have a sausage for lunch' or 'mental image of a completely bare white room with no windows' or 'toothache', could not have been generated as a post-investigation-of-brains bestowal of a type-term upon perceived similarities of properties of brain processes. For we have at no time first noted neurophysiological similarities in a number of brain processes and then bestowed on such processes a generic or 'type' label or description such as 'the thought that I'll have a sausage for lunch' or 'toothache'. The reason for this is simply that our mental terms and descriptions have, and must have, arisen in complete ignorance of human neurophysiology. Such mental or psychological terms and descriptions have long pre-existed what knowledge we do now have of human neurophysiology. They certainly date from the time of Plato and Aristotle, and most of them probably go back far beyond their time. That the generation of most of our mental vocabulary and of our mental descriptions, aeons ago by our ancestors, perhaps in part by old *Homo Habilis*, could *ipso facto* have generated a way of picking out types of brain process would be scientific serendipity of a stupendous sort. It would be simply incredible.

To put this point another way. That 'cypress' names a type of tree is not a speculative assumption. It is simply the steady, assured and uncontroversial process of first finding similarities of leaf, branch, sap, and so on in a number of trees, and of then linguistically marking that noted similarity with a generic term, 'cypress'. On the other hand, saying that 'the thought that I'll have a sausage for lunch' or 'consciousness of my *faux pas* this evening' is the name of a particular identifiable brain process is highly speculative and very controversial. For it is not the culmination of a simple and straightforward process of first observing similarities in brain processes and then agreeing a description or label for that type of process defined in terms of just those similarities. It is a shot in the dark. Arguably, given current knowledge in the brain sciences, it is increasingly looking like a shot in the dark that has continually failed to hit any target. For the more we learn about human neurophysiology and about how we generate our mental terminology, the more the two drift apart, and the more controversial such an identification becomes.

'Out of date, eliminate'

There are a number of other responses that one could make on finding that the hoped-for identity of mind and brain had not been supported by neurophysiological research. However, one of the more suprising responses was that made by a group of philosophers who have subsequently been labelled 'eliminative materialists' or simply 'eliminativists'. The eliminativists regarded the failure of the identity theorists to find identities as grounds for suggesting that there was something radically wrong with the identity theorists' account of one side of the putative identity, namely the mind or mental descriptions side. The eliminativists suggested that there never could be any identity between what is picked out by our ordinary commonsense mental descriptions of humans and what is picked out by neurophysiologists' descriptions of the human brain, because the former, the mental descriptions, *did not pick out (or refer to) anything at all.* When investigated thoroughly, it will be found that mental descriptions are not real descriptions *of* anything, no matter how they might present themselves linguistically. They are pseudo-descriptions masquerading as real descriptions. That being so, they are worse than useless, they are misleading. So they should be eliminated.

The germ of this idea was first cultivated by that philosophical dadaist, the Austrian-American philosopher of science, Paul Feyerabend (1924–94).[31] During the Second World War Feyerabend saw war service with the German army on the eastern front. He was severely wounded and for the rest of his life was able to walk only with the help of a crutch. After the war Feyerabend became a student of physics, astronomy and mathematics at the University of Vienna but became interested in philosophy of science. Afterwards he became a graduate student at the University of London, supervised by Karl Popper (1902–94), who was himself Viennese, and, while not a member, sympathetic to many of the aims of the Vienna Circle. After a brief period as Lecturer in Philosophy at Bristol University, Feyerabend took up a post at the University of California at Berkeley in 1958 and spent the rest of his life in and out of America.

In 1963 Feyerabend published a paper entitled 'Materialism and the Mind–Body Problem'. In that paper, in the course of defending materialism about the mind, he began to develop the idea that any argument against a materialist view of mind that depended upon 'common usage', that is, in particular upon our commonsense talk about purely mental events, is simply irrelevant. Such an argument is irrelevant because, when looked at closely, our commonly employed descriptions of mental events (such as descriptions of or first-person reports about our thoughts, sensations or feelings) lack any real, testable, objectively observable content. As Feyerabend himself put it:

> Thus, the statement 'There is a table in front of me' leads to predictions concerning my tactual sensations . . . Failure of any one of these predictions may force me to withdraw the statement. This is not the case with statements concerning thoughts, sensations, feelings; or at least there is the impression that the same kind of vulnerability does not obtain here. The reason is that their content is so much poorer.[32]

Others were soon eager to develop this line of argument even further. In a characteristically witty and stylish paper, 'Mind–Body Identity, Privacy, and Categories' (1965), the American philosopher Richard Rorty (1931–) put forward what he called 'the disappearance form' of the identity theory. By this he meant that, unlike the identity theory of, say, Smart, where mental descriptions were to be retained alongside neurophysiological descriptions, even in parts of psychology, he felt that mental descriptions should disappear from any scientific enterprise, precisely *because they had no real use, at least as scientific descriptions.* At one point in the paper, he puts his position in terms of an analogy:

A certain primitive tribe holds the view that illnesses are caused by demons – a different demon for each sort of illness. When asked what more is known about these demons than that they cause illness, they reply that certain members of the tribe – the witch-doctors – can see, after a meal of sacred mushrooms, various (intangible) humanoid forms on or near the bodies of patients. The witch-doctors have noted, for example, that a blue demon with a long nose accompanies epileptics, a fat red one accompanies sufferers from pneumonia, etc., etc. They know such further facts as that the fat red demon dislikes a certain sort of mold which the witch-doctors give people who have pneumonia. (There are various competing theories about what demons do when not causing diseases, but serious witch-doctors regard such speculations as unverifiable and profitless.)

If we encountered such a tribe, we would be inclined to tell them that there are no demons. We would tell them that diseases were caused by germs, viruses, and the like. We would add that witch-doctors were not seeing demons, but merely having hallucinations. We would be quite right, but would we be right on *empirical* grounds?[33]

Rorty goes on to say that a sophisticated witch-doctor could still argue that 'the demon theory' is not at variance with the empirical facts. Because it would be possible for the sophisticated witch-doctor to correlate any discovery of a particular germ with the name of a particular demon from his demonology, and also suggest that the role of the sacred mushrooms was merely to present admittedly elusive 'sightings' of admittedly intangible things to specially chosen subjects, witch-doctors.

However, Rorty's point is that even such 'theory saving' manoeuvres on the part of the witch-doctor would not incline us, or most of us, to adopt 'demon talk'. This would be so for reasons of simplicity. We would, or should, employ the Principle of Parsimony or Ockham's Razor and preserve only the descriptions of empirical facts as presented by modern science. Equally, since the facts behind our ordinary commonsense mental descriptions are as elusive as the facts behind the witch-doctors' talk of demons, then

Sensations [to take an example from our ordinary mental descriptions] may be to the future progress of psycho-physiology as demons are to modern science. Just as we now want to deny that there are demons, future science may want to deny that there are sensations.[34]

Does this mean, according to Rorty, that we should excise all talk of mental states and events, such as talk of thoughts, feelings and sensations, not merely from our scientific descriptions but from our ordinary discourse? Should we give up telling not only our doctor but also our next-door neighbour about how we felt queasy after eating the Chinese 'carry out' last night? Rorty is in no doubt that, *theoretically*, we could do so.

> Elimination of the referring use of the expression in question ('demon', 'sensation') from our language would leave our ability to describe and predict undiminished.[35]

But Rorty does not believe that, *practically*, we could or even should try to do so. For the elimination of our ordinary talk about thoughts, sensations, feeling, and the like, would be so inconvenient as to be impractical.

If Rorty drew back from this final step, others did not. Famously, or notoriously, the husband and wife team of eliminativists, the Canadians Paul and Patricia Churchland, did not. They advocated the damnation of mental discourse and all its works in all contexts. Paul Churchland (1942–), in his uncompromising article, 'Eliminative Materialism and the Propositional Attitudes' (1981), argued that our commonsense conception of psychological phenomena is not a 'folksy' way of talking which is both useful and harmless if limited to our ordinary social discourse. It is, he argued, a radically false theory in the way that talk about demons as the cause of epilepsy or talk about *phlogiston* (according to eighteenth-century chemistry, a flammable substance present in all things able to be consumed by fire) as the cause of combustibility, are radically false theories. Just as the vast majority of people, including ordinary people in ordinary contexts, now, rightly, no longer talk of demons as the cause of epilepsy or phlogiston as the cause of combustibility, so, for exactly the same reasons, we should no longer talk about minds and mental events as the cause of anything.

Our ordinary mental descriptions are usually described by Paul Churchland as our 'folk psychology'. This, of course, as it is meant to, immediately calls to mind 'folk medicine' or 'folk science', both of which are pejorative terms. In the case of 'folk medicine', we do not merely think of it as false but as positively dangerous. To get a priest or witch-doctor to treat epilepsy by exorcism is not merely to act on a false theory, it is to put the patient in mortal danger. In the same way, we should think of 'folk psychology' as not merely false but potentially dangerous.

Paul Churchland brushes off any suggestion that our 'folk psychology' does not really aspire to be a psychological theory by pointing out that we, ordinary folk, constantly use it as a basis for explanation and prediction. That is to say, we constantly use it as if it were a real empirical theory, a real theory about what is really going on psychologically. For we might explain why we or someone else did something in terms of what we or someone else believed or desired. For example, I might excuse my loss of temper by saying, 'I lost my temper with Fred because I truly believed at the time that it was Fred who had told the Provost that I had cancelled my lecture in order to go to the Leonard Cohen concert.' Or we might predict what someone else is likely to do, on the basis of our knowledge of that person's beliefs and desires. For example, I might predict Mary's future behaviour by saying, 'We cannot count on Mary's vote because she will almost certainly not turn up to the Faculty meeting, because she believes that Fred will be there and she just cannot stand Fred.'

Paul Churchland maintains that it is incredible that we take our 'folk psychology' seriously and consider it a rival for modern neuroscience. After all, our 'folk psychology', in terms of its belief–desire explanations, has not really altered in any substantial way since the time of the ancient Greeks, if not before. If we would not, even for ordinary 'talking over the fence' purposes, think of retaining the astronomical or cosmological or biological accounts of, say, Homer or Euripides or even Aristotle, why then should we retain their psychology? If we no longer talk of the sun as a fiery chariot being driven across the sky nor of the stars as being fixed upon the transparent spheres of the heavens nor of the generation of frogs by the action of solar heat upon river slime, why should we still talk about humans believing and desiring, or hoping or wanting, or wishing or intending? Why should we still think of humans as possessing mental states in their heads?

Paul Churchland's answer to these rhetorical questions is that we should not retain any part of our obsolete, false and wholly misleading 'folk psychology' for any purpose. In the all important scientific context, we should immediately set about the task of replacing our 'folk psychology' with the explanations and predictions of the brain sciences:

> The thesis of this paper may be summarized as follows. The propositional attitudes [i.e. the attitudes of believing, desiring, etc.] of folk psychology do not constitute an unbreachable barrier to the advancing tide of neuroscience. On the contrary, the principled displacement of folk psychology is not only richly possible, it represents one of the most intriguing theoretical displacements we can currently imagine.[36]

If this substitution of the theories and explanations of neuroscience for those of current 'folk psychology' also implies the demise of most of current cognitive psychology, then Paul Churchland would say, 'So be it.' If some, or perhaps eventually all, psychologists are to be out of a job, then we have no more grounds for regret than we have for the redundancy of the practitioners of medieval witchcraft.

If the eliminativists have their way, then philosophy of mind itself would also have to alter radically. For, according to the Churchlands, it too could and should no longer propose theories or carry on debates in terms of the ascription to humans of beliefs and desires and other mental states. For belief and desire, and other such mental-state concepts, are obsolete and misleading concepts. A philosophy of mind worth preserving would have to translate everything into the language of the brain and behavioural sciences. Thus Patricia Churchland (1943–) entitled her first book *Neurophilosophy* (1986) and the flaps of the jacket of the hard-back edition included endorsements from Francis Crick, the co-discoverer of the double helical structure of DNA (deoxyribonucleic acid which stores the 'genetic code' in the nuclei of all cells), and Rodolfo Llinás, the Thomas and Susanne Murphy Professor of Neuroscience at New York University School of Medicine, who has produced important research on the biophysical properties of nerve membranes and synaptic transmission. For philosophy of mind, in Patricia Churchland's scheme of things, is to become the handmaiden of the brain and behavioural scientists. Its task is to produce 'a synoptic vision [of the brain and behavioural sciences], transcending disciplinary boundaries',[37] a task which has seemed to some critics to be little more than science journalism in relation to the brain and behavioural sciences. In keeping with this scheme of things, Paul

Figure 3.13
The Canadian
philosopher,
Patricia
Churchland –
the first neuro-
philosopher?

Churchland's latest book is entitled *The Engine of Reason, The Seat of the Soul: A Philosophical Journey into the Brain*, and the 1997 MIT Press philosophy catalogue described the book thus:

A new picture of mind is emerging, and explanations now exist for what has so long seemed mysterious. Philosopher Paul Churchland, who is widely known as a gifted teacher and expository writer, *explains these scientific developments* in a simple, authoritative, and entertaining fashion . . . [emphasis mine].

Seen against the background of the previous half-century, eliminative materialism could be seen as the apotheosis of the logical positivist programme of translating mental descriptions into physical ones. For, in effect, it has advocated something even stronger, namely the bypassing of any work of translation in favour of the complete elimination or liquidation of mental descriptions. With this liquidation of even any mention of mental states or events, eliminative materialism has performed a sort of philosophical 'disappearance trick' with the 'problem of privacy'. When *Le Penseur* is sitting in contemplation upon his rock, all that is going on, and so all we should ever talk about, are neurophysiological processes, and neurophysiologists are increasingly able and willing to tell us about them.

'The labelling fallacy'

I was once told about a teacher who believed that the best way to teach Latin to school boys and girls was to treat it as if it were a living language rather than an ancient code needing to be deciphered. She felt that if she could get her pupils to think in Latin and even to talk to one another in Latin, they would get a better sense of Latin as a language. She also felt that it would be more fun, both for them and herself, and in consequence they would learn more quickly. To that end, she used to write the Latin names for things her pupils would come across in the school yard on large pieces of paper and pin them on the appropriate objects with drawing pins. Thus she pinned *arbor* to the large oak tree outside the sports pavilion, *porta* to the school gate post, and scattered *herba* on various parts of the grass verges. She even pinned a piece of cardboard, with the words *circus maximus* on it, to a stake and placed it in the middle of the school playing field.

While her pupils rapidly increased their Latin vocabulary, and did so with eagerness, the system was by no means foolproof. For when the end of the year examinations arrived, a number of her pupils revealed that they had taken the words *cave canem*, on the gate to the Headmistress's Lodge, to mean 'elaborate wrought-iron gate'. In fact it is to be translated as 'Beware of the dog'. To slip into some jargon for a moment, those pupils had fallen victim of what might be called 'the labelling fallacy'.

They had presumed that all the pieces of paper that were pinned to things were labels bearing the names for those things. Generally speaking, names gain their meaning by picking out or referring to things. *Arbor* means 'tree' because, when spoken or written down, it draws the hearer or reader into thinking of or looking for a real tree. This understanding of the word is probably based, at least some way back, on the fact that someone, say a parent or teacher, at sometime, had pointed at a tree and said 'Tree'.

Now it seemed, and still seems, to many philosophers of mind that just as the Cartesians themselves had, so both the identity theorists and eliminative materialists had committed some form of the labelling fallacy. The identity theorists and the eliminativists had become Cartesian materialists. For the identity theorists could be taken as, in effect, arguing that since mental terms, such as 'a feeling' or 'a sensation of yellow', or even the very word 'mind' itself, did not pick out or refer to any detectable mental events or any mental substance, then they must be referring to detectable physical events and to a physical substance. They must be referring, for that is the obvious candidate, to the brain and its processes. And the eliminative materialists could be taken, in effect, as arguing that since mental terms, such as 'mind' or 'a feeling' or 'a sensation of yellow', did not pick out any mental substances or mental events, and were of no use in picking out anything scientifically relevant in regard to brain states or processes, then they must be regarded as completely misleading and so useless labels. They are labels which purport to refer but in fact fail to do so. They are labels which should be discarded.

At any rate, many philosophers of mind felt that a richer view of language, and so a richer view of how our psychological words and sentences gain their meaning, would show that at least some of the most common mental (psychological) terms were not employed as labels (or naming words) at all. In turn, this would show that there was no need to go in the direction of eliminating our psychological explanations, if these psychological explanations included mental terms which failed to *name* anything, whether these be mental 'things' or physical 'things' such as brain processes.

As philosophy of language has been as active a part of philosophy in the twentieth century as has philosophy of mind, there was no shortage of relevant research to draw upon in seeking alternative employment for our mental terms. Indubitably, the preeminent source, acknowledged or unacknowledged, for the strength of the ensuing linguistic counter-attack against the identity theory and eliminative materialism was the work of Ludwig Wittgenstein. His name came up earlier, in Chapter 2, in connection with the discussion of the Vienna Circle, logical positivism and its links with philosophical behaviourism. Since Wittgenstein is such a commanding figure in twentieth- century philosophy, I should say a little more about him before referring to his work in philosophy of language.

Wittgenstein was born in Vienna in 1889, of a wealthy and cultured family who, while of mostly Jewish descent, were practising Christians. After first studying engineering at the Technische Hochschule in Berlin-Charlottenburg, Wittgenstein then went to Manchester, England, to study aeronautics. Subsequently his interests changed first to mathematics, then to mathematical logic and philosophy of mathematics, and finally to philosophy. Towards the end of this journey from engineering to philosophy, on the advice of the German logician and mathematician Gottlob Frege, Wittgenstein went to Cambridge to become a student of the great English philosopher Bertrand Russell (1872–1970), who was awarded the Nobel Prize for Literature in 1950. Wittgenstein was duly enrolled at Cambridge in the autumn of 1912. Russell tells us this story about Wittgenstein coming to visit him at the end of his first term at Cambridge:

> At the end of his first term at Cambridge he [Wittgenstein] came to me and said 'Will you please tell me whether I am a complete idiot or not?' I replied 'My dear fellow, I don't know. Why are you asking me?' He said, 'Because if I am a complete idiot, I shall become an aeronaut; but, if not, I shall become a philosopher.' I told him to write me something during the vacation on some philosophical subject and I would then tell him whether he was a complete idiot or not. At the beginning of the following term he brought me the fulfilment of this suggestion. After reading only one sentence, I said to him 'No, you must not become an aeronaut.'[38]

During his lifetime, Wittgenstein published only one book, the *Tractatus Logico-Philosophicus*, in 1921. Much of this work was written after Wittgenstein had volunteered to serve in the Austrian army during the First World War. After the war, which

Figure 3.14
An Austrian
postage stamp
issued on the
occasion of
the hundredth
anniversary of
Wittgenstein's
birth.
Wittgenstein
became a
towering
influence on
mid-to-late
twentieth-
century
philosophy.

ended with him as a prisoner of war in Italy, and having completed the *Tractatus*, Wittgenstein gave up philosophy and took
on a variety of jobs such as school teaching and gardening.
However, after attending a lecture by the great Dutch mathematician Brouwer, in 1928, Wittgenstein rekindled his interest in
philosophy. He was persuaded to return to Cambridge in 1929
and the following year he was made a Fellow of Trinity College.
In 1936 Wittgenstein began to write what became Part I of the
posthumous *Philosophical Investigations* (or, simply, *Investigations*), his major work and the book to which, until his death, he
devoted the major part of his philosophical labours. In 1939 he
succeeded G. E. Moore to the Chair of Philosophy at Cambridge

but resigned soon after, believing that a formal academic life was inimical to good philosophy. He died in 1951 and the *Investigations* was published in 1953.

In the *Investigations* one of Wittgenstein's targets is a version of 'the labelling fallacy'. The very first words of Part I of the *Investigations* is the following quotation from Augustine's *Confessions*:

> When they (my elders) named some object, and accordingly moved towards something, I saw this and I grasped that the thing was called by the sound they uttered when they meant to point it out. Their intention was shewn by their bodily movements, as it were the natural language of all peoples: the expression of the face, the play of the eyes, the movement of other parts of the body, and the tone of voice which expresses our state of mind in seeking, having, rejecting, or avoiding something. Thus, as I heard words repeatedly used in their proper places in various sentences, I gradually learnt to understand what objects they signified; and after I had trained my mouth to form these signs, I used them to express my own desires.[39]

Wittgenstein's point in quoting Augustine is that if someone were to think that this was how we learn to use *all* words or, more strongly, that this is the way language in general operates, then this would be an egregious error.

Wittgenstein went on to contrast labelling words, like 'table', 'chair', 'block', 'pillar', 'slab', 'beam', with obvious non-labelling words, like 'Away!', 'Ow!', and 'Help!' It is no accident that each word of the second list, of non-labelling words, has an exclamation mark following it. This is so in order to signify that they should be considered as being part of an actual speech act or utterance. For this reference to the context of utterance is central to Wittgenstein's view of language and the words in it. Words, Wittgenstein suggested, were like tools in a tool box. The tool box has a variety of tools, and the tools have a variety of *uses*. We only find out their use by seeing them used appropriately. Thus the tool box might contain a hammer, a chisel and a saw. We use the hammer to hammer in things, like nails into wood. We use the chisel for such tasks as tapering wooden pegs or smoothing wooden planks. We use the saw for cutting wood. By analogy, we use the utterance 'Away!' as a command to someone or some animal to get out of the way, the cry of 'Ow!' as an expression of pain, and the cry 'Help!' as an urgent request for aid.

In a very famous passage in the *Investigations*, by way of contrast with a labelling account of meaning, Wittgenstein defines the meaning of a word in the following way:

> For a *large* class of cases – though not for all – in which we employ the word 'meaning' it can be defined thus: the meaning of a word is its use in the language.[40]

Wittgenstein's employment of the word 'use' in that passage implied that a host of what might be called 'background considerations' also had a part to play in the use and so in the meaning. Some of these 'background considerations' were described by Wittgenstein as '*language games*', that is, the techniques or procedures we learn in order to use words and so understand them correctly. To take an example, to use the word 'five' correctly, you must be able to count. You must know 'the numbers game'. Another 'background consideration' was *grammar*, though, on the whole, Wittgenstein tended to think of grammar as more liable to mislead us about the meaning of words rather than enlighten us. For example, the sentence 'That is a good hat' is, grammatically speaking, very like the sentence, 'That is a yellow hat', but nevertheless the meaning of the word 'good' operates in a completely different way from the meaning of the word 'yellow'. 'Good' is a term of approval or commendation. 'Yellow' is a descriptive term. Other 'background considerations' were the *context* in which a sentence is uttered and the *tone of voice* with which it is uttered. 'That was a nice shot', spoken in a neutral tone of voice, about Bradman's cover drive to the offside fence 'for four', is praise. 'That was a nice shot', spoken in an ironic tone of voice, about my cover drive, which lifted the ball directly into the hands of the fielder at cover point, is condemnation.

For Wittgenstein, this general purview about the nature of language applied no less to our use of psychological terms or mental words than to any other part of a natural language. You should no more jump to the conclusion that psychological words gain their meaning as labelling words than you should jump to the conclusion that 'Away!' or 'five' gain their meaning by being labelling words. Thus Wittgenstein explained our psychological term 'toothache', allegedly the *name* of some inner mental state called 'a feeling', in the following way:

'What would it be like if human beings shewed no outward signs of pain (did not groan, grimace, etc.)? Then it would be impossible to teach a child the use of the word "toothache".' – Well, let's assume the child is a genius and itself invents a name for the sensation! – But then, of course, he couldn't make himself understood when he used the word. – So does he understand the name, without being able to explain its meaning to anyone? – But what does it mean to say that he has 'named his pain'? – How has he done this naming of pain?![41]

The point, of course, is that we neither use nor learn to use the word 'toothache' through some naming procedure, and *a fortiori* through some private naming procedure. Whatever it is, 'toothache' is not the *name* in the sense of *label* of some inner private mental state. If it was, no one could ever know that his or her inner private mental state merited the same name as your or my inner private mental state. Psychological words, and so psychological explanation, would be impossible.

More positively, Wittgenstein believed that to learn to apply the word 'toothache' correctly, you need to observe a whole 'toothache performance' over time. You need to observe the person struck down with toothache groan and grimace, and you also need to observe, or at least have a good guess at, what caused the groaning and grimacing, and perhaps know how it comes to be relieved, and so on.

Wittgenstein argued the more general case about our psychological terms not being labelling terms, in the following way:

Suppose everyone had a box with something in it: we call it a 'beetle'. No one can look into anyone else's box, and everyone says he knows what a beetle is only by looking at *his* beetle. – Here it would be quite possible for everyone to have something different in his box. One might even imagine such a thing constantly changing. – But suppose the word 'beetle' had a use in these people's language? – If so it would not be used as the name of a thing. The thing in the box has no place in the language-game at all; not even as a *something*: for the box might even be empty. – No, one can 'divide through' by the thing in the box; it cancels out, whatever it is.[42]

The point is if you substitute any 'inner mental state or process', or for that matter any 'inner, wholly individual brain process', for the word 'beetle', you get another version of Wittgenstein's argument that our psychological terms cannot be labels for inner, private *anythings*. Whatever we are doing when we describe other people in psychological terms, we are not doing so by means of labelling their inner private states or processes. For that is not possible. Therefore such 'inner private things' can have no place in our psychological language games.

At any rate, it was against this background that new, subtle, rich and often highly ingenious versions of what exactly we are doing when we describe people psychologically arose. Wittgenstein's own positive account was not the one which came to be generally accepted, because it was thought to be too behaviouristic, but his arguments against the 'labelling view' were enormously influential. More generally, the infusion of a more sophisticated philosophy of language came to be crucial in all future developments in philosophy of mind, and the very nature and status of our 'folk psychology' or commonsense mental descriptions and explanations came to be a central topic of discussion.

CHAPTER FOUR

Computers to the Rescue

Computers come of age

The word 'computer' comes from the Latin word *computare* which means 'to calculate or reckon together'. One of the earliest machines for calculating or reckoning was designed and built by the French philosopher and mathematician Blaise Pascal (1623–62), while still in his teens, to assist his father who was a tax collector.[1] This machine comprised a series of metal cog wheels, pegs and ratchets, and was housed in a wooden box. It was able to perform both addition and subtraction. Pascal's 'calculating box'[2] stirred up considerable interest so that he decided to advertise it to the public in the following words:

Figure 4.1 Pascal's 'calculating box' built in 1642.

I submit to the public a small machine of my own invention, by means of which you alone may, without any effort, perform all the operations of arithmetic, and may be relieved of the work which has oftentimes fatigued your spirit when you have worked with the counters or with the pen.[3]

IBM's sales department could hardly have done better.

However, historically, it is the inventions of the Englishman Charles Babbage (1791–1871) that inaugurated the modern age of the computer, for it was he that made the calculating machine both much more sophisticated and more or less automatic. The machines of Pascal and others, such as the German philosopher and mathematician Gottfried Leibniz (1646–1716), who had added the functions of multiplication and division to Pascal's 'calculating box', required continual setting and resetting of dials, the cranking of handles and the recording on paper of intermediate results on the part of the operator. Babbage, on the other hand, produced a series of detailed designs for a machine that could carry out much more sophisticated calculations without any of this continual human intervention.

Babbage was the Lucasian Professor of Mathematics at Cambridge from 1827 to 1839 and is the envy of all modern academics who are weighed down by the need to teach ever increasing numbers of students. Babbage managed to avoid delivering even a single university lecture during his entire tenure of the chair. It should not be inferred from this that he was either

Figure 4.2 Replica of Leibniz's calculator, invented in 1673.

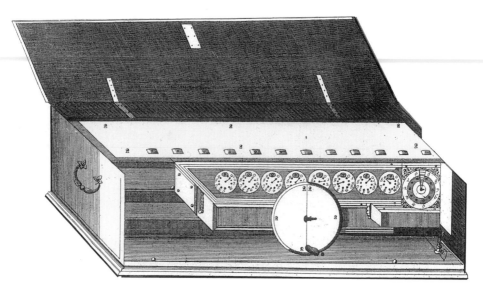

Figure 4.3 English mathematician, Charles Babbage – many of the ideas incorporated in his Analytical Engine were influential in the invention of modern computing machinery.

lazy or reclusive. Far from it. He spent his enormous energy on a wide variety of tasks. Indeed it was only after he had eventually suffered a nervous breakdown that he was offered the sinecure of a chair of mathematics at Cambridge. Among other things, he stood twice for parliament, involved himself in helping to found the Royal Astronomical Society, tried to reform the Royal Society and the working practices of the British Post Office, did research into the operating costs of various industries such as those of the pin-makers and printers (and, in consequence, wrote an influential text on political economy, *On the Economy of Machinery and Manufactures*), and produced reliable tables for various purposes such as actuarial tables about human life expectancy.

Indeed Babbage himself records how, around 1812, he came to invent his first automatic calculating machine in order to avoid the drudgery involved in producing such tables:

> The earliest idea that I can trace in my own mind of calculating arithmetical tables by machinery arose in this manner: One evening I was sitting in the rooms of the Analytical Society, at Cambridge, my head leaning forward on the table in a kind of dreamy mood, with a table of logarithms lying open before me. Another member, coming into the room, and seeing me half asleep, called out, 'Well, Babbage, what are you dreaming about?' to which I replied, 'I am thinking that all these Tables (pointing to the logarithms) might be calculated by machinery.'[4]

Babbage first produced blueprints for a special-purpose automatic calculating machine, which he called a 'Difference Engine'. This name was quite apt as it was a machine designed to calculate and print out automatically a table of various 'differences'. In the first place it was designed to calculate the different values of a variable, y, given a known input value for the other variable, x, which was related to y by means of a complex mathematical function. Thus Babbage's Difference Engine might be set to calculate the values of y given known input values for x in the quadratic function: $y = 2x^2 + 3x + 4$. Thus, for example, if $x = 3$, then $y = 2(9) + 3(3) + 4 = 31$. The machine was designed also to produce, as part of the table, a column of 'first differences', that is, the differences between the values of y produced for each successive value of x (i.e. where $x = 0$, $x = 1$, $x = 2$, $x = 3$, and so on, then $y = 4$, $y = 9$, $y = 18$, $y = 31$, and so on, giving a 'first difference' column of, respectively, 9 minus 4 i.e. 5, 18 minus 9 i.e. 9, 31 minus 18 i.e. 13, and so on). Finally, the machine was designed to produce a column displaying the constant interval, or 'second difference', between these 'first differences' (in this case the constant difference between 5 and 9, 9 and 13, and so on, namely 4). Thus the 'constancy' appearing in the final or 'second difference' column is a quick and easy test of the accuracy of the tables produced. It also enables all other values of y, given an initial value, to be recovered by comparatively simple addition using that initial value plus the 'first' and 'second differences'. In turn this suggests comparatively simple ways of mechanising the computation of the values of y.[5]

With some considerable financial help from the government of the day – for it was thought that his invention would be useful

Figure 4.4
A reconstruction
of Babbage's
Difference
Engine, first
developed by
Babbage
between 1822
and 1833.

to the navy in relieving the tedium in the preparation of its
copious nautical tables – Babbage and his associates built the
first Difference Engine. It is not clear when his first Difference
Engine was built but it is known that he demonstrated a model
to some members of the Royal Society in 1822.

In 1832 Babbage began work on what he called his Analytical
Engine, which, he intended, would be capable of automating any
calculation whatsoever. This machine was to be his most important contribution, indeed extraordinary contribution, as its design
anticipated almost all the essentials of the modern general purpose
or universal computer. Babbage envisaged the main parts of his
Analytical Engine as follows:

1. An input device or way of introducing both a set of instructions and set of values into his machine in a way that could
   be 'understood' by the machine.
2. A main control unit, which would receive the input instructions and values, and then ensure that the machine carried
   out the calculations in the correct sequence as instructed.
3. A calculating unit, which Babbage called 'the mill', which
   did the mechanical calculations.

4. A memory, which Babbage called 'a store', which would hold both the initial numerical data for use in the problem to be solved and any intermediate data generated in the course of the calculations.

5. An output device for publishing the solution to the problem or result of the calculations.[6]

Babbage had quite definite ideas as to how this blueprint for a universal calculating machine would be realised mechanically. As regards the *input device* and *control unit*, he was greatly influenced by the automated looms of the Frenchman Joseph Marie Jacquard (1752–1834), which had revolutionised the silk-weaving industry at the beginning of the nineteenth century. When the Jacquard looms were in operation, the intricate patterns of the resulting cloth were controlled by a series of holes punched out on paste-board cards. These cards were fed into the looms by being strung together in sequence and then smoothly fed into the machines over a drum. As each card was pressed against the rods which held the warp threads, any rod lying opposite a hole was left as it was, while a rod not opposite a hole was lifted so that the shuttle carrying the weft thread passed underneath it. Thus the intricate dance of the rods and shuttle, as choreographed by the holes in the cards, laid down the pattern in the threads. Babbage himself was so impressed by Jacquard's use of punched cards as an input and control device for automated operations that he kept a portrait of Jacquard, woven on a Jacquard loom, on the wall of his own drawing room. Jacquard's fellow weavers, who still wove their silk cloth by hand, with great patience, skill and labour, were less impressed and on one occasion they attacked his machines with such violence that Jacquard himself barely escaped with his life.

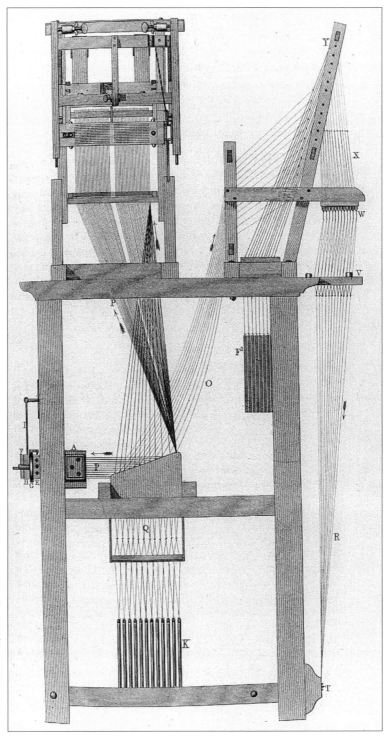

Figure 4.5
The semi-
automated
loom of
Joseph Maria
Jacquard, with
the punched
cards
displayed
opposite.

In regard to these punched cards Babbage envisaged, first, a set of *operation cards* that would carry the punched-hole instructions as to what calculations (addition, multiplication and so on) the machine was to make, and thereby, in effect, for a period, would turn the general purpose Analytical Engine into a specific purpose Calculating Engine. Then Babbage proposed a set of *variable cards* that would supply mechanically, from *memory* or 'store', the values of particular variables (as well as the value of any constants) involved in the calculations.

Babbage was less certain and so less clear how the other parts of his Analytical Engine would be incarnated in machinery. The central *calculating unit* was envisaged, at least initially, as involving gears, rods and linkages in more or less the manner of the then current industrial machinery, such as the Jacquard looms. The *memory* or 'store' of the Analytical Engine was to be composed of stacks of wheels, each with ten positions, and so capable of representing a decimalised number system. He had not decided what form his *output device* should take. However he toyed with the idea of hooking up his Analytical Engine to a printing machine or at least to a machine which could make moulds from which printers' blocks could be made.

Indeed it seems that Babbage called his mechanised computer 'an engine', and its calculating unit 'a mill' and its memory unit 'a store', in order to suggest an analogy with the machines of the newly mechanised and much admired printing and weaving industries. It is said that Babbage also intended that his calculating machines would be powered by the recently invented steam engine and so thereby be made fully automatic.

Babbage himself never succeeded in building a completed Analytical Engine. Each time he would begin, reach a certain stage, and then abandon the whole attempt in favour of what he believed was a better way of going about it. The lack of precision engineers capable of meeting his exacting requirements for machine parts, plus his own perfectionist and irascible temperament, probably made such failure inevitable during his own lifetime.

In a quite literal sense, it was, in part, yet again Jacquard's punched cards that led to the next great advance, namely the electrification of the computer, and so to the modern era. This advance occurred in the last two decades of the nineteenth century, when John Shaw Billings (1839–1913), Superintendent of the US Bureau of the Census, and his younger colleague at the

Bureau, Herman Hollerith (1860–1929), set out to automate the gathering of census data. A fellow worker in the Census office recorded the following inaugurating event:

> While the returns of the Tenth (1880) Census were being tabulated at Washington, Billings was walking with a companion [Hollerith] through the office in which hundreds of clerks were engaged in laboriously transferring items of information from the schedules to the record sheets by the slow and heartbreaking method of hand tallying. As they were watching the clerks he said to his companion, 'There ought to be some mechanical way of doing this job, something on the principle of the Jacquard loom, whereby holes in a card regulate the pattern to be woven.' The seed fell on good ground. His companion was a talented young engineer in the office who first convinced himself that the idea was practicable and then that Billings had no desire to claim or use it.[7]

Soon afterwards Hollerith left the Bureau in order to devote himself completely to the task of inventing a machine for automating the gathering and tabulating of information. In particular he worked on the design for an *electromechanical* machine which could operate with punched cards. Hollerith realised that just as a hole in a card can cause a mechanical effect, such as allowing a rod to pass through the hole, so it can cause an electrical effect, such as allowing a current of electricity to pass through the hole. He also realised that this latter effect *ipso facto* provides a binary or two-place 'machine language', namely 'open' (with current flowing freely through) or 'closed' (with current blocked), which, in turn, could be interpreted, as in the case of a census questionnaire, as the answers 'yes' or 'no'.

It was machines based on Hollerith's designs that were in fact used in the first automated census in the United States, the now famous Eleventh Census of 1890. Strictly speaking, Hollerith had designed a cooperating collection of machines: one for making the cards with the 288 locations for possible punched holes, another for punching the holes, another for sorting the now-punched cards, and finally, and most importantly, the machine for tabulating the data. This Census of 1890 was an enormous success and proved to be an astonishing demonstration of the power of Hollerith's electromechanical machines. Soon afterwards, on the back of this extraordinary success, he set up the Tabulating Machine Company to exploit his designs commercially. In 1911 Hollerith sold this company, which then became the Computer Tabulating Recording Company. In 1924, after merging with two other companies, it in turn became the International Business Machines Corporation, now known simply as IBM.

With hindsight, that most powerful of our senses, it is easy to see how the next and final series of advances came about. They resulted from the marriage of the basic design of a general purpose analytical device as envisaged by Babbage with the 'hands on' electronic 'savvy' of entrepreneurs like Hollerith. The products were, first, the sophisticated electromechanical calculator and then the general purpose, all-electronic computer.

In 1937, while still a graduate student in physics at Harvard University, Howard H. Aiken (1900–73), in collaboration with George R. Stibitz, a mathematician at Bell Telephone Laboratories, wrote a paper outlining how the rudimentary punched-card electromechanical calculators, then being produced by IBM, could be turned into quite sophisticated, if still electromechanical, calculators. Aiken approached IBM and, in 1939, began the collaboration which ended with the construction of the Automatic Sequence Controlled Calculator. This was hailed, in a 1946 issue of the preeminent science journal, *Nature*, as the 'realisation of Babbage's project, although its physical form has the benefit of twentieth century engineering'.[8] Among the advances employed by Aiken and his collaborators was the use of punched tape on a continuous roll, with the complete programme or set of instructions in very precise sequence, as the *input device*. This idea was first used by T. H. Flowers (1905–98) when building 'Colossus', arguably the first fully (or almost fully) electronic computer, a code-breaking machine at Bletchley Park in Buckinghamshire, England, during the Second World War. Aiken and his collaborators also made use of electrical accumulators (or storage batteries) as part of the 'store' or *memory*, of an electromechanical relay system similar to what was then in use in telephone exchanges as part of both the *memory* and the *calculating unit*, and of typewritten sheets as one form of *output*. Furthermore, all the parts, input, memory, calculator and so on were integrated into a single, albeit rather large, machine.

The resulting machine contained some three-quarters of a million parts and more than five hundred miles of wiring. Besides the basic arithmetical functions of addition, subtraction, multiplication and division, it could calculate such things as logarithms,[9] and trigonometric tables.[10] An indication of its speed was that it took about five or six seconds to perform even a quite complex multiplication and about twelve seconds for division. By the standards of contemporary computers that is very slow. At that time it was simply astonishing.

However Aiken's machine had barely become operational when it was superseded by ENIAC, America's first electronic computer, in December 1945. ENIAC or the Electronic Numerical Integrator and Computer was a wartime project financed by America's War Department. It was designed and built by John Presper Eckert, Jr (1919–95), and John William Mauchley (1907–80), together with their associates in the Moore School of

Figure 4.6 An early, modern, room-sized computer, ENIAC, developed in America during World War II by John Presper Eckert, Jr., and John William Mauchley.

Electrical Engineering, at the University of Pennsylvania. ENIAC was more than a hundred times faster than Aiken's machine at Harvard and just as reliable (or, by current standards, just as unreliable). It could do in an hour what took Aiken's machine a week. This gain in speed was a result, especially, of the fact that, excepting for its input and output devices, which still involved switches and made use of punched cards, there were no mechanically moving parts whatsoever. In particular, this was brought about by Eckert and Mauchley's substitution of electron vacuum tubes (or thermionic valves) for the comparatively ponderous electromechanical relays of Aiken's machine. Just as a relay, like a gate or switch, can be 'on' or 'off', so can a vacuum tube. It is 'on' when electrons are flowing through the tube (as in an ordinary household battery, from the negative electrode, or *cathode*, to the positive, or *anode*). It is 'off', when there is no such flow. Like Aiken's machine, ENIAC was physically a giant. It was 100 feet long, 10 feet high and 3 feet wide and arranged in a U-shape. It contained 18,000 vacuum tubes, 70,000 resistors, 10,000 capacitors and 6,000 switches.

ENIAC, and its immediate successors, were built for special scientific work. ENIAC's first commercial offspring was the UNIVAC (or Universal Automatic Computer), built by the newly formed Eckert-Mauchley Computer Corporation, which in turn became soon afterwards part of the Remington Rand Corporation. The UNIVAC achieved fame by predicting the result of the 1952 US presidential election, won by Dwight D. Eisenhower, and by predicting almost exactly the number of electoral votes won by both candidates, Eisenhower and Stevenson, on the basis of less than 7 per cent of the votes tallied.[11]

For the time being, I have deliberately passed over Alan Turing's wartime work on computerised code-breaking at Bletchley Park, and his subsequent work on automatic computing machines at Teddington and Manchester. The reason is that his work has had a greater influence on psychology and philosophy of mind than has the work of any other person in computing, so I want to discuss it, with that influence in mind, in the next section.

Major technical advances since the 1950s include the replacement of the unreliable valves with very reliable transistors,[12] the replacement of punched cards with keyboard terminals and of cumbersome programming languages with user-friendly ones,[13] the substitution of mass-produced printed circuit boards for laboriously hand-wired circuits and, in general, the progressive miniaturising of practically everything associated with computers. However, arguably the greatest advances over the same period have been in terms of the social and economic impact of the computer upon the community. The computer is now commonplace and inhabits every aspect of the culture of developed countries, because technical advances have brought about not merely an enormous decrease in the size of computers but also an enormous decrease in their cost. In the twenty-first century the most permanent and valued workers in most offices in developed western countries are the computers on the desks.

Humans, at least those not employed in the computer industry, often feel threatened by the computer. Many factories have already laid off workers in favour of computer-controlled manufacturing processes or robots. Human traffic police, telephone operators and bank tellers have all but disappeared. Whole industries, especially old-fashioned communication industries such as the postal or telephone service, are in danger of being rendered completely obsolete by personal computers linked by e-mail.

However, there is a deeper sense of threat that has been produced by the inexorable advance of the computer. Put bluntly, in regard to many tasks, the computer seems to be cleverer than we are. Its brain is better than ours. It performs highly intellectual tasks, such as sophisticated calculations, much faster and much more reliably than we can. In 1988 a supercomputer, with specialised hardware for playing chess and operating on a program called 'Deep Thought', defeated the Danish grandmaster, Bent Larsen, in tournament play. This computer had two processors working together or 'in parallel' which enabled it to analyse 750,000 chess positions per second. In 1989 the computer and its program were improved by having six processors working together which could analyse 2,000,000 positions per second.

Over the following years both the computer and the chess program were improved even more, and renamed 'Deep Blue'. In February 1996 'Deep Blue' defeated the then world champion, and arguably the greatest human chess player of all time, the Russian Gary Kasparov, in the opening game of the ACM Chess Challenge held in Philadelphia. When, after some difficulty, Kasparov finally defeated 'Deep Blue' to win the series 4–2, he declared afterwards that it was extremely important that he had won as he had been battling on behalf of the human race.

In May 1997, in the presence of more than two hundred

journalists from around the world, Kasparov entered into a second, six-game, chess challenge in New York with an improved 'Deep Blue'. By now 'Deep Blue' had been programmed with the knowledge of every grandmaster game from the last hundred years and could analyse about 200 million positions per second. At stake was more than one million dollars in prize money and what one commentator described as 'the dignity of the human race'. As Kasparov himself put it, 'A victory by "Deep Blue" would be a very important and frightening milestone in the history of mankind.'

With a win apiece and three games drawn, 'Deep Blue' won the final, deciding game. The *Boston Herald* ran the headline, 'You lose, Man'. While IBM shares rose on the New York Stock Exchange to a 52-week high, Gary Kasparov's stocks were at their lowest point. He seemed to be a broken man. In his own words:

> We [he and his advisers] faced a machine that made moves that were beyond anybody's understanding . . .
> Because I'm a human being and after game two [which 'Deep Blue' won], I had major, major problems of getting back into the match. I proved to be vulnerable. When I see something that is well beyond my understanding, I'm scared.[14]

In recent years, over articles by science correspondents in newspapers, we have become used to headlines such as, 'Researchers build silicon chip that acts like human brain cell', 'Roboprof sees rise of the evil androids' and 'The superiority of the human mind is under threat: scientists predict that within 50 years machines will think for themselves.' In 1997 newspapers had the front-page headline, '39 die in computer cult suicide'.

Computer programs and human intelligence

In the section immediately above, I have concentrated almost exclusively on advances in the design and construction of computers. Strictly speaking this is a very one-sided view of computing. A full and proper account of an operational computer must include, besides its design and construction, an account of its programming. An account of a computer's program is an account of the task or tasks it is carrying out and of the menu or recipe that instructs the machine so that it can successfully carry out that task or those tasks.

39 dead cult members were packed and ready to go

Tim Cornwell
Rancho Santa Fe

The 39 cult members whose bodies were found in a mansion were well prepared for their journey to outer space, where they apparently believed they would fly on a UFO in the wake of the Hale-Bopp comet.

The 21 women and 18 men had their passports and IDs tucked in the top pockets of their matching black shirts.

They were equipped with $5 dollar bills and small change and had their suitcases close to hand. San Diego County police

and doctors said yesterday that all indications were that the cult members died in a mass suicide, using a mixture of alcohol and phenobarbitol and plastic bags over their heads.

They killed themselves in three waves over a period of days, with the last survivors removing the bags of the earlier dead and draping them with purple scarves.

According to "recipes" they held, they were directed to swallow their drugs with pudding or apple sauce. Each one had video-taped a statement saying they were "going to a

better place".

As post mortem examinations got under way, documents retrieved from the World Wide Web appeared to confirm that the victims killed themselves in a ritual timed to coincide with the arrival of the Hale-Bopp comet, and possibly with Holy Week. They believed they were "angels" who would "shed their containers" to join a UFO.

One passage from the Internet read: "We are happily prepared to leave 'this world' and go with Ti's crew."

Internet angels, page 3

Figure 4.7 A newspaper article about the notorious Hale-Bopp suicides near San Diego, California, in 1997.

Just as computers needed engineers to bring them into existence, so they need programmers to make them operational. Historically, just as there was a Babbage or a Hollerith or an Aiken, so there were those who invented and advanced the art of programming. Indeed it was Babbage's assistant, the mathematician Augusta Ada Byron (1815–52), daughter of the poet Lord Byron, and later Lady Lovelace, who is given the accolade of being the first programmer. With remarkable foresight, she speculated that, one day, a Babbage-type machine might be programmed to play chess or compose music. Babbage himself left no systematic account about how exactly his Analytical Engine was to be programmed. However, Lady Lovelace's extensive notes to the account of the Analytical Engine, published by the Italian military engineer Luigi Menabrea,[15] are in effect a quite detailed manual for programming Babbage's engine. And Lady Lovelace herself has succinctly described the importance of the programmer's task, 'The Analytical Engine has no pretensions whatever to originate anything. It can do whatever we *know how to order it* to perform.'[16]

Originally programming was fairly primitive and amounted to making machine connections by hand, such as opening and closing switches, setting dials or putting plugs in sockets and pulling

Figure 4.8
Babbage's
collaborator,
the English
mathematician,
Ada, Countess
of Lovelace,
who is
sometimes
called the
world's first
computer
programmer.

them out again. Now complete programs of instructions are stored inside the computer and are merely activated by the person who happens to be using it at the time. The programmer's art is to produce these stored programs by making use of the basic operations that are built into the hardware of a computer by the engineers. To keep it simple, let us say that a computer's hardware is only capable of addition. The programmer could still produce a program for multiplication for this computer. For the task 'Multiply 7 by 7' becomes, in the programmer's instructions, the task 'Add 7 to 7 to 7 to 7 to 7 to 7 to 7'. In general, for someone to make use of the computer's hardware, at some point this hardware must be capable of being instructed in its own terms. A modern computer receives instructions by having a processing unit that has a program which can translate the user's instructions into its basic machine operations.

However the influence of computing on philosophy of mind and theoretical psychology came about, at least initially, through the work of two very different people who found themselves working with machinery in the interests of the Allied war effort during the Second World War. The first of these two people is the British philosopher turned psychologist Kenneth Craik (1914–45). As an undergraduate student at the University of Edinburgh, Craik studied philosophy. On completion of his undergraduate degree, with great distinction, Craik studied psychology for a year at Edinburgh before going to Cambridge to continue his graduate work in psychology. He obtained his Ph.D. at Cambridge in 1940. Subsequently, as war work, he engaged in research on such things as night vision and adaptation to glare, the design of radar display panels and of anti-aircraft range-finding equipment. In 1945, at the age of 31, Craik was killed in a road accident, while riding his bicycle in Cambridge, on the eve of VE (Victory in Europe) Day.

It was during the war, in 1943, that Craik's one and only book, *The Nature of Explanation*, was published. It is, strictly speaking, a work of philosophical psychology, and more read and admired these days by philosophers than by psychologists. Its central theme is that human thought, or some of it, has close similarities to the activities of those machines which model aspects of the world and then make action-guiding predictions on the basis of those models or analogues. For example, a machine might be capable of predicting, on the basis of a theoretical model, that an aeroplane, which has been observed travelling at such and such a speed, at such and such an altitude, and coming from such and such a direction, will be in range of an anti-aircraft battery in three minutes' time at coordinates so and so. On the basis of that prediction, the gun crew of the anti-aircraft battery might fire into the night sky in a particular direction in three minutes' time.

We humans do much the same sort of thing on many occasions. Indeed that is the core of our mental life. We avoid danger, at least sometimes, by first imagining what would happen if we were to do so and so, and then by predicting that what would happen would turn out to be dangerous. In turn, we sometimes

Figure 4.9
Scottish
psychologist,
Kenneth Craik,
who published
the influential
book, *The
Nature of
Explanation*,
in 1943.

bolster our imagination by remembering or reconstructing a model of just what happened when I, or someone of my acquaintance, did just that sort of thing on a previous occasion, and by then adjusting this model to the new circumstances. Or an engineer designs a bridge on the basis of building a scale model, out of wood or on paper or on a computer screen or in his or her mind. In terms of the model, and without having to go to the expense of constructing a full-scale bridge and engaging in a long process of trial and error, he or she can predict what would happen if the bridge were to carry such and such a load. As Craik himself summed up at the end of *The Nature of Explanation*:

Assuming then the existence of the external world I have outlined a symbolic theory of thought, in which the nervous system is viewed as a calculating machine capable of modelling or paralleling external events, and I have suggested that this process of paralleling is the basic feature of thought and of explanation. The possessor of a nervous system is thus able to anticipate events instead of making invariable empirical trial.[17]

The most famous name associated with the design and programming of computers in Britain this century is that of Alan Turing (1912–54). After graduating in mathematics at King's College, Cambridge, he was elected soon afterwards, in 1935, to a Fellowship at King's on the basis of a thesis on a particular theorem in probability theory. Probability theory is a mathematically-expressed theory about the likelihood of some circumscribed event occurring in comparison with the other possible outcomes. For example, a professional gambler might find it useful to know the exact probability, expressed as a precise percentage, of a double six coming upon two tosses of a dice with six sides numbered one to six.

After obtaining his Fellowship, and prompted by a letter from one of his teachers at Cambridge, Turing was then invited to become a graduate researcher at Princeton University in New Jersey, where he collaborated with the philosopher and logician Alonzo Church (1903–95). Almost immediately on returning from Princeton, Turing, like Craik, was drawn into war work at the outbreak of the Second World War. It was only some thirty years or so after the end of the war, and long after his death, that what was for so long top secret could be revealed and the supreme importance of Turing's war work could be made known.

Turing was a master code-breaker who helped to design the decoding device, the 'Bombe', at Bletchley Park in Buckinghamshire. With this machine and Flowers's 'Colossus', and aided by the fortuitous capture of a German encoding machine, an Engima machine, the Bletchley Park cryptanalysts were able, eventually, to read all the German secret codes. At the end of the war Turing joined the National Physical Laboratory at Teddington in Surrey and worked on the design of the experimental machine, the Pilot Model ACE (Automatic Computing Engine). When it was completed, some years later, it became one

Figure 4.10
The English
mathematician,
Alan Turing.
He outlined the
principles of a
multi-functional
'Turing
machine' and
so laid the
foundations for
modern digital
computing.

of the earliest, stored-program, electronic computers in Britain. In 1948 Turing was appointed Deputy Director (there was no director) of the Royal Society Computing Machine Laboratory at Manchester University. Turing, a homosexual, committed suicide in 1954, at the age of forty-one, some three years after he had been arrested by the police and charged with gross indecency.

However, from the point of view of Turing's influence on philosophy of mind and cognitive science, it is his work of the mid-1930s that is of most relevance. In 1936 Turing had published a paper, 'On Computable Numbers, with an Application to the *Entscheidungsproblem* [decision problem]',[18] in the *Proceedings of the London Mathematical Society*. In the course of that paper, Turing developed what has subsequently become known as the Turing Machine.[19] This machine is not a design for a particular sort of electronic computer but an idealisation of the design for any general purpose computer. Though there are no grounds for thinking that Turing was directly influenced by Babbage's work, a Turing Machine can be seen as the continuation of Babbage's basic aim of designing a general purpose Analytical Engine.

While it was strictly speaking just an abstract conception, that is, abstracted from any particular sort of hardware, Turing allowed that one could visualise his Turing Machine in the following way. Input would be in the form of an infinitely, or at least indefinitely, long tape made up of discrete squares. Each square would be either blank or have some symbol printed on it. The 'mill' or calculating unit would be that part of the machine which could, among other tasks, 'read' (in the sense of 'be causally affected by the symbol or lack of symbol' on it) one square at a time, move the tape forward or backward one square at a time, and erase or print a symbol on a square. Output, like input, would be in the form of a tape with symbols on it. The central idea was that a machine capable of such step-by-step procedures, brought about by instruction through a language or set of symbols, was *ipso facto* capable of solving any problem (or, it is now thought, almost any problem[20]) whose solution could be reduced to a series of instructable step-by-step procedures.

For our purposes, it was certain consequences of this concept of a Turing Machine that gave further weight to Craik's suggestion that human mental activity was to be identified, not with the brain, but with its functions, or, at least, with some of them. Turing went on to suggest, in perhaps his most famous paper, 'Computing Machinery and Intelligence', 1950, that we should equate human intelligence with certain sorts of functions (such as answering questions intelligently, playing intellectual games, being able to learn, and so on) rather than with a certain sort of hardware, such as our brain and central nervous system.

To illustrate this point, Turing proposed what he called the Imitation Game. He proposed two versions, with the first version being merely employed as an easy stepping-stone to the second, important version. The Imitation Game, in its first version, involves three people, A (a man), B (a woman), and C (an interrogator). The aim of this first version is for C, who is in a room apart from A and B, to try and find out which of the two, A (pretending to be a woman) or B, is the woman, simply by asking questions. In order that the interrogator may not be influenced by tones of voice, the questions and answers are to be communicated through a teleprinter.

Now it is the second version of this game that Turing is really interested in. For it involves substituting a computer for A. The aim of this version of the game is for C to try and discover whether it is A or B that is the machine. Nowadays this version of the game is known as the Turing Test and the game is in fact played out every few years. Recently annual contests have been held in the Boston Computing Museum. As with the programs for chess computers, ever more sophisticated programs for intelligent conversation are being developed, so that it is becoming more and more difficult for C to win.

The important point, or one of the points, that Turing was emphasising by means of the Turing Test, was that 'the new problem [of finding out which one was the machine] has the advantage of drawing a fairly sharp line between the physical and intellectual capacities of man'.[21] In a literal manner, the physical presence of A and B is shielded from C, and C is only able to contact their intellectual capacities through a question and answer procedure. Furthermore it will be clear in a very

Figure 4.11 The Turing Test. It remains hotly disputed whether a computer that could pass itself off as a human in this type of test would really be intelligent.

concrete way that if and when a machine passes the Turing Test, then intellectual capacities are independent from their physical realisation or, for that matter, their spiritual realisation. It will have been shown, Turing believed, that intellectual capacities, and perhaps mental capacities in general, are realisable in any number of forms, neurophysiologically and electronically being just two, obvious, well-known incarnations.

The mind as the computer's software

It will come as no surprise, then, that contemporary philosophy of mind and theoretical psychology have been deeply influenced by the computer. In particular, it is this distinction between computer 'software' (or its programming) and computer 'hardware' (or its physical construction) that has suggested to philosophers a new and attractive solution to the mind–brain problem itself.

Just as an operating computer behaves in accordance with a user's instructions which tap into a certain program or set of programs realised in and implemented by a computer's electronic hardware, so the human mind can be described as a particular set of, mainly cognitive, 'programs' realised in and implemented by the brain's neural hardware. Biological evolution has both developed the brain's hardware, namely the sophisticated and complex neuronal architecture of the brain and central nervous system, as well as its basic 'programs'. A combination of genetic inheritance and individual maturation, from foetus to adult, is the programmer of any particular individual's mental capacities. Input into 'the human computer' is often, though not always, the information that comes into the human machine by means of the human senses, such as those of hearing, taste, touch, or sight. In turn this information will set in motion some particular 'program' or part of a 'program' which we think of as that person's psychology. The output of this human computational machinery is human behaviour in all its forms, including action or inaction, verbal thought and behaviour, facial expression and bodily gesture, and emotional passivity or perturbation.

To align the mind with a computer's software and the brain with a computer's hardware immediately avoids certain things worth avoiding and produces certain results worth having. For a start, such an alignment clearly obviates the need, even for the most materialistic and scientific of theorists, for any crude mind-to-brain identification. On the analogy of a computer, the mind is no more to be identified with the brain than a computer's program is to be identified with its mechanical or electronic hardware. The mind is the brain's (and central nervous system's) 'software' and so clearly distinct from its 'hardware'. Furthermore, there is also no need to postulate the existence of a special non-physical 'stuff' or substance with which to identify the mind and thereby to guarantee its independence.

Another clear gain that accrued from viewing the mind as the brain's 'software' was a new and seemingly impregnable autonomy for psychology and psychologists. Just as programmers are absolutely essential to the computer industry and could not be passed over in favour of just employing electronic engineers, so psychologists could never be ousted from their jobs in favour of neurophysiologists. Psychologists have the essential and unique job, not of programming the brain, but of working backwards to discover the 'program' or set of 'programs' that have been created by evolution, plus, in the case of particular individuals, individual development. Thus, in viewing the mind as the brain's 'software', the autonomy of the science of psychology was also assured.

The philosopher who made most capital out of this parallel between machine computation and mental activity, and made particular reference to Turing, was the American Hilary Putnam. Putnam was born in 1926, went as an undergraduate to the University of Pennsylvania, and obtained his Ph.D. in 1951 at UCLA (the University of California at Los Angeles), with a thesis on the concept of probability under the supervision of an émigré from the Vienna Circle, the German philosopher of science Hans Reichenbach (1891–1953). After a number of posts, teaching both philosophy and mathematics, at various American universities, Putnam was appointed Walter Beverly Pearson Professor of Mathematical Logic at Harvard University in 1976.

The seminal paper, in which Putnam developed a fully articulated functionalist account of mind from a consideration of the concept of a Turing Machine, was 'Minds and Machines' (1960). In that essay, after elaborating upon the concept of a Turing Machine, he wrote:

> It is interesting to note that just as there are two possible descriptions of the behaviour of a Turing machine – the engineer's structural blueprint and the logician's 'machine table' [the table setting out in a purely formal or logical way the functional relation of input data to internal states and to

Figure 4.12
American
philosopher,
Hilary
Putman, who
introduced
Turing's ideas
into modern
philosophy of
mind.

output] – so there are two possible descriptions of human psychology. The 'behaviouristic' approach . . . aims at eventually providing a complete physicalistic description of human behaviour, in terms which link up with chemistry and physics. This corresponds to the engineer's or physicist's description of a physically realized Turing machine. But it would also be possible to seek a more abstract description of human mental processes, in terms of 'mental states' (physical realization, if any, unspecified) and '[sense] impressions' (these play the role of symbols on the machine's tapes) – a description which would specify the laws controlling the order in which states succeeded one another, and the relation to verbalization (or, at any rate, verbalized thought). This description, which would be the analogue of a 'machine table', it was in fact the program of classical psychology to provide![22]

In short, Putnam is saying that psychology as a subject is free from any worry about being taken over by neurophysiology, because it deals with something, the brain's 'program', which is independent from the subject matter of neurophysiology, the brain. The task for psychologists, or at least cognitive psychologists, is to provide a detailed description of 'the human program', that is, 'the machine table', of the human machine, while, presumably, physiologists and biochemists, together with, perhaps, some unreformed psychological behaviourists, are to provide the equivalent of the 'engineer's or physicist's description' of the human machine. In calculating the human 'machine table', a psychologist need only take account of a human as an information-processing machine, and so need only take account of input information (sensory impressions), internal processing of that information (thinking), and output of information (the verbalisation of thought).

In a real sense, Putnam concluded, the analogy between the relation of our mental life to our bodily life (including, in particular, to our brain's processing), and the relation between a computer's 'machine table' and its electronic or mechanical realisation, deflates the importance of the mind–body problem. It shows that the realisation of the mind, that is to say, 'the human psychological program', in the neurophysiological stuff of the human brain rather than in the spiritual stuff of a soul is just as *ad hoc* or contingent as the realisation of a program for alphabeticising names in your IBM computer rather than my Apple Mac or Babbage's Analytic Engine.

In 1973, as part of a symposium on 'Computers and the Mind' at the University of California at Berkeley, Putnam presented a paper 'Philosophy and Our Mental Life'. In this paper he returned to the central theme of 'Minds and Machines', again emphasising the importance of making the distinction between the functional description of a computing machine (its program) and the physical description of such a machine (its construction) and so, by analogy, the distinction between the psychological description of a human (the functional description) and the neurophysiological description of a human (the physical description). Again he also emphasised that it makes no more sense to identify the mind with the brain than it does to identify a computer's program with its physical realisation.

There were two things in the paper which were new and important. The first was that Putnam offered a caution about taking the analogy between human psychology and a computer's program too literally and so too far. There were important differences. The most important being, perhaps, that all humans were able to learn from experience and 'so change their own program' but very few computers could do that unaided. But even to speak of a single 'program', or of a particular human being in a particular state at a particular time which in turn was describable in tabular fashion, was too Procrustean as regards human psychology. Human psychology is more complex.

The second novelty in this paper was Putnam's additional argument for the autonomy of our mental life and our descriptions of it. This argument took the form of arguing not merely against identifying psychological events with neurophysiological events, but against the very attempt to reduce explanations of human behaviour in psychological terms, which was the right level for worthwhile explanations, to explanations at any lower level, such as that of biochemistry or physics, because *ipso facto* such explanations would be at the wrong level. As usual he argues by analogy. Consider our usual explanation of why a square wooden peg, whose length of side is x, will not go into a round hole in a plastic base, where the diameter of the hole is x. This explanation is at the level of solid geometry. We explain that the surface area of the square on the top of the square peg can be shown to be greater than the surface area of the round hole into which someone is trying to insert the peg. Or, less technically, we say that if you place the square peg at the entrance to the hole, you can see that the corners of the peg stick out and stop the peg going into the hole. Now it must be admitted that one could give another 'deeper' explanation of why the square peg will not fit into the round hole. It is conceivable, just, that a very clever physicist and his or her team at MIT, with the aid of the world's largest computer, could give an explanation in terms of the actual configurations of the sub-atomic particles comprising the wooden peg and the plastic base with the hole in it and the interplay between the two. But it would take an inordinate amount of time to produce that explanation and, when it had been produced, few if any people, other than those in the MIT team, would be able to understand it or would even be interested enough to go through the interminably long series of mathematical equations and formulae in order to gain some understanding. To put it paradoxically, such an 'explanation' would not give any useful explanation.

So, to give another example, while it might literally be possible, at some time in the future, to give a physical explanation at the neurophysiological level, or even at the micro-level of sub-atomic physics, as to why I crossed the road just now, the useful and informative explanation will always be because I *believed* that I *saw* my old friend Carol *looking* into a shop window on the other side and I *wanted* to have a *chat* with her. That is, the useful and informative explanation will always be at the psychological or 'software' level. Even in the unlikely event that one could bring it off, it would not be useful to try and reduce this explanation to any explanation at a lower, physical or 'hardware' level, because such a physical explanation would not explain in any useful sense.

Putnam points out that psychology is not special or peculiar in resisting the reduction of its explanations to lower-level explanations. The same is true, for example, of economics. It would be absurd to try and derive the laws of economics from, say, just the laws of physics. To attempt such a reduction would be to mistake the level of description at which explanations in economics work. It would be futile to try and reduce talk about, say, money supply, inflation and unemployment to, say, talk about neutrons, protons and electrons.

Functionalism becomes the orthodoxy of the day

This account of a human's mental life as the operational 'software' of the human machine became so attractive that subsequently it has been developed into a complete philosophy of mind. In the vanguard of this enterprise has been Jerry Fodor. Fodor was born in New York City in 1935 and pursued his undergraduate studies at Columbia College. He received his Ph.D. in philosophy from Princeton University in 1960. Until comparatively recently, when he was made State of New Jersey Professor of Philosophy at Rutgers, he had spent all of his academic life at the Massachusetts Institute of Technology, where he held a joint appointment in philosophy and psychology.

In 1981 Fodor presented functionalism to the discerning readership of the *Scientific American* as both the solution to the mind–body problem and as a philosophy of mind for the new Age of Information. Functionalism was presented as solution to the perennial problem of how to relate mind to body because it alone was able to occupy that *via media* between the unworkable Cartesian dualism of mental and physical substances and the crude monistic materialism of the behaviourists and identity theorists. Furthermore it was not difficult to see how functionalism, based as it was on the software/hardware distinction in computing,

Figure 4.13 American philosopher, Jerry Fodor, arguably the best known exponent of functionalism in modern philosophy of mind.

fitted in with the new computer-based sciences which were contributing so much to the revolution in information technology and, especially, to the comparatively recent and exciting research programme called 'artificial intelligence'. As Fodor himself summed things up:

> In the past 15 years a philosophy of mind called functionalism that is neither dualist nor materialist has emerged from philosophical reflection on developments in artificial intelligence, computational theory, linguistics, cybernetics and psychology. All these fields, which are collectively known as the cognitive

sciences, have in common a certain level of abstraction and a concern with systems that process information. Functionalism, which seeks to provide a philosophical account of this level of abstraction, recognizes the possibility that systems as diverse as human beings, calculating machines and disembodied spirits could all have mental states. In the functionalist view the psychology of a system depends not on the stuff it is made of (living cells, metal or spiritual energy) but on how the stuff is put together.[23]

As Fodor was eager to point out, functionalism seemed to occupy the best of all possible theoretical worlds. For example, it obviated any problems about the causal interaction between mind and body, because functionalism was not a dualism of mental or spiritual substance and physical substance but a much more subtle dualism of abstract function (or 'software') and its realisation (or 'hardware'). Thus causal interactions were always and entirely at the one level of functions-already-realised-in-some-sort-of-hardware. Functionalism also gave a very clear and attractive answer to the nagging problem about what exactly *Le Penseur* was doing as he sat there on his rock contemplating. *Le Penseur*, according to the functionalist, could be clearly and unequivocally described as engaged in that part of a 'program' of the human brain that, in ordinary parlance, we call thinking. The more knowledgeable we are about the human psychological 'program', the more detailed will be our final answer to the question as to what exactly *Le Penseur* is doing. Functionalism also made redundant many of the questions we used to ask about mind and body, such as, for example, 'Should the mind be identified with the brain?' or 'Should our mental descriptions be translated into or eliminated in favour of physical descriptions of brain states and processes?' Functionalism made clear how nonsensical was any move in the direction of reducing mind to body or mental talk to physical talk, for one could no more do that than one could reduce the functional or 'software' description of some machine to a description of its hardware. Finally, functionalism made clear that it made perfectly good sense to attribute such adjectives as 'intelligent' and 'thinking', in a perfectly straightforward way, to machines or, for that matter, to Martians, as well as to humans. To be thinking or to be acting intelligently was merely to be engaged in a particular part of a particular sort of program and, in turn, such a program could equally well be run on a computer as in a Martian or by a human brain. After all it was already abundantly clear that machines, such as chess-playing or code-breaking electronic computers, could do some mental tasks at least as well as or, in many cases, better than humans.

Where Fodor significantly advanced the functionalist account of mind was in taking the computer metaphor one step further. Fodor pointed out that the core of the mental life of adult humans were mental states that we ordinarily, that is, in our everyday commonsense or 'folk psychology', refer to as beliefs, hopes, decisions, desires and so on. These mental states are often called the 'propositional attitudes' by Fodor because their most common grammatical expression is of a verb, which expresses some attitude, operating over or governing a content which is in the form of a proposition or 'that clause'. For example, typical expressions of our mental life are 'He *believes* that he left his hat on the train' or 'She *hopes that* the exam will go okay tomorrow' or 'They *decided* that Mary should get the Cognitive Science Prize.' In other words a great deal of our mental life is expressed in terms of doing things with propositions.

The next important step is to realise that not merely is that core part of our mental life best *expressed* in terms of doing things with propositions, it is the very *nature* of our mental life. If Fred has left his hat on the train, such an act is a physical act, a behavioural performance. Fred took his hat off when he got on the train and put it on the rack above his head. Then he got off the train, and did not take his hat with him. But when Fred believes that he has left his hat on the train, irrespective of whether he did or not, this time all the action is inside Fred's head. To keep it simple, let us suppose that Fred's belief takes the form of expressing to himself, in his own language, English, something like the following, 'Damn. I believe I've left my hat on the train.' In that act of believing, Fred has not performed anything like an internal behavioural act, such as some miniature version of placing a hat on a rack above a head while on a train followed by a miniature version of leaving the train and leaving behind the hat. In his head, there are no trains or hats or racks or heads or leavings behind. So Fred can only have worked with 'stand ins', that is, symbols or representations for hat, train, rack, head and leaving. Symbols or representations 'stand in for' something beyond themselves. This is made clear when we consider ordinary language symbols or representations. If I say 'hat' to an English speaker, then that is a world of difference from my saying a nonsense word, 'blat', to an English speaker. In the former case, the listener, Mary, knows what I am talking *about*. Whether or not she imagines a hat, or calls to mind her father's Homburg, is not really relevant. All that is important here is that Mary, the listener, in some way was caused to think of a hat when she heard the word 'hat', and did not just passively receive in her head the phonemes (voiced letters) 'h', 'a' and 't', in a string, in the way she might passively, if amusedly, receive in her hand, from a child, three pebbles.

This capacity of symbols or representations actively to prompt their receiver to do something, such as draw them into thinking of something or into behaving in a certain way, is called their semantic property. The word 'semantic' comes from the Greek word, *semainein*, to mean or signify. Since digital computers operate in terms of symbols, and the causal powers of those symbols, then this means that in the computations of a computer we have a model for human thought. As Fodor put it:

> Associating the semantic properties of mental states with those of mental symbols is fully compatible with the computer metaphor, because it is natural to think of the computer as a mechanism that manipulates symbols . . . In fact, the analogy between minds and computers actually implies the postulation of mental symbols. There is no computation without representation.[24]

For Fodor, then, both brains and computers operate in terms of symbols. They are both 'symbol crunchers'. Moreover such operations are controlled and directed by what the symbols signify or are about. How this can be so, in a purely physical system, such as a brain or an electronic computer, depends, says Fodor, on the notion of syntax. Syntax is the bridge between the significance or meaning of a symbol and its power to cause something to happen. As Fodor himself explains, in *Psychosemantics* (1987):

> Here, in barest outline, is how the new story is supposed to go: You connect the causal properties of a symbol with its semantic properties *via its syntax*. The syntax of a symbol is one of its higher-order physical properties. To a metaphorical first approximation, we can think of the syntactic structure of a symbol as an abstract feature of its shape. Because, to all intents and purposes, syntax reduces to shape, and because the

shape of a symbol is a potential determinant of its causal role, it is fairly easy to see how there could be environments in which the causal role of a symbol correlates with its syntax. It's easy, that is to say, to imagine symbol tokens interacting causally *in virtue of* their syntactic structures. The syntax of a symbol might determine the causes and effects of its tokenings [its actual physical realisations in some computer or brain] in much the same way that the geometry of a key determines which locks it will open.[25]

The way to understand how symbols work, whether the symbols be in the 'machine language' of a computer or in the 'language of thought' (that is to say, 'the machine language of the human brain'), is by analogy with how a key works. Different keys have different shapes, that is, in this context, different ways in which the part that goes into the lock is cut into serrations. The differences in serrations determine which locks the keys will open. The serrations in the metal at the lock-end of a key are like a gap-and-no-gap code. If this particular serration code fits, in mirror image, the serrations in the barrel of this particular lock, then the key can be turned, the bolt withdrawn, and the door opened. Thus the serrations, and their proper order, could be called the syntax of the key. Clearly, then, it was by means of the causal powers of the serration-syntax that the door could be opened. Fodor might have used as an illustration for the causal power of syntax, Jacquard's punched cards by which he controlled the movements of the shuttle and rods in his looms. For the syntax of holes and no holes, on the punched cards which were tied together and drawn smoothly over drums, was what caused the loom to operate in a certain way and so produce a particular pattern on a cloth or carpet.

It will come, then, as no surprise that Fodor called this view of mind, at whose core was this view of symbols, the Representational Theory of Mind. It will also come as no surprise that Fodor's first book was entitled *The Language of Thought* (1975) and that subsequent titles, all published by the MIT Press, include *Representations* (1981), *The Modularity of Mind* (1983) and *Psychosemantics* (1987).

Let me give, finally, a more panoramic view of this fully developed Fodorian functionalism. Central to it is the claim that the interplay of belief, desire, hope, hate, decision and despair, and all the other mental items in our commonsense or folk psychology, is mirrored at the level of brain functioning by the interplay of the symbolic items that make up 'the language of the brain'. It is because our commonsense or folk psychology is realised in the brain that we can and do predict the behaviour of humans, continually and in quite remarkable fashion, by means of this commonsense psychology of the 'propositional attitudes'. Indeed we cannot predict or satisfactorily explain human behaviour to anywhere like the same degree of accuracy by any other method. To take an example, if you ring up and say that you will be on the five o'clock plane from London which arrives at Dublin airport at six o'clock, and I believe that you are sincere and not joking, and believe that the airport is not closed and that you did not miss the plane, then lo and behold, when I arrive at Dublin airport at five minutes to six, I see your aeroplane touch down and meet you soon afterwards coming out of the arrivals' exit. Certainly the task of a professional or scientific psychology is to tidy up our commonsense psychology, and see it as a coherent programme with psychological laws that govern the interplay of belief and desire and the other attitudes, but at base it still remains true that our mental life is captured in a remarkable way by our perennial commonsense psychology. We function as regards our mental life, even at a scientific level, in more or less the way that our commonsense psychology describes. As Fodor himself has said, in a moment of triumphalism, any attempt to give up the firm basis of psychological explanation in our common-sense belief–desire accounts would be 'beyond comparison, the greatest intellectual catastrophe in the history of our species'.[26]

Chinese puzzles

Functionalism is undoubtedly a clever and attractive account of the nature of mind. As we have seen, it solves so many of the problems thrown up by its predecessors, substance dualism, behaviourism, the identity theory and eliminative materialism. It is clear and concise. It is technical and tough-minded. It resonates with our times. However, there is now a significant number of philosophers – and it is mainly the philosophers who are show-ing this lack of faith – who have doubts about the adequacy of functionalism as a complete account of mind. Seen from one angle, functionalism is warmly liberal. Unlike the chauvinism of the identity theory, it allows that the mental life of humans may be shared, at least to a significant extent, by some computers, robots, and perhaps by some as yet unknown life-forms on planets in other solar systems. Seen from another angle, functionalism is chillingly minimal. The mental life of humans is depicted as being no different from the cold, machine-dark mental life of some human artifacts. The philosophers' doubts have arisen from this latter viewpoint.

Doubts about functionalism have been expressed, very memorably, in the form of two thought-experiments. These thought-experiments, for differing reasons, have both been presented as items of *chinoiserie*. The first thought-experiment might be called the 'Great Mind of China'. With this title I am referring to a passage in a very trenchant and by now well-known article, entitled 'Troubles with Functionalism', published in 1980 by the American philosopher Ned Block (1942–). That Block is the author of such an article seems perversely fitting, given that most of his academic life has been spent as Professor of Philosophy in that hotbed of artificial intelligence and robotics, the Massachusetts Institute of Technology. In that article, Block supposes that

> We convert the government of China to functionalism, and we convince its officials that it would enormously enhance their international prestige to realize [i.e. incarnate] a human mind for an hour. We provide each of the billion people in China (I chose China because it has a billion inhabitants) with a specially designed two-way radio that connects them in the appropriate way to other persons and to [an] artificial body . . . [equipped with a] radio transmitter and receiver connected to the [body's] input and output neurons . . . [Finally] we arrange to have letters displayed on a series of satellites placed so that they can be seen from anywhere in China.
>
> The system of a billion people communicating with one another plus satellites plays the role of an external 'brain' connected to the artificial body by radio.[27]

Block is asking us, in effect, to think of how our brain functions as a mind, according to functionalism. Once information is received in the brain from the sensory organs, say, from our eyes, then it is processed in computational fashion by the brain's billion (in fact it is far more) neurones. Finally, most often, something like a summary of all the incoming and then internally processed information reaches the output neurones of the brain and central nervous system, and the limbs are moved to act in some appropriate fashion. In like manner, according to this thought-experiment, some piece of information is first received by the billion inhabitants of China, supported by a central transmitter-receiver plus satellites. Then, with the billion Chinese acting as an organised system, the received information is processed in computational fashion and then used as the basis for a command to an artificial body that it carry out some appropriate behaviour. For an hour, the billion Chinese perform the same mental functions as an ordinary human brain. They, the 'Great Mind of China', have become, for an hour, the mind/brain operating an artificial body.

The point of this thought-experiment, of course, is that, strictly speaking, if taken on its own terms, functionalism has to admit that the 'Great Mind of China' is indeed as real a mind as any other. A mind is just a certain way of processing information. A mind is just some system's software (of a higher, cognitive sort) and its ensuing functioning. Block, on the other hand, and a growing number of other philosophers believe that a theory which allows for such a conclusion must be a bit dotty. Or, to put it in logician's jargon, this thought-experiment is intended to be a *reductio ad absurdum* ('a reduction to absurdity') of function-alism. Moreover, if you allow the conclusion that the 'Great Mind of China' is indeed a mind, then you will probably have to allow that a good many other, functionally similar, systems are also minds. For example, if it is only a matter of functioning as a mind for an hour, then you could probably, in principle, with a few crucial alterations, substitute a very large number of trained pigeons for the billion Chinese. An army of dedicated Skinnerian behaviourists from Harvard could probably train ten billion pigeons, each stationed in front of a pre-set two-way radio, to peck, and so depress, the button on their radio when-ever it lit up (indicating that it was receiving). In this way, in response to any incoming signal, the correct output signal would be sent automatically by the relevant pigeon and, globally, over an hour, the 'Great Pigeon Mind' would be functionally the same as the 'Great Mind of China'.

In 'Troubles with Functionalism', Block himself gave yet another example of the possibility of the human mental 'program' being realised in an unusual way but still, according to function-alism, meriting the title 'mind'. He speculated that, one day, to his great surprise, an x-ray might reveal that, inside his own head, the tasks which previously had been carried out by neurones were now being carried out by thousands of fleas, trained by a joint subcommittee of the American Philosophical Association and the American Psychological Association.

The second problem for functionalism was first aired by the American philosopher John Searle (1932–), in an article, appropriately entitled 'Minds, Brains and Programs', in the journal *Behavioral and Brain Sciences*, in 1980. Its publication caused immediate and prolonged discussion.[28] His expression of the problem took the form of a thought-experiment which has since become known as 'The Chinese Room'. The version I give below is slightly adapted.

In this thought-experiment, Searle announces, first, quite truthfully, that he knows no Chinese whatsoever. He suggests that we also take it that he would not even be able to distinguish Chinese characters from Japanese ones or, for that matter, from meaningless squiggles. Then he supposes that he himself, Searle, is locked into a room after being given a large batch of Chinese symbols (that is, characters of written Chinese) plus a set of rules, written in English, for systematically supplying, as output, appropriate Chinese characters in response to whatever Chinese characters are given to him as input. We could imagine that there is a two-way letter-box in the door of the room which acts as the avenue for both input and output.

Figure 4.14 John Searle's Chinese Room thought experiment. An alleged counter-example to the claim that passing the Turing Test would prove that real understanding was present. According to Searle, a person in the Chinese Room could respond appropriately to inputs in Chinese without understanding any Chinese.

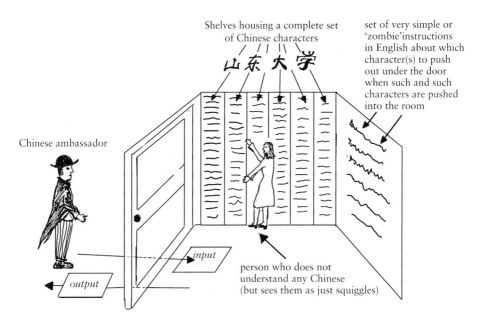

Shelves housing a complete set of Chinese characters

山东大学

set of very simple or 'zombie' instructions in English about which character(s) to push out under the door when such and such characters are pushed into the room

Chinese ambassador

input

output

person who does not understand any Chinese (but sees them as just squiggles)

After a while Searle gets quite adept at this symbol manipulation, pushing out the appropriate string of Chinese characters just a few seconds after a string has been sent in. Also the set of rules, according to which he manipulates the strings of symbols, is gradually refined by whoever wrote them in the first place, so that the strings of Chinese characters sent out through the letter-box are ever more subtly meaningful replies to what, in fact, have been a series of questions in Chinese. Eventually Searle's responses would fool any Chinese speaker outside the door into thinking that he, Searle, could understand Chinese.

However, as we learnt above, Searle understands no Chinese. None at all. The Chinese characters do not mean anything to him. Strictly speaking they are not, from his point of view, even symbols. They are just meaningless shapes. His recognition of them is purely by shape. His manipulation of them entirely by rules linking together one shape with another, and one string of shapes with another. His manipulation is, in computer jargon, entirely syntactic. Searle is just 'a shape butler' who, with impeccable zombie-like service, implements the instructions to carry one set of shapes in a certain order to the output letter-box whenever another set of shapes in a certain order arrives as input. Eventually, most probably, Searle would become quite bored and, after a while, barely notice what he was doing.

The point of this thought-experiment, of course, is to show that any account of human mental life in terms of mere machine-like computation or symbol manipulation cannot be adequate. In the Chinese Room, we have someone who knows no Chinese but carries out perfectly, in the manner of a computer, the procedures for providing appropriate Chinese language output for any given Chinese language input. To put this another way, 'The Chinese Room' would pass the Turing Test, for no one could tell whether or not there was someone with a real understanding of Chinese in the room. Therefore it follows that an account of the human mind in terms of computation according to a program must leave out something essential, namely understanding. The mind as computer software is a mind without understanding, which is not really a mind at all. Thus functionalism must be wrong and the Turing Test must be inadequate as a way of testing whether a respondent has human mental abilities.

Searle believes that this thought-experiment also exposes the absurdity of the claims of what he calls 'strong AI [artificial intelligence]'; indeed, in the original article, this was Searle's immediate target. 'Strong AI' is described by Searle as any research programme in artificial intelligence which, among other things, maintains that a computer that could simulate some human mental ability, say, the ability to play chess well, would *ipso facto* realise, in the sense of incarnate, that mental ability. Moreover, if playing chess is an intelligent thing to do, then a chess-playing computer is, literally, intelligent. To make such a claim in the light of 'The Chinese Room' thought-experiment is, Searle believes, to misunderstand the distinction between mere *simulation* (of output in the light of input) and *duplication* (of the human capacity to understand input so as thereby to provide appropriate output). The important bit, the core of human mentality, according to Searle, concerns how input is processed in order to arrive at appropriate output. Zombie-like syntactic procedures are just not good enough. There must be processing at the level of the symbols *having* meaning for the subject whose mind it is. In terms of the jargon, there must be *semantics* as well as syntax, that is, semantic manipulation (or understanding) and not merely syntactic manipulation.

If a functionalist is fanatical enough, he or she can probably make light of the above objections. He or she would probably agree, without loss of any sleep, that if we take the billion Chinese plus their two-way radios, satellites, and transmitter-receiver, *as one system*, then this system should count as being the realisation of a mind no matter how counter-intuitive or even shocking this recognition might be. A computer's *perfect simulation* of, say, the moves of a chess grandmaster in game after game is all the evidence you need for concluding that the computer *understands* chess. Understanding some task is no more nor less than *knowing how to do it successfully*. In similar fashion a fanatical functionalist will be quite prepared to accept that the Chinese Room *as a system* – that is to say, the whole package of locked room, Searle inside, 'program' or book of symbol-manipulation rules, set of Chinese characters, and input–output device – also incarnates or realises a mind, albeit a very peculiar instance of one. After all, the kernel of functionalism is that 'a mind' is really just a set of capacities to do certain sorts of things, especially certain sorts of cognitive tasks. So it should follow quite logically from that standpoint that anything, whether an evolved organism or an artificial system, that realises those capacities is a mind. What is more, in holding such a view, functionalism comes across as a very forward-looking and liberal viewpoint. As we have already seen, it avoids the chauvinism associated with a standpoint that allows that humans alone can have a mind.

Absent qualia, inverted spectra and blindsight

However there is a deeper problem that worries even the most fanatical of functionalists. Indeed, in his 1981 article in *Scientific American*, Jerry Fodor admitted as much when he wrote:

> Many psychologists who are inclined to accept the functionalist framework are nonetheless worried about the failure of functionalism to reveal much about the nature of consciousness. Functionalists have made a few ingenious attempts to talk themselves and their colleagues out of this worry, but they have not, in my view, done so with much success.[29]

In the very next sentence, Fodor referred to yet another thought-experiment which illustrates the problem functionalists have in finding room for consciousness in their account of mind.

This new thought-experiment is very succinctly expressed by Jaegwon Kim (1934–), an American philosopher who is at present William Perry Faunce Professor of Philosophy at Brown University in Rhode Island:

> Moreover, we can imagine a system, like an electromechanical robot, that is functionally – that is, in terms of inputs and outputs – equivalent to us but to which we have no good reason to attribute any qualitative experiences. This is called the 'absent qualia problem'. If . . . absent qualia are possible in functionally equivalent systems, qualia are not capturable by functional definitions, and functionalism cannot be an account of all psychological states and properties. This is the qualia argument against functionalism.[30]

The term 'qualia' is a neuter plural form of the Latin interrogative pronoun or adjective (depending upon the context), *qualis*, *qualis*, *quale*, meaning 'of what sort or of what kind'. By means of this term, philosophers are drawing attention to the fact that, in being conscious, humans (and, presumably, some other animals) have subjective experiences associated with at least some of the psychological functions they perform. For example, generally speaking, humans have conscious experiences when they have sensations. Thus when I am smelling a newly concocted perfume by Givenchy, someone might say, 'What is it like?' She is not asking me for information about its chemical composition or information about its packaging or price or its power to attract me but about the qualities or what-it-is-like-ness of my experience when smelling the perfume. So I might reply, 'It smells mainly like a bunch of roses on a hot heavy humid day, with a hint of citrus and perhaps, in the background, something I cannot quite place. Though this sounds odd, it might be seaweed.' She would get little or no idea of the actual smell of the perfume from such a description. At most, if she had in the past smelt and could now recall the aroma of roses, oranges and seaweed, and if I had indeed accurately guessed that the perfume had been made mainly from these ingredients, then she might get some sort of idea of the smell. However, strictly speaking, I should reply to her question by saying, 'You'll just have to smell it yourself.'

Talking about qualia, then, is a method in philosophy of mind of referring to aspects or qualities of the here-and-now, subjective, conscious experience associated especially with each of the senses. This point can be made most starkly in terms of examples where someone is lacking one or other sensory capacity. A blind person, for example, can never, ever, have the experience of seeing red, such as seeing the redness of a London bus or of a ripe tomato. No matter what descriptions I use, a blind person will never know what red is. It seems perfectly feasible that a team of technicians might invent an apparatus, which included a television camera that was connected to a device which made different bleeps whenever it was focused on different colours, and which could be worn by a blind person. When wearing this apparatus, a blind person, by taking note of the different bleeps, could say such things as 'I am now standing in front of something red' or 'I am now standing in front of something green.' In short, by means of this apparatus, the blind person could make colour discriminations. On the other hand, we would not even be tempted into claiming that the blind person could see colours.[31] Because a blind person can never experience the qualia which can be obtained only by undergoing the actual experience of seeing something which we call 'red' or 'green' as the case may be. Such 'knowledge through actual conscious experience', in regard to sight, is forever foreclosed to a congenitally blind person. In similar fashion, of course, a person born deaf will never hear the peal of bells or the song of a blackbird or even the less savoury sound of traffic. Such a person might be able to read a music score but will never 'read' it in the 'language' of sounds.

Let us now move to a more detailed look at the 'absent qualia' argument against functionalism which was outlined by Kim. Consider, for the sake of this argument, that it is really possible, now, to construct an electromechanical, perhaps even a neurophysiological, Replicant who is not conscious but is in every functional respect exactly the same as a particular human. I and my Replicant function exactly the same in all respects in all circumstances. We say the same things, do the same things, appreciate the same things, and so on. Indeed no one can tell us apart. Nevertheless, psychologically speaking, there is a world of difference between me and my Replicant: the world of consciousness. When awake, or when dreaming, I will have a stream of internal, private, wholly subjective, conscious experiences, while my Replicant does not. My consciousness – my wealth of inner experiences with their qualia – is not an additional function which I have and my Replicant does not. According to our psychological flow charts of functions, according to our psychological '*program*', according to our 'machine table', we are identical. If consciousness were merely another sort of function, then, in principle, it would be describable in terms of the steps required to accomplish the goal of that function and so would appear on my functional flow chart and thereby be replicable in my Replicant's program. Qualia are not additional, furtive, special psychological functions, over and above the usual, readily recognisable ones, such as seeing, hearing, tasting and so on. They are the *awareness* that most often accompanies those usual functions. In not being functions themselves, it follows that qualia must forever escape any functional account of humans.

Functionalism's difficulties in coping with qualia have sometimes been illustrated in the philosophical literature by another, fanciful, thought-experiment, called 'inverted spectra'. We are asked to imagine a world parallel to ours, in which there are humans who are exactly the same as us, both physiologically and functionally. The one and only respect in which they differ from us is that some of their colour experiences differ from ours in a strangely inverted way. They experience red things as green and green things as red, yet act and react, neurophysiologically, verbally, behaviourally, indeed in all respects and in all contexts, in exactly the same way as we do. When, for example, they look at a tomato, though they say 'That tomato is red', in fact, as regards the colour of the tomato, their private conscious experience is the same as ours when we are looking at something green in normal sunlight and with normal sight. Likewise, when they look at something such as a French bean, though they say 'That French bean is green', as regards the colour of the bean, they have the same conscious experience as we have when we look at a ripe tomato under normal conditions. In fact we could never tell that, as regards their qualia, they have an inverted red-green colour spectrum. Only an omniscient God would know about it. We could never tell because, in all respects, including their brain processing, their use of colour words, and their powers of discrimination, they act and react in exactly the same way as we do. Functionally (including neurophysiologically) they are the same as us, yet, and this is the point, we, the God-like thought-experimenters, know that they are not the same psychologically. They have inverted qualia experiences in relation to our experiences of the same objects under the same conditions.

As it happens, we do not have to resort only to 'thought-experiments' to make good the point that there is an important distinction to be made between a psychological function and its being conscious. In recent decades, philosophers of mind and psychologists have been able to refer to a rare and severe, visual deficit called 'blindsight' or 'cortical blindness'. This condition was first described by Ernst Pöppel of the University of Munich and his colleagues and later, in the 1970s and 1980s, in great depth, by Lawrence Weiskrantz and his team at the University of Oxford.[32] Blindsight can be described as a condition wherein a patient has suffered a lesion or other severe damage to the primary part of the visual cortex, called 'area V1', but has suffered no damage to other parts of the visual system, such as the eye, the retina or the optic nerve. Visual information is being received by the eye and retina, and then travelling along the optic nerve and reaching the brain areas that enable some residual visual discrimination. However, at the same time, this information is bypassing area V1 of the damaged visual cortex. The patients are blind and so will correctly reply that they cannot see, yet they can make some visual discriminations.

Under laboratory conditions, when prompted by questions, patients with blindsight can provide answers, or produce hand movements, which indicate that they can discriminate fairly well between certain visual stimuli. For example, a patient with blind-sight might be able correctly to indicate the direction of movement of some object or to indicate whether or not some object is present in the visual field. Because they are not conscious of making any visual discriminations, the patients think that they must be just guessing. In fact, while not always 100 per cent correct, their answers are much better than random guesses. They consistently and correctly, and sincerely, deny seeing what they have correctly given visual information about. As they are able to make these circumscribed visual discriminations, they can truly be said to function visually in these limited areas, but they have no visual experiences, no visual qualia, no visual consciousness. In short, we have here the rare and curious, and tragic, case of humans who possess residual visual functions which have been severed from the consciousness of those functions.

Let us return once again to the matter of absent qualia. This time not to make the negative point that a functional account cannot capture conscious experiences or qualia but to make a positive point about the importance of qualia. Consciousness, with its qualia, may not be crucial to our survival in an evolutionary sense,[33] but it is crucial to our life as humans. It may be the most important part of it. For example, it is arguable that without consciousness there could be no moral life. Without consciousness, while there could be damage, there could be no pain or hurt. If our fellow humans could suffer no pain or hurt of any sort, then we would have no need of sympathy for them if they were damaged, any more than we would for our water-logged computer or our crashed car. If we were unable to feel sympathy for them, we would not include them among the objects of our moral concern. One of the arguments, indeed one of the good ones, for including animals within the circle of our moral concern is that they do, incontrovertibly, feel pain in much the same way as we ourselves do and so can be hurt in various ways by what we do to them.

If, in a fit of frustration, I throw my computer out of the window on to the concrete patio below and it is smashed into little pieces, I will not feel morally guilty. If it was not my computer or if, in its nose-dive to the patio below, it just grazed the head of a passing pedestrian, then I might feel guilty. But in such cases my moral concern would be for the humans concerned – the owner of the computer or the passing pedestrian – not for the computer. If I could not afford to replace the computer, I might regret what I had done in my moment of frustration. But in this case my feelings would be directed to myself, not towards my computer. If my computer was the very latest slimline laptop designed by Italia Oggi, I might feel ashamed at having destroyed such a beautiful piece of machinery. But here, again, the feelings are directed towards myself.

If, in a fit of frustration, I throw my Replicant out of the window on to the concrete patio below and it is smashed into little pieces, I will no more feel morally guilty about this than I did about my computer. Again, such an action may cause a variety of feelings to arise in me, including ones of uneasiness associated with the fact that the Replicant so closely resembles me physically and functionally, and people often think it is me, but none of

Figure 4.15 The 'strong AI' view, that one day machines will be able to do anything humans can do, including replicate their mental acts, has long been popular in science fiction. In the cult film *Blade Runner*, based on a science fiction novel by Philip K. Dick, 'Replicants' are virtually indistinguishable from humans. The still from *Blade Runner*, opposite, shows a female 'Replicant', Pris.

them will include moral guilt or concern directed towards the Replicant. Notice, too, that in a context where its lack of consciousness is emphasised, it seems natural to refer to the Replicant as 'it' rather than by means of the masculine personal pronoun, 'he', even though, among other things, it perfectly replicates my male characteristics. Though it would take me too far from the main street of our discussion to argue for it here, it may also be the case that being a conscious creature is essential, though not sufficient, for meriting the title 'person'.[34]

Not so long ago, a Senior Freshman student came into my room and asked me what was the meaning of life. Though his colour was heightened and his skin was perspiring, I do not think that he was on drugs, though he may have had a few pints for lunch. I am ashamed to say that, in regard to his question, I let my dry lecturer's reflex have its way. I proceeded to explain to him that, strictly speaking only representations, such as words or signs, have meaning. Only things which are made to stand for or be 'about' something beyond themselves have meaning in a literal sense. For example, 'P' in a circle, and crossed by a diagonal line, means, in some countries, 'No parking here'. Life, I said, is not like a road sign. It does not have meaning beyond itself. It just is the biological, and perhaps psychological, course that a particular organism runs.

On reflection, some days later, I realised that I had replied very badly. What he was really asking me was about how he might give meaning to his own life. I should have replied that humans are remarkable in being conscious in a way that enables them to decide how they should live their lives and so make plans for the future. By means of consciousness, they are able to give meaning to their own lives. They are, as Sartre so often reminds us, beings *pour-soi*.

What should come as no surprise by now is that, since the 1990s, consciousness has been at the centre of discussions about the nature of mind in both philosophy of mind, psychology and the brain sciences. One manifestation of this has been the organisation of annual interdisciplinary conferences on consciousness at the University of Arizona at Tucson, the founding of interdisciplinary journals such as the *Journal of Consciousness Studies* and *Consciousness Research Abstracts*, and a veritable avalanche of books on consciousness. It will not seem out of place, then, if I devote the next chapter exclusively to philosophy of mind's attempts to come to terms with consciousness.

CHAPTER FIVE

The Bogey of Consciousness

The case of the guillotined head

A striking, if grisly, illustration of the close liaison between the brain, and in particular the brain stem,[1] and consciousness is what might be called 'the case of the guillotined head'. It is recorded that, in 1880 in Paris, a Dr Dassy de Lignières

> [c]onducted an experiment with the head of a guillotined murderer named Menesclou. Pumping blood from a living dog into the human head which had been severed some three hours previously, he recorded a reddening of the face and a swelling of the lips which was followed by a sudden and unmistakable stammering and a twitching of the eyelids.
>
> His conclusion was that the transfusion of dog's blood had restored thinking processes to the criminal's brain.[2]

Other, equally grisly, experiments, conducted some twenty-five years later by Dr Beaurieux, involved shouting the name of the guillotined victim at his freshly decapitated head and noting the result. The good doctor recorded that 'I then saw the eyelids slowly lift up . . . and the pupils focused themselves.'[3]

By way of technical commentary on such cases, in his modern neurophysiological textbook, *Human Neurophysiology*, Oliver Holmes writes that

> Most of the methods used for the execution of convicted criminals leave the brain stem and cortex intact so that consciousness persists for a short time. The guillotine, used in the French revolution, may not result in as instantaneous a death as one might expect, since the neural substrate of consciousness is not immediately destroyed. This may account for contemporary reports that, when, after performing his duty, the executioner held up the head for the crowd to witness, the eyes of the severed head surveyed the crowd for a few seconds before asphyxia [lack of oxygen] killed the brain. Although these eye movements may have been merely reflex, there is no reason to assume that consciousness was immediately lost.[4]

Over the ensuing years since the French revolution, scientists have discovered a great deal about consciousness, in particular a great deal about the relationship between consciousness and the brain. For example, neurophysiologists and psychologists have gained knowledge about the physiological basis of consciousness from studying the differences in the brain while a person is asleep and while awake. When a person is awake and alert, all the neural circuitry in the brain is switched on and functioning normally. Being asleep, however, is not simply a case of the brain being switched off. Rather the brain is still functioning but in a different way. Some of the connections between it and other areas of the nervous system are disconnected. Thus, when a person is asleep but dreaming, the circuitry in the outer rim or cortical areas of the brain, and the connections between it and parts of the brain stem, remain switched on and active. Indeed they are unusually active. However, the links between this circuitry and

Figure 5.1
The head of the French king, Louis XVI, executed by guillotine in 1793, is displayed to the watching crowd.

our limbs and, via the sense organs, the outside world, remain by and large disconnected. That is to say, in more academic terms, during dream sleep some of the usual waking links between the *central nervous system* (the nerves of the brain, brain stem and spinal chord) and the *peripheral nervous system* (the nerves connecting the brain, brain stem and spinal chord to other parts of the body) are disconnected. In consequence, during such dream periods, consciousness is limited almost entirely to this dream world and suffers no interference from what is happening in the world outside. Also, fortunately, this dream-world consciousness is by and large disconnected from the system that controls our limbs, so that when, in a dream, we run away in terror from the tiger that is chasing us, we do not in fact run out of the bedroom, along the street and into the nearest police station (though, in rare cases, this has happened). In technical terms, during dreaming, those subsets of the peripheral nervous system called the *somatosensory* (concerning sensations) and *motor* (concerning muscular movements) *nervous systems* are more or less functionally inactive.

Figure 5.2 Experiments on a sleeping subject in a psychological laboratory.

Sometimes, when asleep, there are periods of little or no dreaming. During those periods, those parts of the brain associated with the maintenance of consciousness of any sort just jog along.

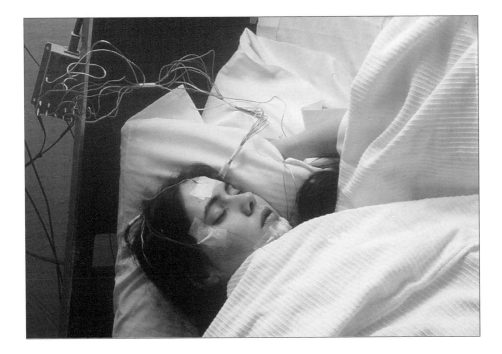

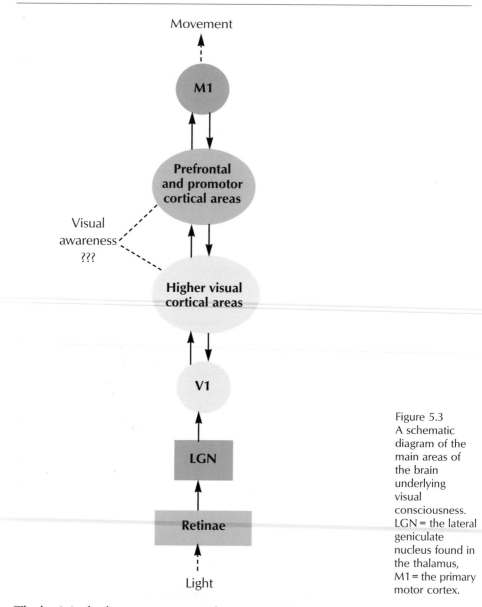

Figure 5.3
A schematic
diagram of the
main areas of
the brain
underlying
visual
consciousness.
LGN = the lateral
geniculate
nucleus found in
the thalamus,
M1 = the primary
motor cortex.

The brain's rhythms or waves can be measured by an electroencephalograph or EEG, a machine designed to record the rate of
the rhythmical electric currents that pass through the brain.
When so measured during non-dream sleep, those parts of the
brain associated with consciousness register extremely slow
rhythms. But even then, the brain itself is not asleep. It is always
active to some degree. For it must still oversee and maintain in
good working order such essential bodily functions as heart beat,

the circulation of the blood, digestion and respiration. We would be dead if it did not do these things. So those parts of the brain that maintain these essential, automated 'bodily services', and the connections between the brain and the basic organs that provide those services, namely the *autonomic nervous system*, must remain active.

Another great source of knowledge about the intimate relation between the brain and consciousness is the study of the effects of drugs. As far as we know, humans have always used drugs to put themselves to sleep or to keep themselves awake, to dampen down their conscious states or to enhance them. In modern times, the variety and sophistication of such drugs for medical use has increased enormously. With increasing knowledge of the biochemistry of the brain, for example, the exact effects on the brain of such common drugs as nicotine, caffeine and alcohol, and of such specialised drugs as valium, morphine and benzedrine, can be tracked. Yet another source of knowledge about the relation of the brain to consciousness comes from the study of the diseases and injuries which affect the brain. Some diseases, such as, for example, some forms of encephalitis, have a narcotic or sleep-inducing effect, others, such as some types of fever, can produce hallucinations. Injuries to the spine can eliminate all consciousness relating to any ensuing contact with or movement

Figure 5.4 EEG (electroencephalogram) readings showing the patterns of brain waves throughout a whole day – the upper, left-hand side records the sleep period. Dreams are mainly associated with REM (rapid eye movement) periods of sleep. Stage 1 = lightest form of sleep, stage 4 = deepest form of sleep.

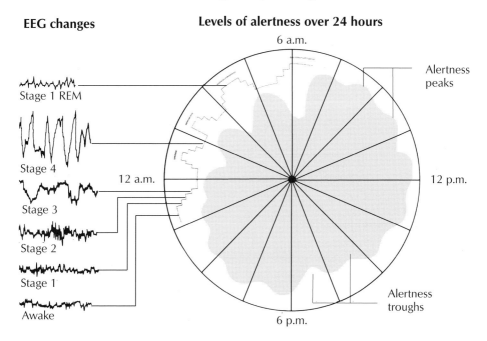

EEG changes

Levels of alertness over 24 hours

Stage 1 REM

Stage 4

Stage 3

Stage 2

Stage 1

Awake

6 a.m.

12 a.m.

12 p.m.

6 p.m.

Alertness peaks

Alertness troughs

in one's own limbs. Injuries to the head can induce unwanted consciousness. For example, injuries can produce unwanted sounds, such as a ringing in one's ears, or unwanted sights, such as a distortion of one's vision. Injuries anywhere, almost always, as any torturer knows, involve that most unwanted of all conscious states, pain.

One of the best clues to current thinking about the physiological basis of consciousness lies in the fact that, nowadays, a medical practitioner or a brain scientist will equate death with *brain death*. In turn, he or she will equate brain death with the irreparable breakdown in the functions of the brain stem. The brain stem sits atop the spinal chord and acts as the junction box that allows electrical activity to flow backwards and forwards between the main bulk of the brain and the rest of the body. More importantly, for our purposes, the brain stem also seems to be essential to the very maintenance of consciousness itself. While the brain stem needs to liaise with the more sophisticated areas of the cortex if the ensuing states of consciousness are to be focused and organised, and needs to liaise with the peripheral nervous system if consciousness is to control behaviour, the brain stem itself makes possible the very state of being conscious. It is the engine of consciousness. So that, even though the very complex areas of the cortex are intact, and even though the heart still beats, the blood still flows and the lungs still breathe, if the consciousness-maintaining function of the brain stem is irreparably damaged, the patient is declared dead. Brain-stem death is the death of consciousness. The only life that remains for a body with brain-stem death is that of an animated corpse.

However, all brain scientists would agree that the brain sciences are only at the very beginning of the project of mapping those parts of the brain that are involved in initiating and maintaining conscious states, and of providing a flow chart of the interplay between those parts. Many discoveries are still to be made and many problems still remain to be solved.

Of bats and eels

Philosophers suggest that, in regard to consciousness, there is another sort of problem that awaits solution, if there is a solution. A problem of a different sort altogether and one which seems systematically to evade any explanation by any of the relevant sciences.

In 1974, in his now famous essay, 'What is it Like to be a Bat?', published in the senior American philosophy journal *Philosophical Review*, Thomas Nagel (1937–) began by declaring that

> Consciousness is what makes the mind–body problem really intractable. Perhaps that is why current discussions of the problem give it little attention or get it obviously wrong.[5]

In that essay Nagel mischievously let a bat into the philosophical fly-bottle and even now, in the twenty-first century, the flies have not settled. After Nagel's essay it became no longer possible for philosophers to 'solve' the relation of consciousness to our brain simply by asserting the reduction of consciousness to brain processes, or the reduction of talk about consciousness to talk about behaviour, on the grounds of simplicity and parsimony or on the grounds that reduction seemed the scientific way to go.

Nagel put his central point in a memorable way. What was unique to that part of an organism's psychological life, which we label as 'conscious', he wrote, was its being the source of 'there being something it is like to *be* that organism'.[6] For the clause, 'there is something it is like to be that organism', we can read,

Figure 5.5
The American philosopher, Thomas Nagel: He argued that no account of mind could be complete if it ignored the question, 'What is it like to be X?'.

'there is something it is like to be conscious in the way that organism is'. By this he meant that consciousness is the source, for example, of our own *feeling* of what it is like to be a creature which is able to employ a pair of arms situated on either side of its torso and to walk in a bi-pedal way, of what it is like to hear the sounds of its own voice emitting linguistic noises and to see bifocally with two eyes, both of which are placed at the front of its head, and so on. In short, what it is like to be some organism is what it is like to have that organism's various senses and so in turn its own peculiar stream of consciousness or interior life.

It is in so far as it is a conscious organism that every organism has an interior life. This interior life is private, and exclusively so, to the subject of that interior life. If, for example, you hit the 'funny bone' of your elbow (so called, with black humour, because its medical name is the *humerus* bone) on the edge of the desk, then, in normal circumstances, you will experience a sharp, tingling and sometimes excruciating pain. Neither I nor anyone else besides you can ever share precisely that experience of yours. The conscious moments of that experience are private to your stream of consciousness. Of course, to some extent, I can make a good guess at what your pain is like. Since I am of the same species, and share your anatomy and biology quite closely, then, given also that at some time in the past I have hit my 'funny bone' on some hard object, I can at least 'half remember' what my pain was like and so 'half imagine' what your pain might be like. However, since we are all individuals and have individual differences, your pain will never exactly resemble mine.

Nagel's point is made especially vivid by his taking this lack of exact resemblance a step further. Take the case of an organism which is not even of the same species as ourselves, he suggests. Take, for example, the case of a bat. Furthermore, take the case of the bat's ability to navigate by echolocation. For, in effect, that ability amounts to the bat's having a sense organ we do not have. For a bat can locate the wall or roof of the cave in which it dwells in complete darkness by sending out ultra-sonic, high-frequency sound waves, namely its own high-pitched shrieks. The bat can then interpret the 'interference' or 'bounce back' if and when these sound waves strike some object. In other words, a bat locates things somewhat in the manner a convoy-escorting naval vessel, such as a destroyer or frigate, can locate a submerged submarine by means of sonar. Quite clearly, argues Nagel, we do not have any idea about what it is like to be a bat because we do

DE VESPERTILIONE.

Figure 5.6 Nagel's famous example of a radically alien consciousness was bats.

not have any idea about what it is like to find our way around the world by echolocation or sonar. A bat's interior life, a bat's consciousness, and so what it is like to *be* a bat, is for us, humans, therefore, forever outside our experience.

I am not completely convinced that we do not have any idea at all of the stream of consciousness associated with navigation by echolocation. We do have ears and can hear echoes. The naval rating who hour after hour operates the sonar equipment in a destroyer or frigate must have something approaching an echolocating stream of consciousness near the end of his or her shift. Let me take another example; one from my own experience. Some years ago I visited the Ailwee caves in County Clare in Ireland. These caves penetrate deep down under the hills around Ailwee. To find one's way, one needs experienced guides and to carry a torch. For the entertainment of tourists, mid-way in the tour of the caves, the guide asks everyone to put out their torches and to keep deathly silent. The darkness is complete and eerie, and even the slightest sound is unusually sharp and isolated. In an unaccustomed way one is aware even of the sound of people shifting about on their feet to readjust their weight, of the brush of clothed arm against clothed thigh, and of the occasional slight clearing of some throat. Then the guide suddenly demonstrates the caves' echoes by shouting. In the comparative silence one experiences the echo with unusual sharpness. At the time there seemed to me to be no doubt that, to some extent, one could differentiate the different time-lapses from emission of shouts to return of echoes. In some directions the shout was 'returned' quite quickly as an echo, presumably because there was a wall or boulder or bunch of stalactites close by, in others less so. I recall imagining, probably because I had read Nagel's essay, that if someone lived for a long time in the caves, he or she might be able to learn the trick of finding their way around the caves by echolocation. Admittedly, this would be a matter of 'learning the trick' over time, while the bat does it naturally and from birth. However, it certainly did not seem impossible.

So I then thought about the possibility that there were indeed creatures who had conscious experiences which we could *never, ever, duplicate* or even simulate in any way whatsoever. After some rummaging in zoological texts, I came up with the example of the gymnotid eel who creates its own magnetic field around about itself and is sensitive, presumably in a conscious way,[7] to any interference in the field when fish stray into it. This, surely, is so foreign to any sense we have that we cannot even guess at or imagine *what it is like* to detect an object by feeling, if that is how it should be put, the interference to one's own self-generated magnetic field. Quite simply, while we do generate our own magnetic field, we are neither aware of it nor of interference to it. In relation to us, humans, the subjective life of a gymnotid eel is unique to it. Its magnetic-field qualia (instances of 'what it is like to be conscious of interference to its magnetic field') are unique to its stream of consciousness.

However, it is Nagel's example of the bat that has passed into the philosophical as well as the non-philosophical literature. There is a reprise of Nagel's ruminations on the difficulties of comprehending the qualia of a bat in the American writer Jay McInerney's splendid comic novel, *Bright Lights, Big City*. The anonymous young writer, who is the protagonist of the novel, has been working in the Department of Factual Verification on the staff of a prestigious cultural magazine which bears a close resemblance to *The New Yorker*. Because he had failed to check a number of factual claims in an article about the recent French elections, and because the article has now gone to press full of errors subsequently discovered, he has just been sacked. While musing on the impossibility of his colleagues (even his good friend Meg) ever being able to share, intimately, in his predicament, he recalls something his blind date of last night, Vicky, had said. She is a graduate student in philosophy at Princeton University:

They're wondering: *Could this happen to me?* and you would like to reassure them, tell them it's just you. They're trying to imagine themselves in your shoes, but it would be a tough thing to do. Last night Vicky was talking about the ineffability of inner experience. She told you to imagine what it was like to be a bat. Even if you knew what sonar was and how it worked, you could never know what it feels like to have it, or what it feels like to be a small, furry creature hanging upside down from the roof of a cave. She said that certain facts are accessible only from one point of view – the point of view of the creature who experiences them. You think she meant that the only shoes we can ever wear are our own. Meg can't imagine what it's like for you to be you, she can only imagine herself being you.[8]

Subjectivity

It is this very subjectivity of the qualia of consciousness, Nagel argues, that creates all the problems. Given that the aim of science is to be as *objective* as possible, then something subjective must elude its grasp. A scientific explanation is always 'from the outside looking on', so to speak, but here we have a whole way of life which is of itself *subjective* or 'from the inside looking out' and, sometimes, 'from the inside looking in'. It follows, then, that an objective account of consciousness looks like a contradiction in terms or an impossible research project in science. It also follows that any attempted reduction of consciousness to brain processing, or, for that matter, any reduction of consciousness to anything else described from an objective point of view, has failed to see the impossibility of reducing what is essentially subjective to something objective.

Nagel is not, of course, denying that conscious experiences may have a causal role, and in that respect could be given a functional, and so in part an objective, characterisation. For example, it may turn out that consciousness has evolved as the arena where creatures, who have consciousness, produce a unified view or sensory *gestalt* (single unified form) for whatever is providing information to their various senses. Thus, in perception, we see *and* hear the bus coming at one and the same time, and perhaps smell its diesel fumes as well. The information from eyes and ears and nose come together in unity. Though we may be said to process the information from eyes and ears and nose in separate but parallel systems, the results are brought together in a single, though still complex, conscious experience. Doing this 'unifying trick' in regard to the multiplicity of our neuronal systems may be the function of consciousness, or one of its main functions. But Nagel's point is that talk about the function of consciousness, and indeed any other sort of objective characterisation of consciousness, does not and cannot capture an additional aspect of consciousness, its subjectivity. For it could have turned out, evolutionally speaking, that our brains could pull off this 'unifying trick' while not having the ability to do so consciously. Our brains might simply have summated the information from all of our senses, which in turn might have enabled us to perform, including verbally, in accordance with this summary information bulletin. That being so, the subjective qualia of consciousness – the 'what it is like to be, consciously, in that state' – must be something over and above, or beside, any such unifying function that consciousness might perform.

Another function which consciousness seems to perform, and again one which may not be possible without consciousness, is providing the subject of consciousness with a sense of his or her own minimal existence as a particular consciousness. It seems that without the 'point of view' which our sensory systems provide, continuously, to consciousness, it is likely that we could have no sense of our own existence. Even if, sadly, through Alzheimer's disease or some other terrible degenerative illness, we lost our memory, we would not thereby forfeit the whole of our sense of ourselves as an independent entity. Certainly we would lose our sense of continuity with the person or point-of-viewer who witnessed the events of yesterday, and so with ourselves of yesterday. In addition, most likely, we would lose our sense of what people think of us, and of what social roles we once filled, and so lose our sense of a social self with a history and personality. But we would still retain, at least while we are conscious, a momentary, focused, living 'point of view'. We would be reduced to a consciousness that remains, at least for a moment or two, a unified subject's view of what is happening, a seeing, a hearing, and perhaps a tasting and a feeling as well, focused into one point of view. At this moment, for example, at the most fundamental level of consciousness, I am my seeing of a reddish-orange sunset over the rooftops of the city of Dublin, my feeling that my feet are very cold, and my hearing of the wheezing sound of my almost superannuated *Laser Writer Select* printer mixed in with the sound of the wind outside my room. Usually this leads on to my forming some view about these sensations, that the sunset is unusually vivid for this time of year, that if I put my coat over my knees maybe my feet will warm up, and that my printer must be nearing the end of its life-span. From a number of my points of view about a number of things, one overlapping upon the next like ripples at the water's edge, I am borne along on my complex tide of consciousness.

Now it is interesting to speculate what it would be like if our life was reduced to immobility and all that was left to us was a consciousness into which fed just one sensory system, say, sight. This, it would seem, would present to us a single and simple sensory point of view. In turn this would reduce our subjectivity and self-consciousness to the barest minimum, to an *ur-self*. In a footnote to his chapter on 'The Consciousness of Self', in the first volume of his *Principles of Psychology*, William James briefly describes an actual case which approximates to this hypothetical one. In this footnote James is referring to the casework of a German professor, Strümpell.

> This boy [one of Strümpell's case studies] ... was totally anaesthetic without and (so far as could be tested) within, save for the sight of one eye and the hearing of one ear. When his eye was closed, he said: '*Wenn ich nicht sehen kann, da BIN ich gar nicht*' – I no longer *am*.[9]

This sense of losing his existence when his one operative eye was closed (even though his one ear remained 'open') arose, presumably, from the fact that Strümpell's boy no longer had a subjective point of view. Having no longer any visual experiences whatsoever, he had lost all sense of being a subject viewing the world. Though I do not know of any empirical work that corroborates this, it must be the case that our auditory experiences, our hearing of sounds, if they give us any sense at all of being a subject with a point of view upon the world, must do so in a much weaker manner than do visual experiences.

The case of Strümpell's boy reminds me of Jean-Paul Sartre's alleged comment, when he was suffering from a most painful earache, 'I am my ear.' There is also Roald Dahl's rather unsavoury story, entitled 'William and Mary', in his collection *Tales of the Unexpected*, where William allows for scientific

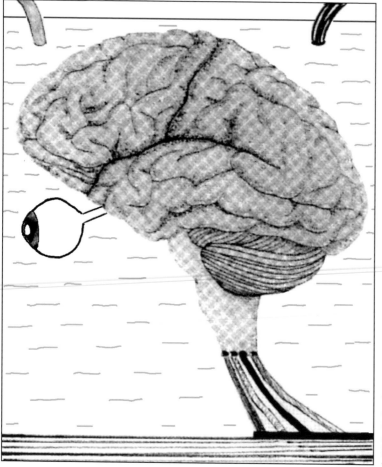

Figure 5.7
In Roald
Dahl's story,
'William and
Mary', a brain,
along with just
one eye, is
kept alive in a
vat of fluid.

purposes that after his death, his brain, with just one eye attached, be kept alive and conscious with constant transfusions of blood.[10]

However, as Nagel was at pains to remind us, it is this same remarkable subjectivity of consciousness, whether it be simple or complex, momentary or sequent, that is a continuously baffling barrier to the success of our orthodox research projects about the nature of mind in both science and philosophy. This is so because this subjectivity is fundamental to consciousness. It pervades consciousness. In the jargon of philosophers, consciousness is both *ontologically* and *epistemologically* subjective. 'Ontological' means of or pertaining to existence, and is derived from the ancient Greek word for being or existence, *ontos*. 'Epistemological' means of or pertaining to knowledge, from the ancient Greek word for knowledge, *epistēmē*. Thus a conscious experience, such as my present experience of an excruciating pain in my 'funny bone', is ontologically subjective because this pain only exists, ever exists, as a feeling, which in turn is a momentary, or more long-lasting, experience in some subject's private stream of consciousness. The same excruciating pain is also epistemologically subjective because only the person in pain, the subject whose pain it is, can have immediate or direct knowledge-by-acquaintance of that pain. Only the person whose feeling it is can *know it as a feeling*.

Nagel is not denying that consciousness is physical. If conscious experiences, and indeed all mental events, have physical causes (brain events) and physical effects (other brain events plus, very often, behaviour), then it makes sense to think of conscious experiences as being in the same line of business as their causes and effects. As Nagel himself put it,

> Suppose a caterpillar is locked in a sterile safe by someone unfamiliar with insect metamorphosis, and weeks later the safe is reopened, revealing a butterfly. If the person knows that the safe has been shut the whole time, he has reason to believe that the butterfly is or was once the caterpillar, without having any idea in what sense this might be so. (One possibility is that the caterpillar contained a winged parasite that devoured it and grew into the butterfly.)[11]

In the analogy, consciousness is the butterfly and brain events the caterpillar, and we, scientists and philosophers, are the person who is unfamiliar with insect metamorphosis from caterpillar to butterfly.

The appearance of the Djin

Since Nagel's essay, the central and most baffling problem about consciousness has become the problem of how it is that consciousness, which generates subjectivity, could evolve out of something so down to earth and material and objective as brain processing. Though this problem has loomed large recently, it is not a new problem. The greatest biologist of all, the Englishman Charles Darwin (1809–92), the designer (with Alfred Russel Wallace) of the theory of the evolution of species by natural selection, pondered on this problem or something very like it. And he pondered on it a great deal, at least in his notebooks. I suspect that he did not write about it in his published works because he had no solution to proffer. In the final analysis he seemed as baffled as anyone else and resigned to the fact that 'our knowledge of matter is quite insufficient to account for the phenomena [the conscious appearance] of thought',[12] and referred to the origin of consciousness as 'mysterious'.[13] Darwin's bulldog, Thomas Henry Huxley (1825–95), who vigorously championed Darwin's theory of evolution against the objections from both the clergy and the scientific community of the time, expressed this same bafflement but in his characteristically pungent way:

> We class sensations along with *emotions*, and *volitions*, and *thoughts*, under the common head of states of *consciousness*. But what consciousness is, we know not; and how it is that anything so remarkable as a state of consciousness comes about as the result of irritating nervous tissue, is just as unaccountable as the appearance of the Djin [or genie] when Aladdin rubbed his lamp in the story, or as any other ultimate fact of nature.[14]

Recently, this problem (of how consciousness can be generated by brain processing) has been brought to the very front of the queue of problems about consciousness by an Australian, David Chalmers (1966–). As an undergraduate, Chalmers studied mathematics at the University of Adelaide. After going to Oxford as a Rhodes Scholar to continue his work in mathematics, he became preoccupied with puzzling over the nature of consciousness and, as he put it, decided 'to switch fields and . . . switch continents'. After studying philosophy, together with some cognitive science and artificial intelligence, for his doctorate at the University of Indiana in the United States, and while holding a two-year McDonnell Fellowship at Washington University, he began to write what became *The Conscious Mind* (1996). In the Introduction to that book, he reiterated the thoughts of Darwin, Huxley and Nagel:

> Consciousness is the biggest mystery. It may be the largest outstanding obstacle in our quest for a scientific understanding of the universe . . . It seems utterly mysterious that the causation of behaviour should be accompanied by a subjective inner life.
>
> We have good reason to believe that consciousness arises from physical systems such as brains, but we have little idea how it arises, or why it exists at all.[15]

Figure 5.8
The Australian
philosopher,
David Chalmers.
He sees the
'hard problem',
about how
consciousness
is generated
by brain
processing,
as a major
challenge for
both philosophy
and the brain
sciences.

Chalmers then went on to distinguish this problem, which he called *the hard problem*, from what he called *the easy problem*. The easy problem is not, of course, easy. It is easy only in comparison with the hard problem. The easy problem is the problem of giving an account of the intricate physical processes that form the neurophysiological and biochemical basis for each and every particular form of consciousness. Take, for example, a person seeing a bluebell or, to narrow it still further, seeing blue. There is reason to think that, one day, in the probably not too distant future, there will be a complete account of the physiological and biochemical processes that underlie the subjective experience of seeing blue. Scientists will know everything about the relevant structures of the eye, the optic nerve and tract, and the cortical areas associated with seeing. Scientists will also know everything about the relevant connections between these structural elements. And they will know everything about how the light waves striking the eyes are refracted by the lenses of the eyes and, on entering the retina, begin the process of being changed into electrical impulses which then carry information about the frequency, amplitude and angle of entry to the eye of the light waves of the blue spectrum. And about how this electrically-embodied information is transmitted to the lateral geniculate body (part of the thalamus), then, via the optic tract, to the primary visual cortex at the posterior pole of the occipital lobe, and so on. Then they will be able, also, to tell a similar story about the parts of the brain and nervous system which maintain consciousness during visual perception, as the experience of seeing a bluebell is, of course, a conscious one. The story will be immensely complicated and will take a very long time to complete, and only experts will be able to understand it. But it does not seem impossible. It just seems to be a matter of time, patience, good instrumentation and good luck. In that sense the easy problem is easy compared to the hard problem. As Chalmers put it in his article in the journal *Scientific American*, which appeared the year before the publication of *The Conscious Mind*:

> The hard problem, in contrast, is the question of how physical processes in the brain give rise to subjective experience. This puzzle involves the inner aspect of thought and perception: the way things feel for the subject. When we see, for example, we experience visual sensations, such as that of vivid blue. Or think of the ineffable sound of a distant oboe, the agony of an intense pain, the sparkle of happiness or the meditative quality of a moment lost in thought. All are part of what I am calling consciousness. It is these phenomena that pose the real mystery of the mind.[16]

To illustrate the distinction between the hard problem and the easy problem, Chalmers describes a thought-experiment[17] about Mary, a neuroscientist of the twenty-third century. As a scientist Mary is extraordinarily gifted. She knows everything there is to know about the neurophysiology and biochemistry of our visual system, and her speciality in this area is colour vision. She is *the* world expert on colour vision. As regards the physiology of seeing a bluebell, Mary is in the position of being able to tell you the whole story, if you are prepared to wait around for it. However, unfortunately, unlike you or me, Mary cannot actually see the blueness of a bluebell, because she was brought up, and indeed has subsequently spent her whole life, in a totally black and white environment. She has answered the easy problem about seeing blue but not the hard problem, because she does not even grasp that there is a hard problem. More accurately, given her environment, she is not even in a position to grasp the nature of the hard problem, let alone solve it.

In more general terms, the easy problems about consciousness are often problems about the structure and function of various neurophysiological and biochemical bits and pieces which underlie our conscious states. However, as we saw when discussing the functionalist approach to mind, consciousness cannot be reduced without residue to something with a known structure which performs known functions. For its phenomenal or qualia aspect is something over and above any function. At other times the easy problems about consciousness are problems about how to analyse something complex, say a biochemical compound, into its constituent elements and thereby to gain an understanding of

Figure 5.9 A newspaper report about a previously colour-blind boy who was enabled to see colour. Intuitively, we would say that his private, subjective experiences had changed radically.

Teenager sees colour after life in black and white

A teenager told yesterday how he cried when he saw in colour for the first time, thanks to revolutionary contact lenses developed by British scientists.

Kevin Staight, 18, was born with a rare eye defect, affecting one in a million people, which meant he saw everything in black and white. Now he is learning about colour, after his grandparents Don and Dorothy Staight saved up for the special lenses.

"After I put them on I went for a walk and slowly saw the world in colour for the first time," said Kevin (above), from Cheltenham, Gloucestershire. "Up until then I didn't have any idea what colour was because I couldn't see it.

"I couldn't stop crying because the world looked so different to what I was used to. The reds just kept on jumping out at me and I had to ask my grandparents which colours were which because I didn't have a clue."

"It has opened up a whole new world for me. I never realised just how beautiful things like trees and flowers are."

Mrs Staight, Kevin's grandmother, who raised him, said: "He is a completely changed person. I don't think anybody realised just how gloomy his world has been up until now.

"The opticians had told us there was nothing that could be done because he was so severely colour blind. When we heard about these lenses we decided

to give them a go to see if they would work for Kevin and the results were amazing.

"He dragged us outside and was rushing around pointing at things and asking what colour they were. It was all very emotional because he was crying."

Mrs Staight said that Kevin's girlfriend, Sarah Gill, had been nervous about his reaction, as she is half Vietnamese and wasn't sure how he would react to her skin.

"It has made absolutely no difference to Kevin because we explained to him beforehand that people have different colour and textures to their skin," Mrs Staight said.

Kevin's career prospects have also been aided by the new lenses. As a result of being able to see on-screen colour, he has secured a job working with computers.

The lenses, called CromaGen, have only been available at six opticians in Britain since they were released last July at £540 a pair. They were supplied by Bristol optician Roger Spooner, who said: "Kevin's case was very dramatic because he lived in a totally grey world. He was the first person I have come across who was totally colour blind.

"The whole practice was in tears when he came here to try on his lenses but it was a very rewarding experience to help him."

— Jojo Moyes

the behaviour of the compound in terms of the behaviour of its individual elements according to the basic laws of physics and chemistry. Again this way of solving a problem does not seem to be of use in solving the hard problem about consciousness. For there do not seem to be any fundamental laws of physics or chemistry which could shed light on how the subjectivity and phenomenal qualities of consciousness arise out of its physics and chemistry. Or, to put it another way, you cannot extract subjectivity out of a heap of micro objectivity.

Thus advances in solving the easy problem are not advances or, at least, not *ipso facto* advances in solving the hard problem. To solve the hard problem, Chalmers suggests, we need to strike out in a new direction. First, Chalmers suggests, we must take consciousness as a fundamental element of the universe, in the sense that it is one which cannot be subsumed and so explained within our current physical science. The best we can do will be to find laws which correlate elements of our conscious states, such as features or structures within them, with elements of the brain and its processing. These would be psychophysical laws. Thus one might be able eventually to formulate, for example, a principle which correlated the different colours that a person sees with the different three-dimensional representations in the cortical areas of the brain that neurophysiologically underwrite those visual experiences. There would be no question here of *reducing* the colour experiences to their neurophysiological substrates but merely of *correlating* them. More speculatively, Chalmers suggests that one might then try to produce an overview of these psychophysical principles in terms of a double-aspect theory of information. What makes it plausible to postulate psychophysical principles or laws is the fact that consciousness and its correlative neurophysiological substrate are both informational states. Perhaps, then, one could say that the fundamental thing that could unite these two correlated things more closely is information. A particular conscious state and the relevant brain process which underpins it are but two views or two aspects of the one coin, information. Viewed from one side, information is objective (neurophysiological), viewed from the other, it is subjective (consciousness). Information is known by us as objective physical states (as revealed by science) or subjective conscious states (as revealed to the subject of consciousness). Furthermore information is, presumably, *the* fundamental aspect of the universe, and the one and only substance. This being so, the psychophysical principles or laws might be expressible, eventually, purely in terms of information.

I would be surprised if many philosophers, psychologists or brain scientists considered such a 'double-aspect' information account to be a viable solution to the hard problem. Chalmers's double-aspect account claims to find common ground between brain processing and consciousness by suggesting that, despite appearances, these two things are really but *two aspects of one thing*. The 'one thing' is a universal substrate, information, which only becomes tangible and knowable through its two surface aspects. Given this common grounding in information, in principle there can be psychophysical laws that will make sense, not merely of the causal interplay between consciousness and brain processing but, especially, of how consciousness could arise from brain processing. That is to say, these psychophysical laws will solve the hard problem by translating both psychological processes (including conscious ones) and physical processes (including brain processes) into informational processes. Then, how consciousness arises from brain processing will be merely the question of how information viewed under one aspect arises out of information viewed in another way.

However, if the two aspects, brain processing and consciousness, are not really two different kinds of things, but really just two aspects or points of view of one and the same kind of thing, namely information, then the interaction problem disappears, at least in principle. But it disappears at a price. The price is that the reality of any causal interactions between consciousness and brain processing also disappears. Just as it does not make sense to talk about a causal interaction between a house seen from the front garden and the same house seen from inside the lounge, so, for a double-aspect theorist, it will not make theoretical sense to speak of any causal interaction between two aspects of information, consciousness and brain processing. Unfortunately for the theory, it does make sense to talk about causal interaction between consciousness and brain processing. We do it all the time, and make perfectly good sense in doing so. It does make sense to talk about our thoughts or desires or feelings, via our brains, causing the bodily movements we call 'actions'. It does make sense to talk about our thoughts and desires and feelings, via our brains, occurring as the result of blows to our bodies or of hugs or kisses. It does make sense to say that it was anxiety about losing his job that caused Fred's hair to fall out or that the appearance of a lump on her breast caused Jane to become anxious. A theory that entails that such accounts of causal interaction are illusory is a poor theory.

There is, unfortunately, also a dilemma for anyone who proposes a double-aspect theory in which the *aspects* are consciousness and physical processes, and *what they are aspects of* is the one and only substance, information. For now it must be pointed out that it follows from this *either* that everything in the universe has a conscious aspect to it *or* that only some things do. If everything in the universe has a conscious aspect to it, then we are lumbered with a primitive form of animism in which even stones are conscious. One would need a very strong philosophical stomach to digest that.[18] If only some things have a conscious aspect to them, then consciousness cannot be simply an aspect of information as such. It must at the very least be an aspect of information *plus some further mysterious ingredient.* Consciousness must be information 'only viewable when . . . [and at this point there must be posited some mysterious additional ingredient which makes consciousness possible]'. In short, the original double-aspect theory – one ingredient or stuff with two aspects – collapses.

Though, apparently, others do not find it so, I have difficulty even in thinking of information as a substance or stuff. I think of information as the meaning conveyed by some stuff, usually tangible stuff such as marks on paper or sounds uttered by a human. I do not think of information as another variety of stuff, tangible or otherwise. Thus, when you send me a note, a piece of paper which has the following sentence written on it in blue ink, 'Let's meet for lunch at 12 noon at the Crown and Anchor', the piece of paper can be said to contain information about where Fiona would like us to meet for lunch. The English words convey that information to me in so far as I am an English-speaker who knows what the words mean and can read. Information is the message not the medium. To call information a substance or substrate that can be viewed under two aspects seems to be what Ryle would have called 'a category mistake'; like noting where the Cheshire cat's ears, eyes, nose, mouth and whiskers are but wondering what part of its head is its smile.

Epistemological pessimism

Some have suggested that the solution to the hard problem is that

Figure 5.10 English philosopher, Colin McGinn. He believes that consciousness may never be scientifically explicable.

it cannot be solved. It is a mystery beyond the capacities of human understanding. The person most associated with this pessimistic response is the philosopher Colin McGinn (1950–).[19] McGinn first studied psychology at Manchester University, then philosophy at Oxford. After a period teaching at University College, London, and as Wilde Reader in Mental Philosophy at Oxford University, McGinn became Professor of Philosophy at Rutgers University in New Jersey. One of his most persistent interests has been in the limits to human knowledge. In regard to the study of the mind, McGinn sees the relation of consciousness to the human brain as a mystery beyond the limit of human understanding.

In an article, entitled 'Can we solve the Mind–Body Problem?', in *Mind* (1989), and subsequently in his books *The Problem of Consciousness* (1991) and *Problems in Philosophy* (1993), Colin McGinn has suggested that 'the time has come to admit candidly that we cannot resolve the [mind–body] mystery' for what resists explanation is 'consciousness, the hard nut of the mind–body problem'.[20] McGinn does not doubt that consciousness arises out of the neurophysiology and biochemistry of brain functioning, and that it does so according to the laws of nature. What he doubts is that we, humans, will ever be able to come to know the relevant laws.

To explain why he has come to such a pessimistic conclusion, McGinn introduces the concept of 'cognitive closure'. He defines 'cognitive closure' as the failure of someone's mind to have the ability to form the concepts (that is, to have an understanding which is expressible in language) of the nature of the property and of the theory which would explain how this property arises.[21] Thus a monkey has 'cognitive closure' with respect to an understanding of atomic theory and so of atoms. So has our ancestor Cro-Magnon Man. There is no reason to refuse to believe that there are a number of things, possibly a large number of things, in respect of which humans (human minds) have 'cognitive closure'.

McGinn's next step is to provide reasons why humans have 'cognitive closure' about the production of consciousness by the brain. The first, perhaps the weakest, reason is the longstanding historical failure on the part of brain scientists, psychologists and philosophers to come even close to a solution to the problem as to how consciousness with its inherent subjectivity can arise out of brain processing with its inherent objectivity. McGinn is not simply saying, 'We have not, over many centuries, indeed millennia, found an answer to the question of how consciousness arises out of brain processing, therefore we will never be able to find an answer to this question.' For that would be a poor argument. You cannot argue from our ignorance about something up to the present time to our eternal ignorance about it. For, if that were a good argument, then we should now be arguing, 'Since we have to admit that we have failed to find a cure for cancer after so many decades of investigation, then it must be the case that we will never find a cure for cancer.' But that looks premature. If, around the year 1900, someone had deployed that form of argument in regard to the mechanism for biological inheritance, then he or she would have looked rather foolish when Crick and Watson came up with the final piece of the puzzle about the genetic code, the structure of DNA (deoxyribonucleic acid), half a century later. McGinn's point is different. He wants to point out that, in the case of consciousness, *we never seem to get any closer to a solution* to the problem as to how 'technicolour phenomenology [our "full colour" stream of consciousness] can arise from soggy grey matter [our brains]'.[22] We do not seem to be any closer to a solution than were Plato and Aristotle.

When the Nobel Prize winners Francis Crick (1916–) and James Watson (1928–) began their collaboration, at the Medical Research Council Unit at Cambridge University in 1951, which led to the discovery of the structure of DNA, quite a lot was already known about DNA. It had been known for some years that it was genetic material but biochemists had been unable to pinpoint the properties of DNA which made it the carrier of the 'genetic code'. However, by the early 1950s, there were available ever-improving x-ray diffraction photographs of the structure of DNA, in particular those stemming from the work of Rosalind Franklin and Maurice Wilkins at University College, London. In addition there was the background of work by Linus Pauling and Elias Corey on helical or corkscrew structures, such as occurred in the case of some proteins. And so on. The point is that the nature of the genetic code was discovered bit by laborious bit, not in some epiphany. Not merely in retrospect but even in prospect, scientists could see that they were getting closer and closer to providing a complete answer to the question about the double-helix structure of DNA and so of the nature of biological inheritance. At the other end of the spectrum of scientific knowledge, we have the question about how the subjectivity of consciousness can arise out of brain processing. Here, after so many centuries, all that we can see is that we have made no progress at all, not even one little bit.

McGinn's second reason for thinking that humans must accept 'cognitive closure' in regard to consciousness is that we seem to lack the very possibility of access to the information that might help us formulate an explanation as to how the subjectivity of consciousness arises out of brain processing. When edging closer to the complete picture of the molecular structure of DNA, scientists could employ well-developed means of investigation. They knew how to go about their investigation. They could employ x-ray diffraction photography and chemical analysis, for example. By what means, on the other hand, can a scientist track the generation of the subjectivity of consciousness from brain processing?

A brain scientist can map the brain-processing side of the matter by means of various sorts of scanners, such as CAT scans and PET scans. A CAT scan (a *computerised axial tomography* scan) involves sending a narrow x-ray beam through a subject's head and measuring the differing amounts of radiation that get through. The differing amounts indicate the different structures of different parts of the brain. Given that this is done from a large number of different positions (or axes), then a complete picture of the brain can be built up by a computer. On request, the computer can then print out a cross-section or 'slice' picture (the Greek word '*tomos*' means 'slice') of the brain from any angle. A PET scan (a *positron emission tomography* scan) is a scan of brain activity rather than of brain structure. It depends upon the fact that every cell in the body, including every nerve cell in the brain (or neuron), requires energy to function. The most important source of energy for brain cells is glucose (or sugar) obtained from the bloodstream. A small and harmless amount of a radioactive substance (that emits positively charged electrons called *positrons*) can be mixed with glucose and the mixture then injected into the bloodstream. The result is that each molecule of glucose that is subsequently utilised by the brain's nerve cells will be marked by a speck of radioactive substance. The greater the activity in some area of the brain, the greater the amount of energy that will be needed, and so the greater the amount of 'marked' or 'stained' glucose utilised. A PET scan is a highly sensitive detector of radioactivity (namely, of the positron emissions). Again a computer plays a large part in the production of the resulting pictures, for it builds up a complete picture of the levels of activity in the brain, and can produce on command a cross-sectional or 'slice' picture with different colours representing differing levels of activity.

By analogy, though it is not a close analogy, any healthy adult human can scan the consciousness side of the brain–consciousness divide. The word 'scan' should not be taken literally here. We have no inner eye that can perceive events in our own con-sciousness. We do not need one. The essence of consciousness lies in the subject being aware of the contents of consciousness. Likewise we have no scientific instruments for scanning the events in someone else's stream of consciousness. What we all can do is push aside distractions and thereby attend more carefully to what is going on in our stream of consciousness. This careful nurturing of attention, somewhat misleadingly, is traditionally called *introspection*. For example, I can tell you that, now, I have a rather queasy feeling in my stomach (because I have just eaten a vindaloo curry that was rather too strong for my constitution). It is a burning feeling that waxes and wanes in intensity. Then, when I shift my attention (the focus of my consciousness) to writing about that queasy feeling, I can tell you that I am 'speaking to myself' as I write this. I try out first one phrase then another. Where I have written 'burning feeling' above, I had first toyed, in consciousness, with the phrase 'searing feeling', but decided against it, thinking that 'searing' was associated too closely with being burnt by fire and was too strong a word for the context of a queasy stomach. Then, later, I catch myself, first rather absentmindedly, then more carefully, surveying the scene outside my window. There are some striped flags on an office building opposite. The flags are flying about in quite a brisk wind. There are some cumulus clouds in an otherwise blue sky, and so on.

So, incontrovertibly, we can scan the brain areas that support consciousness, and we can introspect in a direct way our own streams of consciousness. But McGinn's point is that we cannot scan or introspect, or in any way observe or detect, the latter arising out of the former. We cannot, so to speak, see the interface or the junction point but only see the two sides, separately, by very different yet appropriate means. That being so, it looks as if we will never be able to fashion the concepts that could furnish us with an appropriate explanation of the *generation* of consciousness from brain processing. If the facts are closed to us, then understanding cannot follow. Our 'cognitive closure' on this matter looks permanent.

McGinn has not finished with his downbeat message. He points out that, whether we like it or not, we are going to have to admit that there has always been and will always be limits to human knowledge brought about by limits to human capacities for gaining knowledge and so limits to the human capacities for forming explanatory concepts. Just as certain longitudinal pressure waves in the air are at too high a frequency to be detected by the human ear and so do not produce sounds for us, and just as some electromagnetic radiation waves are outside the visible spectrum for human eyes so that objects reflecting only them cannot be seen by us, so there will be things which are simply outside our capacities for understanding and explanation. One of those things, McGinn suggests, seems to be the generation of subjective consciousness from brain processing.

Despite his pessimism, McGinn follows Nagel in arguing that, nevertheless, consciousness is a natural product of natural evolution. We must not, in other words, think of consciousness as mysterious in the sense of being *super*natural and so miraculous. Consciousness, in all its aspects, including that of its subjective point of view, is generated according to the laws of nature. The point is that our current or future grasp of the laws of nature will always fall short of completeness. A God's-eye-view or God's-mind-grasp of the laws of nature may produce a perspicuous explanation of the generation of the subjectivity of consciousness from brain processing, but we are not gods.

Knowing how and knowing why

Many years ago, in a dentist's waiting room, while idly scanning a magazine published for fans of the motor car, I came across an advertisement for a car in kit form. The idea was that you could buy a kit, which contained all the pieces required to build a particular model of car, and assemble it yourself, or with the help of your local, friendly, car mechanic. I imagined sending in my money and, a few weeks later, a huge lorry pulling up outside my door and unloading a series of boxes marked 'motor-car parts' or, it was some years ago now, a series of boxes marked, say, 'Morris Minor gear box', 'Morris Minor suspension system', 'Morris Minor fascia and instrument panel', 'Morris Minor wheels and axles', and so on. Then, in a separate box, would be a multivolumed set of instructions, with fool-proof illustrations, of which parts were to be connected together to make a gear box, a suspension system, and so on. Finally there would be a large box with a complete set of the tools required to build the car. All I had to do was to follow the instructions carefully and, lo and behold, after a day or so, I would have in my back yard a gleaming new Morris Minor, 'at 50 per cent of the dealer's price' said the advertisement.

I learned from a knowledgeable friend that you were not

expected to build the car from the nuts and bolts upwards. The car arrived in half-built form. What you put together were pre-assembled units, such as the gear box, the suspension system, the steering system, the engine, the body and the chassis. And, even with that head start, the average time of assembly was weeks rather than days. Even when I had learned this, I still did not have the confidence to buy a kit. For I had a vision of my working over a number of weeks, or more likely months, on the job of assembling the systems together and finally producing a beautiful gleaming Morris Minor. But it would turn out that I had made some simple but vital error, for example, that I had inserted the gear box back to front, so that the car had four reverse gears and only one forward gear.

I suspect that if I had attempted assembling a car from kit form, whether completely successful or not, I would nevertheless have learned a great deal about how cars worked. If I had attempted to assemble a car from the nuts and bolts upwards, without a doubt I would have learned a great deal more. From an enormous heap of such things as rods, pipes, hoses, wires,

Figure 5.11 Assembly workers in the automotive industry displaying 'knowledge how' to build a motor car.

rings, cylinders, valves, filters, plugs, nuts, bolts, screws, belts, chains, levers, cogs, wheels, panels, windows, handles and knobs, I would have first assembled a series of working systems. Then I would have learned how each system, designed to perform a specialised function, fitted together to make a vehicle that was powered by the combustion of petrol.

If, for example, I had even successfully assembled a car gear box from gear lever to drive shaft via gear-shift rod, clutch, gearing cogs, input, output and layshafts, differential, and the rest, then I would probably know as much about automobile gearing systems as an apprentice car mechanic. If I went on to assemble a second, third and fourth gear box, then I could claim something like familiarity with the workings of such systems. If, in a moment of hubris, I had offered to look at my neighbour's car when he said he was having trouble with his gears, and had been successful in fixing his gears, then I could claim real knowledge. I could claim, so to speak, that I had sat and passed an exam in gear boxes.

The point is that one form of knowledge is knowing how something works in a 'hands on' way. Such knowledge is gained by knowing how to assemble it correctly, so that it works, and knowing how to repair a damaged or faulty version. Arguably knowing how to produce a working example of something is just as convincing a display of knowledge as being able to produce a theoretical explanation of why it works. Certainly the two sorts of knowledge are different. The lecturer in mechanical engineering may be able to give a marvellous lecture on the workings of a car driven by a petrol-fuelled internal combustion engine, but be unable to assemble or mend a gear box. He may know, for example, about the mathematics of torque or the physics of combustion chambers, yet not know how to assemble the cog wheels of a gear system or the spark plugs, cylinders, connecting rods and crank shafts of the engine.

Knowing how to build something that works well is a very practical but still very deep form of knowledge. It is an explanation of how it works.[23] *Knowing why* something works in terms of mathematical formulae or the laws of physics is a very theoretical and obviously also a very deep form of knowledge. It is an explanation of why it works. It may be the case that we will never arrive at a full theoretical explanation of how consciousness arises out of brain processing. However there seems to be no good reason for thinking that we will never be able to synthesise in the laboratory the bits and pieces that go to make up a working neurophysiological system which generates consciousness. If and when scientists can do that, then they will have a real and deep knowledge of how consciousness arises out of brain processing.

So far I have stressed the differences between *knowing how* and *knowing why*. Now, somewhat perversely, I want to argue that, in some cases at least, an account of *knowing how* is also an account of *knowing why*, and that knowing how to make a working neurophysiological system with consciousness may be just such a case.

Take the case I came across recently in the science and technology section of a daily newspaper. A service run by the editor of this section is 'Science Line', which includes a Dial-a-Scientist service (which in turn includes an e-mail-a-scientist service). Selected questions and answers from this service are printed in the newspaper. A recent question was 'Why don't railway lines buckle in the heat?' The answer was as follows:

> They do sometimes, but are laid to reduce the amount of buckling. There are two types of track: jointed rail and continuous welded rail. Jointed rail comes in 60ft (18m) lengths and is bolted at the ends by a fishplate. Each track end has two holes in it and the fishplate has four. The plate is bolted to the track and the bolts are tightened. However, a small gap is left to allow for expansion and contraction between the ends of each rail. In addition, a technique called 'sun locking' is used, whereby the track is laid, and then on a hot day the bolts are finally tightened fully.
>
> Continuous welded rail comes in a variety of lengths which have about a metre of overlap at each end. The ends are shaped like wedges, so that the track can expand and contract lengthwise without there being any break in the entire length.
>
> Jointed rail track makes the noise we all associate with train travel – clickety-clack, clickety-clack. The continuous welded rail should be quieter.[24]

It is an exemplary answer to the question, clear, precise, informed and explanatory. However my point is that the answer to the Why-Question, the *knowledge why*, is in fact a long account of *knowledge how*. For the scientist explains *how* the tracks are laid in order to show *why* they do not buckle in the heat. With jointed rails, a gap for contraction and expansion is left by means of employing a fishplate at the join. With welded rail, the join involves two wedge-shaped ends which can move slowly over one another with expansion or contraction (presumably, each wedge is sloped in a reverse way to the other, so that the fit is snug).

It seems likely that if scientists could explain how, neurophysiologically and biochemically, the parts of our brain causally relevant to consciousness are put together and function in relation to one another, then *ipso facto* the scientists will have explained how these parts function together *so as to generate consciousness*. In David Chalmers's terminology, it seems likely that if scientists can solve all the easy problems about the conscious brain, then *ipso facto* they will also have solved at least part of the hard problem. Just as explaining the construction of rail track is an explanation of why they do not buckle, so an explanation of the construction (and functioning) of certain systems in the brain will be an explanation of why they generate consciousness. We are only led to think otherwise by imagining, wrongly, that knowledge how and knowledge why are always completely separate.

I have admitted, in the previous paragraph, that solving the easy problem of consciousness may not solve the whole of the hard problem. My reason for saying this is that there is one important difference between the explanation of *how* rail tracks are constructed and then laid, leading to *why* they do not buckle, and the explanation of *how* our neurones are constructed, laid down, interconnected and function, leading to *why* they generate consciousness. Not buckling is the avoidance of a physical defect in rail tracks, namely the avoidance of their buckling due to the heat of the sun. Consciousness is not the avoidance of a defect in brain functioning. It is the emergence of a surprising effect of brain functioning, the emergence of subjective qualia. So no matter how adept scientists may become at producing this effect in the laboratory, we may have to admit that an element of surprise, if not mystery, will always remain. But the mystery that remains may be of the same sort that remains after we have learned, after centuries of endeavour, that heat is the kinetic energy associated with random motions in the small particles of ordinary matter, or that gravity is the force of attraction that can be exerted by every body in the universe with mass upon any other body with mass. As the eighteenth-century Scottish philosopher David

Hume declared, 'The most perfect philosophy of the natural kind only staves off our ignorance a little longer.'[25]

There is more to be said about consciousness, even now, but I shall leave that to the final chapter where I want to draw matters together and give a synoptic view of where exactly we have arrived in our thinking about the nature of mind.

CHAPTER SIX

The Pit and the Pendulum

The pit and the pendulum

The account in the preceding chapters has been an account of how our view of the mind over the last hundred or so years has been heavily influenced by the *Zeitgeist* of each period. The desire to be objective and scientific about the mind, and to see human minds as evolutionary developments of, and so continuous with, animal minds, was an important influence on the development of behaviourism in both philosophy and psychology. The explosion of knowledge about the brain and its crucial role in even the most complex aspects of human thought and behaviour was an important influence on both the identity theory of mind and on eliminative materialism. The astonishing development of the computer and its ever increasing incursions into our lives were important influences in the development of functionalism in philosophy of mind and on the similar view of mind embedded in cognitive science.

The account in the preceding chapters has also been an account of a dialectical process wherein theories about the nature of mind were confronted by objections and thereby forced into making revisions. I have highlighted those points where the objections have been so fundamental and the revisions have been so radical that new theories came into being as a result. The account of this evolution of theories has, I believe, also been an account of progress. In the course of the dialectical process we have learned a lot about the nature of mind. The lessons, or at least some of them, have not always been obvious. The task of this final chapter is to try and make them obvious. On the other hand, it would be absurd of me to claim that we have now arrived at anything like a definitive all-embracing theory about the nature of mind. Rather this final chapter is in the nature of a work-in-progress report – an account of where we have come from, where we now stand, and what has been learned from that part of the journey we have already completed.

One way of summarising much of what has been happening in philosophy of mind over the last hundred years is to describe it as if it were a pendulum oscillating backwards and forwards above two pits: one, on the left-hand side, marked 'internal' theories of mind and the other, on the right-hand side, marked 'external' ones. 'Internal' theories are theories which claim that minds are 'in the head', which in turn is taken to mean either that they are to be identified with souls or that they are to be identified with brains. 'External' theories are theories which postulate that minds are part of the immediately observable world and so are to be identified with the dispositions of human persons to behave in certain ways in certain contexts. Of course, this 'internal/external' distinction is an oversimplification, because, during that same pendulum-oscillating period, there were also theories that did not fit easily into either side of that internal–external distinction. However, like many such oversimplifications, it does make clear an important point. The point in question is the undeniable fact that Descartes, at least in his reincarnation in turn-of-the-century Cartesianism, had 'sold a dummy' to many theorists of mind in the twentieth century. In the manner of a soccer player moving slightly to the left as if to go in that direction and then, when the opposing player has been 'sold the dummy', darting suddenly to the right, Cartesianism had sold much of modern philosophy of mind a dummy. It had done so by seducing many modern theorists of mind into thinking that the mind was a thing that had to be located somewhere quite definite, either in the head or outside of it. It is this 'being sold a dummy', and how modern philosophy of mind eventually learned to avoid it, that I want to discuss in this section.

At the beginning of the twentieth century philosophers of mind and theorists in the field of psychology stood side by side, arm in arm, and both would have accepted William James's definition of psychology as 'the science of mental life'. Being still Cartesian in spirit, both would have held that the mind was more or less coextensive with our interior conscious life and would readily have agreed that the inside of human heads was the most likely place where minds were to be located, though the term 'located' had to be handled carefully in this context.[1] With the coming of behaviourism, psychology was defined as 'the science of human behaviour'. Given that they did not find the question 'Where is the mind?' totally absurd, behaviourists would reluctantly have answered the question by saying that minds were not inside human heads but were to be located on the periphery of the human organism. To refer to a mind was simply a way of singling out certain patterns of human behaviour, and the dispositions to exhibit them in suitable environments, as the bearers of the majority of the terms of our psychological vocabulary. The pendulum bob had moved from inside the head to outside of it.

With the appearance of the identity theory of mind, with its catchcry that the mind is nothing but the brain, the pendulum's bob immediately swung back again to the left-hand, inside-the-head side. For minds were once again inside heads, excepting this time they were not made of mental substance, and so were not to be thought of as separable souls capable of outliving the death of the body. Minds were to be identified with the brains we knew all along were located inside human heads. Moreover they were now to be considered as a body part that died along with the death of the rest of the human body.

With the coming of functionalism in philosophy of mind and psychology, with its view of the mind as a segment of the brain's software, the pendulum's bob should be depicted as remaining stationary on the left-hand side and minds should be thought of as remaining inside heads. However the idea that the mind had to be some sort of stuff, either soul stuff or bodily stuff, had now been given up. Minds were depicted as inside heads in a much subtler way. They were depicted as a series of abstract, functional states, which, in the case of humans, just happened to be realised in brains. In that sense minds were still understood to be part of the physical world but not as a type of hardware. Minds were a segment of the brain's software, that is the brain's higher, cognitive programmes and their operation. This allowed for a liberalism such that these same programmes could be realised in machines and thereby create artificial minds, or at least artificial part-minds or intelligences. Given that machines, or Martians for that matter, exhibited the requisite functions, that is to say the particular sorts of capacities, abilities and skills that we think of as mental, then they had minds. In so far as some of these powers were greater than the similar powers of humans, then these artificial minds or the minds of other species were in those respects more powerful than human minds.

Then there came a confusing period when some functionalists muddied the software–hardware distinction so that minds were depicted as the functioning of brains in a much less abstract way. The functions in question were thought to be realised in a quite literal way at the level of the neurophysiological functioning of brains. Our ordinary language descriptions of what we humans thought about or believed or hoped or decided were also, in a literal way, descriptions of the computer-like functioning of representational states of the human brain. This sort of functionalism in effect became another version of a mind–brain identity theory.

Others rejected that move as being a backwards step and invoked philosophy of language as a way of making clear that to identify the functions that functionalism groups together as mental, literally with brain functions, is to misunderstand the way we learn to apply our mental vocabulary and the way our resulting mental descriptions and explanations are deployed in our commonsense psychological explanations and predictions. These linguistically more sophisticated views eschewed the reduction of mental functions to brain functions and depicted our talk about minds and their activities as talk about functions of the whole human person. With that change of perspective, it might be thought that the pendulum's bob should be depicted as having moved to a neutral position between the left, inside-the-head side, and the right, outside-the-head side. In fact, with that change of perspective, it is probably more accurate to suggest that the whole image of the pendulum had itself been swept aside. Minds were now thought of as neither inside heads nor outside them. Mental descriptions and explanations were descriptions and explanations about how humans as a whole organism, or in some contexts as a whole person, functioned. By analogy, sometimes, in a loose way, we may say that the driver turned left, when strictly speaking we mean that the whole car, including the driver, turned left. In similar fashion, while we may use such expressions as 'Use your brains!' and so think of the brain alone as pondering or problem-solving, strictly speaking it is the whole animated human organism, the human person, that does these things. The lesson had finally been learned that to separate off an *animus* (the Latin word for mind or soul) from the whole animated or living human organism, and to make this *animus* the repository, whether spiritual or material, of minds and their activities, was a grave error. The mind is neither a soul nor a brain. It is the higher, psychological life of the human organism.

Admittedly consciousness has been hard to fit into any version of this new functionalist account of mind. For consciousness is not so much a function as an experience or awareness of functions being carried out. But consciousness does seem, at least to most people, to be firmly inside heads. So, if consciousness is to be part of any account of mind, as surely it has to be, then consciousness seems to force us back to the pendulum picture. As soon as consciousness is mentioned, we seem inevitably drawn into depicting matters once again as if there were a mind-locating pendulum which had swung back to the inside-the-head side. However, this revival of the pendulum picture would only be acceptable if there was also a revival of the Cartesian view that the mind was coextensive with our conscious life but, given Freud's work and contemporary work on the subliminal mind, this is most unlikely to happen.

Equally unlikely is any suggestion that the debates about the nature of consciousness, even if they do not tempt us into reviving the pendulum picture, will force philosophy of mind or psychology back into thinking of minds as souls or mental substances. There will never be a return to the view that minds are souls which merely inhabit the body during life and then at death clap their hands with joy and willingly escape to a better or at least a different world or, in some versions, to a different body. Darwin's doctrine of the evolution of species implied and still implies that everything of a biological nature, absolutely everything, including human minds, has evolved. Moreover this evolution has been a natural, causal process. In that sense minds must have evolved from the same substance or stuff from which our bodies have evolved. Minds are as natural as bodies or, for that matter, bats or bees.

Evolution also brought about a move away from our traditional anthropocentric view of the universe. Within evolution humans have had a similar history to that of all the other animals. Our ancestors were animals and we, members of the species *homo sapiens*, are still animals. We have no preeminent place in the universe excepting that which we have aquired by our power to subdue and subject other species. There can be no return to a pre-Darwinian way of thinking that we alone are God's children and alone have immortal souls which will ensure for us a unique salvation.

In general there has also been a firm and probably irrevocable move away from any suggestion that a mind is a sort of thing, whether immaterial or material. Behaviourism and mainstream functionalism, as well as later versions of the identity theory, in their differing ways, saw the mind as a set of powers which in turn comprised capacities, abilities and skills, rather than as a thing made of a certain unique stuff. This seems to be on the right track. This, of course, throws up a new set of problems, namely which capacities, abilities and skills are to be labelled 'mental' and why. But this does not seem to be an insoluble, just a difficult, problem.

In this section, I have described one very fundamental change of perspective that has taken place from the demise of Cartesian philosophy and psychology to our present post-functionalist era. In the final sections, I look at other, less obvious, themes that can be discerned over the same period.

Avoiding philosophical anorexia

There is no denying that there is and always will be pressure to reduce our larger or macro-level descriptions and explanations to smaller or micro-level ones because that seems 'the scientific thing to do'. In science the best strategy, often, very often, seems to be to reduce an explanation at a higher or larger or macro level to an explanation at a micro level. If you can break up the entities or processes employed as part of a macro-level explanation down into a larger number of smaller entities and smaller processes, then you have, quite likely, explained the larger entities and processes in terms of the smaller ones. Thus we explain the rise in temperature of a large body, such as an iron bar, in terms of a rise in the mean kinetic energy of the particles that make up an iron bar. To take another example, scientists had long known that sons and daughters can inherit characteristics from their parents or grandparents or even uncles and aunts. Contemporary scientists can now explain the inheritance of characteristics from one reproductive organism to another by first explaining that, inside humans, there are chromosomes which are part of the nuclei of living human cells. In turn chromosomes consist of DNA (deoxyribonucleic acid) and protein. The code which directs human development, and so by means of which different inherited characteristics are handed on from mother and father to son or daughter, is expressed by or 'written' in the different configurations of the DNA segment of the chromosome or gene. Hence the term 'genetic inheritance'. The easily observable inheritance of, say, red hair or blue eyes, can be explained in terms, ultimately, of the configuration of something microscopic which is buried deep inside the nucleus of a human cell. The general point being made is that the explanations that produce such marvellous advances in science often turn out to be reductive explanations that reduce macro explanations to micro ones.

Modern analytic philosophy, generally speaking, craves to be considered scientific. Very often this craving takes the form of a craving for reductions. Indeed some philosophers, like anorexics, are addicted to reducing. Besides seeming to be scientific, reducing involves getting rid of things. In philosophy this usually involves reducing one sort of explanation or description or theory to another already existing and better established and more fundamental explanation or description or theory. In turn such reduction has the connotation of a clearing away of rubbish or a getting rid of superfluities or a slimming down. So it has a methodological probity and purity that seems to match the logical probity and purity with which philosophers try to conduct their arguments and speculations.

Philosophers of mind have been no exception. Some of them have craved the satisfaction of their deep-seated reductionist desires. Thus we have seen that a number of philosophers have suggested that 'folk-psychological' explanations of our mental life in terms of the commonsense notions of belief and desire and hope and intention and pity and love and hate, and so on, are obsolete, superfluous and in need of elimination. These eliminative materialists argued that such folk-psychological explanations were nothing but the metaphysical and linguistic detritus of our misbegotten Cartesian heritage, if not of our more ancient Aristotelian one. To try to do professional psychology or serious philosophy of mind in terms of such concepts was like trying to do contemporary physics in terms of such obsolete and discredited concepts as that of the ether, calorific fluid and phlogiston. To remind ourselves of another of their analogies, the eliminativists suggested that our 'folk psychology' is, in comparison to what real psychology should be, what medieval alchemy is to modern chemistry.

But there were less severe and more subtle reductionists than the eliminative materialists. To take just one example, a contemporary American philosopher, Daniel Dennett (1942–),[2] has suggested that our explanations in terms of such psychological attitudes, as belief and desire and so on, are useful explanations for ordinary purposes, but not, at least eventually, for scientific or professional purposes. To put it another way, it is useful in ordinary social intercourse to take up 'the intentional stance' whereby we explain the behaviour of ourselves, or for that matter that of our car or cat, in terms of the 'intentional attitudes' (which phrase, for our purposes, may be taken as a synonym for the psychological attitudes of belief, desire, hope and so on). This 'intentional stance' is nothing but a useful device that enables us to explain human behaviour in a swift, neat and easily comprehensible fashion. But we must not think that we really possess mental states or that there really are attitudes called 'belief' and 'desire', any more than we should believe that there really are an equator and lines of longitude and latitude. We take up 'the intentional stance' to humans in much the same spirit as a chess grandmaster, like Kasparov, might take up 'the intentional stance' to a computer when he is trying to defeat it at chess. Just as Kasparov, when confronted by the latest chess-playing computer, might find it helpful to plan his next move by saying to himself, 'I fear that the computer *realises* that my queen now threatens its king, so I'd better . . .', so, for similar purposes, you might find it helpful to say something like that to yourself when playing chess with your grandmother.

Of course a better explanation and prediction about what the computer will print out, as its next move, given a certain input, would result from Kasparov's taking up what Dennett calls 'the design stance' in regard to the computer, if that were feasible. That is to say, to predict the computer's next move by taking account of its program and electronic design. Kasparov's explanation and so prediction of the computer's responses would be even better grounded if he could take up what Dennett calls 'the physical stance' whereby he would be able to explain matters by reference to fundamental physics. Of course, taking up either of the latter two stances is probably impossible for any ordinary person, and may be so for any single person operating over a reasonable amount of time. So Dennett does not advocate the total elimination of the quotidian vocabulary of our ordinary commonsense or 'folk psychology', he just takes the stuffing out of this vocabulary. In effect, he is suggesting that this vocabulary does not refer to real human attitudes but merely indicates that it is useful to adopt the fiction that humans do have them. At most this vocabulary refers, in a manner reminiscent of behaviourism, to discernible behaviour patterns. And it does enable us to explain and predict human behaviour better than we would otherwise be able to do.

More interestingly, from our point of view, is the fact that there has been a more robust backlash against reductionism. There has arisen a series of philosophical 'refuseniks' or non-cooperative protesters who have refused absolutely to engage in reductionism of an anorexic kind. What is more, I think that not merely time but also the tide of good argument are moving in their direction. The future lies with them.

The 'refuseniks' I have in mind are such philosophers as Donald Davidson, Hilary Putnam, John Searle and, to a lesser extent, Jerry Fodor. While their refusals to go down the usual reductionist path have quite different origins, and while they end up in quite different places, they can be said to be in broad agreement about being against reductionism of an anorexic kind. The American philosopher Donald Davidson (1917–), for example,[3] believes that it is a gross misunderstanding even to imagine that our commonsense psychological vocabulary of belief and desire could be reduced to something else. For this vocabulary arises as a result of our taking up (to assume, for a moment, a Dennettian way of speaking) 'a normative stance' to humans whereby we see them as basically rational, consistent and coherent agents. Furthermore, to view humans as rational is to view them at the level of their planning and shaping their own lives by reference to their own and others' beliefs and desires. Indeed, if we want to understand and so get on with our fellow humans, if we want to be social creatures, then we cannot do otherwise than view them in this generous way. If you know that Judith believes that smoking is bad for her health and if you know from past experience that she has a strong will, then you can predict with something like certainty that she will refuse your offer of a cigarette. This prediction clearly depends on Judith retaining her strength of will and her remaining consistent in her belief about the dangers of smoking and her being sufficiently rational to realise that, in the light of that belief, she should refuse the offer of a cigarette. It also depends upon your being sufficiently rational to predict what a rational Judith will do if offered a cigarette, and so on. But to see human motivation in this way is to realise that such an explanatory and predictive stance is indeed 'normative', that is to say, that it involves a deliberate tidying-up (or artificial regimentation) of our explanations of human behaviour according to the norms of rationality, consistency and coherence. To attempt to reduce these highly complex and highly sophisticated psychological explanations to some sort of explanation at the level of neurophysiology or fundamental physics is a mistake.

It is a mistake similar in kind to that of seeking to reduce a sailor's explanation of why his yacht foundered, in terms of the high wind, the way his boat sat high in the water and his failure to take down his mainsail in time, to an explanation in terms of the particles, wave motions and forces of fundamental physics. The mistake in both cases is a failure to discern the right level of explanation for the phenomenon in question.

Choosing the right level of explanation is not necessarily non-reductionist. It may involve what might be called non-anorexic reduction, that is to say, a reduction down to a lower level which proves to be the right one together with a principled refusal to go further down, precisely because the right level has already been found. An example of this non-anorexic reduction, in the psychological context, might make this point more forcibly. The nearest thing in contemporary psychology and philosophy of mind to an orthodox account of human emotions is the so-called cognitive theory of emotion. A cognitive theory of emotion depicts a human emotional state as a complex psychosomatic process. According to such a theory, at least in simplified form,[4] an emotion is to be analysed in terms of a series of smaller components which causally interact so as to produce the compound process we call an emotional state. Crucial components in these interactions are the cognitive (and appetitive) ones, hence the label 'cognitive theory of the emotions'. Thus your now being afraid of the Rottweiler dog running towards you in the street might be analysed in the following way. First, you perceive and so come to believe that there is a dog running towards you and that the dog is a Rottweiler. Second, this perception triggers a belief, previously formed, that Rottweilers are very aggressive dogs that are given to biting people in a quite savage way. These beliefs lead you, more or less instantaneously, to evaluate or appraise your situation as highly dangerous. In turn, this appraisal leads you to form the desire to escape the danger. By reference to past experience, you realise that the best way to escape immediate danger of this sort is to take to your heels. The urgency of your need to do this is communicated to your physiological systems which are first placed on high alert and then activated. Adrenaline is pumped into your body. Your respiration rate increases as does your heart beat and pulse rate. You break out into a sweat, your bowels become tense and your muscles tighten up. All these heightened bodily changes are reflected in your stream of consciousness as feelings. You feel the quickening of your pulse, the thumping of your heart, the straining of your limbs and so on.

Though it may not seem to be at first glance, this account of emotion is a reductionist account. It reduces an emotion, in this case fear, to a series of component processes that causally interact with one another to produce the finished product. Thus, in a psychology textbook, the account is sometimes depicted in terms of a flow chart that shows how the emotion might begin with a perception, is mediated by some cognitive processes (such as knowledge or belief) and appetitive processes (such as wishes, wants or desires), and then culminates in a medley of physiological changes, feelings, behaviour and other expressions. On the other hand it is not an account which sets out to reduce an emotion to a series of purely physiological processes or, *a fortiori*, to a series of physico-chemical ones. For to do that would be to produce a reductive account at an inappropriately micro level. It would be to fall victim to theoretical anorexia. Such an account of some emotion purely in terms of neurophysiological or physico-chemical processes would be inappropriate because it would not really explain how an emotion is generated nor how it comes to have the composition it has nor how it comes to play in human lives the role that it does. The reason for this is that human emotions are generated, for the most part, at the level of perception, memory, belief, desire, need and so on. In other words they are generated at the level of our commonsense psychology because that is the level at which we humans control, in so far as we can, our own lives. We run away in fear because we believe we are in danger not because our limbic region or associative cortex is in such and such a state. Emotions are part of our conscious life of being aware of our own situation and of trying to cope with it. Hence you are not afraid if you are in a coma or in a state of dreamless sleep or, through the ravages of some degenerative brain disease, completely unaware of your surroundings.

Of course the brain's sense organs and cortical regions and limbic system, and the body's systems that maintain our variable rates of respiration and circulation of the blood, and much else besides, are involved in emotion. Sometimes, though not in general, it can happen that they are the protagonists in the story. For, of course, emotions can sometimes be generated at a purely biological or physiological level. Taking a drug can cause hallucinations which in turn can induce fear. Some forms of manic depression involve switches from mania to depression, and back again, which are so swift, cyclical, context-independent, and so far-reaching and fundamental in their effects, that almost certainly they are caused at a very fundamental biological level. However, generally speaking, emotions are part of our normal adult human life and an emotional state is a concept appropriate to talking about humans as persons, with beliefs and desires and other psychological attitudes, whether conscious or subconscious, rather than as biological systems. As a defendant in court, I might say to the presiding judge, 'Your honour, I turned left because I thought that this was the quickest route to the airport and because I had not realised that it was not permissible to turn left at that junction between the hours of nine to five.' That seems an appropriate, if not necessarily a convincing, defence to a charge of violating a traffic law. On the other hand, if, in the same court and in response to the same charge, I had said to the judge, 'Your honour, I turned left because an electro-chemical impulse from my brain activated movements in the muscles of my left and right arms such that they moved the steering wheel of the car in an anti-clockwise direction thus causing the car to turn left at the junction', I would be cited for contempt of court.

The point is not that reductive explanations are not appropriate in psychology or philosophy of mind, rather the point is that certain sorts of reduction are appropriate while others are inappropriate. For, as we have just seen, by means of the example about the nature of emotion, certain types of reductive explanation are the right way to go about explaining things while other types are not. What the recent history of philosophy of mind has taught us to eschew are those reductions which try to produce an explanation at such a low level as to be useless and so inappropriate. It has taught us to avoid philosophical anorexia. In turn, as we shall now investigate in more detail, this tendency to philosophical anorexia has often arisen among philosophers of mind through their incontinent adulation of the oh-so-glamorous and oh-so-slim theories that strut along the catwalk of the hard, experimental, physical sciences.

Substituting scientia for science

It was the diaspora from the Vienna Circle that put together many of the basic ingredients of modern American philosophy, which, in turn, has put together many, perhaps most, of the basic ingredients of modern philosophy of mind in the analytic tradition. In Britain, which was the other main arena for analytic philosophy, there were other influences at work, or at least in addition, namely the influence of Moore, Frege, Russell, 'the later Wittgenstein' and Ryle.

Now, one of the central doctrines of nineteenth-century positivism, which can be traced right through these historical and geographical gatherings and dispersals to current analytic philosophy of mind, is the belief that the paradigm of proper knowledge is the data and theories of natural science, and that the paradigm of proper procedures for gaining proper knowledge are the procedures of natural science. Moreover, particularly under the influence of the doyen of modern American philosophers, W. V. O. Quine (1908–), who in turn was influenced by one of the great figures of logical positivism, Rudolf Carnap, the paradigm of natural science, and so of exact positive knowledge, has come to be seen as physics. As Quine wrote in 1964, in an approving review of J. J. C. Smart's book *Philosophy and Scientific Realism*:

> Physics investigates *the essential nature of the world*, and biology describes a local bump. Psychology, human psychology, describes a bump on the bump.[5]

In answer to the question that will occur to most people, namely, why this special deference to physics?, Quine replies in another book review (in 1978):

> This is a good question, and part of its merit is that it admits of a good answer. The answer is not that everything worth saying can be translated into the technical vocabulary of physics; not even that all good science can be translated into that vocabulary. The answer is rather this: nothing happens in the world, not the flutter of an eyelid, not the flicker of a thought, without some redistribution of microphysical states. It is usually hopeless and pointless to determine just what microphysical states lapsed and what ones supervened in the event, but some reshuffling at that level there had to be; physics can settle for no less. If the physicist suspected there was any event that did not consist in a redistribution of the elementary states allowed for by his physical theory, he would seek a way of supplementing his theory. Full coverage in this sense is the very business of physics, and only of physics.[6]

This is a very subtle endorsement of the physical point of view. It clearly repudiates some of the earlier, cruder interpretations of the 'unified science' doctrine of the logical positivists of the Vienna Circle, which, in effect, endorsed the view of Lord Rutherford (1871–1937), the Nobel Prize-winning pioneer of sub-atomic physics, that 'all science is either physics or stamp collecting'. For this crude interpretation of the 'unified science' doctrine proclaimed that all science is reducible to physics in so far as the law-like generalisations of any science, say those of geography or biology, ultimately can be derived from the more basic laws of physics. What Quine's view does not repudiate is the evaluative stance behind that crude interpretation. Quine claims, in effect, that physics has a privileged status because it alone investigates the 'essential nature of the world' because its scope alone is 'full coverage' of every event in the universe. In more demotic language, physics alone is 'the business', scientifically speaking. In turn, this has often been taken to mean that the explanations of a subject like psychology are not explanations that get at the essentials. They may produce useful explanations, at least for some purposes, but ultimately they are not explaining what is really happening. Any such view that restricts what really counts as science to the so-called natural sciences, and then adds to this a quasi-religious veneration of physics as the only science that penetrates to the essential nature of the universe, is often called, admittedly by its opponents, 'scientism'.

Quine could reply, with justification, that this view of what counts as doing real science was more or less the accepted view at the time he was writing and continues to be. He was just echoing the modern view of what counts as science, not proselytising on behalf of some artificially restricted view of it. As justification, he could point to the fact that a readily available dictionary of science will include under the label 'science' only physics itself plus the other sciences that are readily relatable to physics, such as, for example, astronomy, chemistry and biochemistry. *The Penguin Dictionary of Science*, 4th edition, 1977, for example, includes under the label 'science' only physics, biophysics, astronomy, chemistry, biochemistry, molecular biology, and mathematics and computing. The latter two, mathematics and computing, are included, presumably, because they are the indispensable instruments of modern science. He could also point to the fact that the central meaning of the word 'science' in *The New Shorter Oxford Dictionary* (1993 edition) is 'now usu. *spec.* [usually specifically] the intellectual and practical activity encompassing those branches of study that apply objective scientific method to the phenomena of the physical universe (the natural sciences), and the knowledge so gained; scientific doctrine or investigation; the collective understanding of scientists'.[7]

During the heyday of the identity theory of mind and of eliminative materialism, philosophers of mind in the analytic tradition were also religiously devoted to this modern, restricted view of science. One result of this piety, as we have already seen, was the tendency to attempt to reduce descriptions of any events at a higher level to descriptions of micro events at a more fundamental level, which, hopefully, at some future time, would result in the ability to give explanations of human actions at the level of fundamental physics or at a level reasonably close to it. Thus we saw a concerted move to show that, at least eventually, we should seek to reduce our ordinary discussions about the nature of mind, in terms of beliefs, desires and the other propositional attitudes, to talk about events at a lower level, which will either be descriptions of mental events in the language of physics or be a way-station, such as a neurophysiological or biological one, on the line to that terminus.

In the last few decades of the twentieth century, this modern, restricted view of science was also championed under a different banner and in a far less obvious manner, even if the end result has been much the same. What I have in mind is what has become known as the 'naturalising' tendency in modern philosophy of mind. The use of the term 'naturalising' in modern philosophy of mind refers to the programme of reducing descriptions of mental events to descriptions in terms of those natural sciences which are deemed appropriate to the scientific investigation of what goes on inside human heads. For that is where, with our naive, folk psychology of mental events, we (correctly, the 'naturalisers' would say) locate mental events. If now we can successfully naturalise our talk about minds and mental events, then minds will have been successfully interwoven with the rest of nature, and a genuine science of the mind will have become a reality. The last vestige of that religious and Cartesian desire to have human souls as something special and transcending the purely natural will have been removed.

The more dogmatic adherents to 'the way of natural science' in philosophy of mind have said, in effect,

Well, we've shown you the direction in which things must go. We've also shown you who are the ones that, professionally speaking, have a licence to travel in that direction, that is, the scientists from disciplines such as biology and neurophysiology and biochemistry and perhaps, ultimately, physics. We shall just have, finally, to admit that psychology and philosophy of mind are now redundant. Their job has been done. Just as in the past the philosophical cosmologists had to hand over their subject to the astrophysicists and astronomers, so now psychologists and philosophers of mind should hand over their subject to these natural scientists of the mind.

However, as we have already seen, in the previous section of this chapter, the last few decades of the twentieth century saw a backlash against reducing the explanations gainfully employed in philosophy of mind and psychology to those that are employed at a lower and supposedly more scientific level. In effect, the reply was that

> Physics and chemistry and biology and neurophysiology have had their chances, for a long time now, to take over philosophy of mind and psychology, but it simply has not happened. The best way of explaining most things in psychology, at least of a higher human cognitive sort, is still to do so in terms of beliefs and desires and the other propositional attitudes. What is more, the redundancy of such explanations, through the advance of neuroscience or some kindred natural science, does not look any more likely to happen in the next hundred years than it looked like happening in the last hundred years. While the physicists each year learn more about physics, and biologists about human biology, and neurophysiologists about the human brain, these gains have had little effect upon human psychology. What light on psychology and philosophy of mind has been shed by the natural sciences – to an extent by neurophysiology and biochemistry but not at all by physics and hardly at all by biology – has been shed, not upon the nature of beliefs and desires and the other propositional attitudes, but upon the relation of brain processes to sleep, memory, and sensation, and the relation of failures in brain mechanisms to organic mental disease or breakdown.
>
> Besides, if the best, because most useful, explanations of human actions and their motivation are in terms of the concepts and categories of psychology and philosophy of mind,

then perhaps we should grant that such explanations are not merely natural but also scientific. What we need to return to is a less narrow concept of what counts as scientific and also what counts as natural.

I want to expand on that last sentence by contrasting the concept of science employed explicitly or implicitly in modern dictionaries of science with an earlier, now largely lost, conception of science which might be called *scientia*. Then I want to suggest that the earlier conception is ultimately the more useful because more true to the facts of the matter.

In the 1773 edition of Samuel Johnson's *Dictionary of the English Language*, first published in 1755, there is a listing for the word 'science'. First Dr Johnson points out that the word 'science' is derived from the Latin word *scientia*, meaning, simply, 'knowledge', via its French translation, *science*. Then he lists the meanings of the word 'science' in his time as follows:

1. Knowledge.
2. Certainty grounded on demonstration.
3. Art attained by precepts, built on principles.
4. Any art or species of knowledge.
5. One [meaning 'any one'] of the seven liberal arts, grammar, rhetorick, logick, arithmetick, musick, geometry, astronomy.[8]

Somewhat surprisingly, Dr Johnson equated science with the liberal arts and so included grammar and music and logic among the sciences. It seems from the other listed meanings that in the eighteenth century what made something scientific was that it was clearly knowledge of something and clearly attained by the most rigorous method appropriate to finding out about that thing. Though the earliest microscopes date from the end of the sixteenth century, and both microscopes and telescopes were comparatively common by the end of the seventeenth century, there is no suggestion in this eighteenth-century account of science that, to count as scientific, knowledge should be confined to some instrument-aided investigation of events. There is also no suggestion that scientific knowledge had to be mathematical in form or experimental in method, though, presumably, both mathematics itself and experimental investigations, such as those carried out by Luigi Galvani, would be counted as scientific. There is also no mention of any special status for 'natural philosophy', the then current term for physics. Indeed the term

T. Trotter del.

Cha. Ino.

Figure 6.1
The famous
eighteenth-
century
lexicographer,
critic and
poet, Samuel
Johnson. His
Dictionary,
first published
in 1755, gives
a very liberal
definition of
the word.
'science'.

'natural philosophy' is not mentioned at all. Quite simply it seems
that any rigorous method which produced certainty via demonstration would count as scientific. As regards 'demonstration', in

his *Dictionary* Johnson defined it as involving 'the highest degree of deducible or argumental evidence' or as involving 'indubitable evidence of the senses or reason';[9] in short, its two meanings coincide roughly with what used to be covered by the old terms 'deduction' and 'induction'. You either arrived at exact knowledge simply by employing valid deductive reasoning on given premises or axioms (this, presumably, was why logic and mathematics were considered part of science) or you arrived at it via both observation and reasoning on the basis of the observation.

This account of science would not merely readily embrace what are now called the social sciences, and so include, for example, psychology and economics, it would also embrace the humanities as well. Let us take history as our example from the humanities. Historical research would be considered a scientific enterprise in the eighteenth century for the good reason that it produced or set out to produce the nearest one could get to exact knowledge about the past events of human history. A historian who employs the best possible methods of investigation when writing about, say, the Battle of the Somme, is being scientific in the fullest sense. The best possible methods for such an investigation would include interviewing any survivors of the battle, no matter which side they were on, as well as scrutinising regimental records to ascertain the age and background of the soldiers in both armies, and medical records to ascertain their physical and psychological state before and after the battle. The historical investigations would also include reference to extant diaries, letters or reports of the combatants, as well as the accounts by journalists and other observers. They would also make use of official maps as well as official lists of the supplies of transport, food, armaments, tents, uniforms, medicines and medical equipment, coffins, recreational materials, and so on. It would also take into account the records of home and field hospitals, of the meteorological office, of courts martial, the pay corps, shippers and suppliers, the cabinet and war office. It would also include visits to the sites of the battles and to museums now housing examples of the uniforms, weapons and other pieces of equipment used by all the armies involved, and, if possible, it would also include witnessing practical demonstrations of the arms and equipment. The historian would also need to study the economic, social, cultural and political aspects of the combatant countries. He or she would also need to compare and contrast the Battle of the Somme with other, earlier battles of the First World War in that theatre of war, such as, say, the Battle of Verdun. And so on. Given that the most exacting investigation and rational consideration of all relevant materials was made, the resulting account would be part of science or *scientia*. Indeed any such exacting and rigorous historical investigation would be a lot harder and much more demanding than the conduct of most experiments in physics or chemistry.

History is also a *natural* science in this wider sense of science. History studies events in the natural world which are just as natural as the interplay of sub-atomic particles or the fusion of chemicals into compounds. The natural events which history investigates just happen to be very large events, in the past, involving humans and often very large groupings of humans such as happens in the case of battles or revolutions or plagues. Just as an entomologist looks down at the world of insects and thinks of himself as a naturalist, so a historian might look down at the world of humans as they scurried into some battle or fell into an economic recession or were decimated by some plague and might be able to think of him- or herself as reporting upon natural events.

In so far as psychology and philosophy of mind are rigorous and exact in the gathering of the relevant facts, and the formation of their theories, explanations and accounts of human actions and motivations, then they are being scientific and so engaging in *scientia*. Given that they have good reason for thinking that the level at which they gather those facts and the level at which they form those theories, explanations and accounts is the most useful level for the task, then they are operating at the appropriate scientific level. As old Aristotle (384-322 BC) put it,

> And we must remember what has been said before, and not look for precision in all things alike, but in each class of things such precision as accords with the subject-matter, and so much as is appropriate to the inquiry. For a carpenter and geometer investigate the right angle in different ways.[10]

Just as was the case in Aristotle's time, we must not look for precision in all things in like manner. Precision in physics or chemistry will take a very different form from precision in history or music. Likewise, the level at which psychology (and, for more theoretical purposes, philosophy of mind) should operate, in a precise and so scientific way, will be quite different from the level at which physics and chemistry should operate.

The right level whereby the nature of human actions and their motivations are explained seems to be the level where explanations are expressed in terms of those human mental attitudes which we call 'believing', 'desiring', 'loving', 'hoping' and so on. For in regard to these attitudes, it seems possible to individuate and understand them only at that level at which we, ordinary folk, encounter them. When we talk about these psychological attitudes (or propositional attitudes), it seems that we are noticing and so talking about 'irreducibly macro slices' of another human's life or of our own life. For example, for us ordinary humans and for psychologists as well, the vicar's proneness to go to church, his readiness to preach to his parishioners about God, his being given to long meditations on divine texts, his saying to himself that God will have mercy on him, and his disposition to pray to God for help especially when things go wrong, is best explained as a belief in God. For that level of whole-person behaviour, overt or covert, is the level at which we encounter vicars or, for that matter, any other humans including ourselves, and seek to make sense of them. Likewise it seems likely, in the matter of human actions and their explanation, that it will never make sense for professional psychology to try to reduce this whole-person level of description to a series of micro-level descriptions, such as ones involving reference to descriptions of brain activities and muscle movements. *A fortiori*, it already seems clear that it will never make sense to reduce such psychological explanations to ones involving reference to events described and explained by sub-atomic physics.

In so far as these psychological items, belief and desire and love and hope, are picked out by explanations of the natural behaviour of natural organisms, humans, then they too are natural. Furthermore, they occur naturally *only* at this macro level. So the natural science that is best able to deal with them will be the one best suited to that level, namely psychology (and, for certain theoretical tasks, philosophy of mind). In the future, psychology, while still seen as a social science and, as it still is in some universities, as part of the humanities, might once again be viewed, incontrovertibly, as also a natural science. Of course, to say all this is not to deny that such psychological items as beliefs, desires and emotions are incarnated and so realised in neurophysiological and biological hardware. It is also not to deny that, for some purposes, such as curing a biologically based mental illness, it might be important or even essential to investigate matters at the level of neurophysiology or biology.

More generally speaking, the debates in philosophy of mind since the 1970s, and in particular the failures of reductionism, seem to be pushing us in the direction of accepting that we should rewiden our perspective on what we are willing to count as both 'natural' and 'science', and so as 'natural science'. We should rewiden our perspective to the one we had in the eighteenth century. We should substitute *scientia* for science. Contrariwise we should look suspiciously upon any reflex assumption that to be scientific about the mind we must operate at the level of the brain sciences or even physics. Those last two sentences might serve as an apologia for the humanities, and psychology's part in it, in this jingoistically scientific and reductive age.

Admitting consciousness into the realm of the physical

What lessons should we take from the recent discussions about consciousness in philosophy of mind, psychology and the brain sciences? Quite a number is the short answer. One lesson is plain enough, namely that consciousness is one of the 'bogeys' not merely of philosophy of mind and psychology but also of any relevant branch of brain science. If only we humans were not conscious, things in philosophy of mind and psychology, as well as in the brain sciences, would be so much easier and smoother. Without consciousness, the common philosophical and psychological 'game plan' of 'naturalising' the mind in a very narrow sense of explaining all its works in terms of the concepts of some natural science such as biology or neurophysiology or physics would be made so much more feasible. But philosophers, psychologists, as well as those involved in the brain sciences, have all had to admit that, in our attempted explanations of human nature, we are completely confounded by that part of us we call 'consciousness'. No scientist has even begun to make sense, say, of how it is that consciousness has evolved, or how it is that consciousness arises out of and is maintained by certain types of brain processing but not others. In a recent book with the confident title, *The Human Mind Explained*, edited by the British brain scientist, Susan Greenfield, the concluding part of the entry on consciousness (in the sense of 'being aware') is very far from being confident about the ability of natural science ever to explain it:

At the heart of the debate is the puzzle of how matter – molecules – and electricity can produce something that is aware of itself. We do not just hear and respond, as a machine does, we hear and know what it is like to hear. Some claim this awareness is just a by-product of the brain's complexity – brains produce minds like clouds produce rain – others say there is a gap there that science as we know it now cannot bridge.[11]

We saw also that an underlying difficulty in ever arriving at a way of interweaving our knowledge of consciousness with our knowledge of the brain was the contrast between the subjectivity of the former knowledge and the objectivity of the latter. The procedures and data of the brain sciences are 'objective' because the procedures involve experiments or observations which are empirical, public and replicable, and the ensuing data are quantifiable and testable by further experiment or observation. Consciousness, on the other hand, only exists as the particular stream of consciousness of a particular person, and so its phenomenal contents are only directly knowable by that same person. That is to say, consciousness is subjective not only in its mode of existence but also in the way in which it can be known. Consciousness confounds our objective enquiries by its intrinsic subjectivity.

Continental philosophers, being in major part the offspring of Cartesian philosophy, as filtered through Brentano and Husserl, are amazed that analytic philosophers are left so dazed and confused by consciousness. Phenomenology, that seminal movement of late nineteenth- and early twentieth-century Continental philosophy, was all about consciousness and what one could learn about and from it. So, in a sense, was its close relative in psychology, introspectionism. In its early pure form introspectionism was seen as the embodiment of a specialist, experimental, sub-science of consciousness.

The analytic philosophers reply that they are dazed and confused by consciousness because they are not interested, as were the phenomenologists and introspectionists, in *describing* the conscious mind or *analysing* its contents. The analytic philosophers are interested in giving a philosophically acceptable *explanation* of the very existence of the subjective reality of consciousness in an otherwise objective world. By 'philosophically acceptable' is meant an explanation that makes it clear that consciousness, though subjective, must still be a part of nature and so continuous with brains, bears and barnacles. On the other hand, the Continental philosophers can reply that this dazed confusion in analytical philosophy of mind, as well as in mainstream psychology, for a very long time led these enterprises into neglecting any discussion whatsoever of consciousness; this neglect dating from roughly the advent of behaviourism in the first quarter of the twentieth century till the beginning of the last quarter of the same century.

As we saw in the previous chapter, in modern analytic philosophy, it was the American Tom Nagel, soon to be aided and abetted by Colin McGinn and John Searle, who reintroduced 'the subjectivity of consciousness' as a crucial fact that analytical philosophy of mind would neglect at its peril. John Searle suggested that modern philosophy of mind had been left for dead by this 'problem of consciousness' and, as a result, had returned the compliment by neglecting it almost entirely. What we needed to do was to bring it back to the centre of our discussions in philosophy of mind. Colin McGinn, on the other hand, voiced a note of despair, by suggesting that no type or style or method of philosophy will ever be able to solve the essential questions about consciousness, namely how it can arise from and causally interact with the undeniably physical commerce of brain processing. Most likely, he suggested, we will be the victims of 'cognitive closure' in respect of these central questions about the nature of consciousness, in much the same way that an infant suffers 'cognitive closure' in regard to any understanding of the Theory of Relativity. However our 'cognitive closure', because it is based on a permanent deficit in regard to the requisite conceptual powers, will be permanent.

In so far as they discussed it, the 'reductionist' philosophers, as one might expect, refused to accept that consciousness was anything special. It was just a product of a clever sort of manipulation of representations by a neurophysiological 'virtual reality' machine, the brain. Or else a belief in consciousness was just an illusion that had been foisted on us by our wilful adherence to an outdated Cartesian vocabulary. Or else a belief in consciousness was a result of a sort of logico-linguistic fallacy, 'the Phenomenal Fallacy', that we can all fall into because of the way we express our ordinary perceptions of the world around about us and subsequently mishandle these expressions for philosophical or quasi-philosophical purposes. We could be seduced by such ordinary expressions as 'I seem to see a red streak in the sky' into adopting the philosophical view that perception involves the possession, somewhere in our head, of 'seeming red streaks' or 'moments of red-streak consciousness'.

What seems certain, however, and should be the most important lesson to be learned, is that 'the problem of consciousness' will not go away. It will not leave philosophy of mind and psychology in peace. One sign of hope for the future is that almost all those who say that an adequate account of consciousness is the most pressing need in philosophy of mind, or for that matter in psychology and neurophysiology, see consciousness as one of the products of the evolution of the purely physical world. Most of those would go further and support the view that consciousness is likely to be itself purely physical. One reason for holding this view is that the more usual alternatives are unpalatable, either a return to the long discarded doctrine of Cartesian substance dualism (which was discussed in Chapter 1) or a return to another dubious, seventeenth-century doctrine, panpsychism (which was discussed in the form of its revival by David Chalmers, in Chapter 5).[12]

More positive reasons for holding that consciousness is physical (though, as we shall see, in a wider sense of 'the physical' than is currently employed) have emerged from recent discussions about consciousness. These might be summed up as follows:

1. Consciousness is a fact.
2. Consciousness has evolved, in a purely causal way, from the basic physical bits and pieces present at the Big Bang, that is, at the beginning of the evolution of the universe.
3. Consciousness is a product of the evolution of biological organisms.
4. In humans and other animals, consciousness is a biological product of the evolution of brains.
5. In humans, consciousness occurs as a result of certain sorts of brain processing.

The propositions above, numbered 1 to 5, do not by themselves lead to the conclusion that consciousness must be physical. For there are philosophers who accept 1 to 5 above but then draw back from concluding that consciousness is physical. The main reason for this retreat are two additional facts, namely:

6. Consciousness is a fact that is subjective both ontologically

(that is, in its mode of existence) and epistemologically (that is, in the manner in which it can be known).

7. The physical world, as studied by natural scientists, is objective both ontologically and epistemologically.

This dual subjectivity of consciousness (fact 6) impresses philosophers as a good reason for holding that consciousness cannot be reduced to events in the physical world as described by the natural sciences, for these are wholly objective (fact 7); that is to say, the dual subjectivity of consciousness is a good reason for rejecting the identity theory of mind as well as eliminative materialism. Unfortunately, this dual subjectivity of consciousness also seems to many people to be a good reason for denying that consciousness can be physical, full stop. However, there is another possibility, an alternative view which reserves a place for subjective physical facts. There is, on this view, the physical world describable by physicists and other natural scientists, and there is the physical world describable only by the subjects of conscious experiences. This view holds that we must not assume that the category of the physical is wholly contained within another category called 'objective facts'. There may be *subjective physical facts*, and the fact of consciousness may be a good candidate for inclusion among them.[13] As a way of putting some flesh on this suggestion, a brain scientist at the University of California, San Francisco, Benjamin Libet, in 1994 proposed that consciousness is indeed physical and forms what he calls 'the conscious mental field'. This conscious mental field is a real physical field but one which differs radically from other physical fields, like electromagnetic or gravitational ones, in being 'accessible only to the individual who has the experience'.[14]

It is on this last point that, in the future, I expect to see philosophers of mind seeking help from philosophy of science. For to make plausible the claim that consciousness is physical, yet not physical in the way that brain states and processes are or, for that matter, in the way that photons, mesons, bosons, fermions and other fundamental particles are, philosophers are going to have to investigate how and whether it might be plausible to widen the concept of the physical beyond its present scope. Put more baldly, theoretical physicists and philosophers of science would have to provide grounds for a rather more catholic view, than is currently on offer, of what can be subsumed under the term 'physical'. In his splendid and splendidly combative book,

Figure 6.2
John Searle,
contemporary
American
philosopher,
who has been
a continued
scourge of the
excesses of
the reductive
materialists
and of the
exponents
of artificial
intelligence.

The Rediscovery of the Mind, John Searle writes that Noam Chomsky, the renowned philosopher, scholar in linguistics and commentator on American politics, once said to him 'that as soon as we come to understand anything, we call it "physical".'[15] Perhaps something like the reverse is also true, that when we cannot understand something, in a very profound sense of not understanding, as seems to be the case with consciousness, then we presume that it cannot be physical.

The obverse of this growing tendency on the part of some contemporary philosophers of mind, such as myself, to be sympathetic to seeing consciousness as just another part, albeit 'a peculiar part', of physical nature is that there will always be some – and these usually with some religious dogma to defend – who will insist on setting human consciousness apart from the rest of the evolved natural world. For this apartness, as we have already seen, is part of the grounds for maintaining that humans are special, because they have a soul, and so grounds for the hope for a special post-mortem destiny for humans that is not open to the rest of the natural world.

Arguably, there are grounds already for believing that the concept of the physical, or matter, could expand further to include consciousness, in the undeniable fact that the concept has already expanded from the time of Newton to the present time. The following passage is the very last paragraph of the entry on 'Matter' in volume six of the *Routledge Encyclopedia of Philosophy*:

> Thus the concept of matter has been altered in such drastic ways that certain contemporary ideas correspond at best only roughly to classical scientific and philosophical counterparts. The sharp contrasts between inert, passive permanence and dynamic activity, ultimate constituency and change, matter and force, fail to appear in quantum-theoretical analogues of classical matter. Indeed, the merely approximate analogy of fermions and bosons to classical concepts of matter, the activity of the quantum vacuum, the character of quantum fields as superpositions of possibilities and many other features of the quantum world, together with the existence of dark matter, all conspire to dictate the reformulation of many traditional problems of philosophy, such as the free will problem, the doctrines of materialism and determinism, the distinction between actuality and possibility, and the topic of matter itself.[16]

Would it be too far-fetched to suggest that when the article on matter is written for a new encyclopedia of philosophy, in the year 2050, added to the list of problems that need reformulation, in the light of the latest theories in theoretical physics, will be 'the distinction between objective and subjective'?

Avoiding double vision

On BBC television, during the years 1969–74, there was a regular comedy programme, consisting of comic skits and sketches, entitled *Monty Python's Flying Circus*. One of these sketches went as follows:

VOICE OVER [17] And now to something completely different.
The office of Sir George Head, OBE.
Large study with maps and photographs on the wall and a large desk at which sits Sir George Head.
SIR   Next please.
Bob walks into the room and up to the desk.

SIR	(*looking up*) One at a time please.
BOB	There is only me, sir.
SIR	(*putting a hand over one eye*) So there is. Take a . . .
BOB	Seat?
SIR	Seat! Take a seat! So! (*looking four feet to Bob's right*) You want to join my mountaineering expedition do you? (*keeps looking off*)
BOB	(*rather uncertain*) Me, sir?
SIR	Yes.
BOB	Yes, I'd very much like to, sir.
SIR	Jolly good, jolly good. (*ticking sheet and then looking right at Bob*) And how about you?
BOB	There is only me, sir.
SIR	(*putting hand over eye and looking both at Bob and to Bob's right*) Well bang goes his application then. (*he tears up form*) Now let me fill you in. I'm leading this expedition and we're going to climb both peaks of Mount Kilimanjaro.
BOB	I thought there was only one peak, sir.
SIR	(*getting up, putting one hand over one eye again and going to large map of Africa on wall and peering at it at point-blank range*) Well, that'll save a bit of time. Well done. Now the object of this expedition is . . .[18]

While in this context it may not have been so debilitating, modern philosophy of mind has also suffered from time to time from double vision. The modern debate about the relationship between mind and body began, ironically, with a vehement repudiation of the double vision of Cartesian substance dualism. With the appearance of first behaviourism, then the identity theory and finally eliminative materialism, modern philosophy of mind entered into a passionate embrace of monism, namely monistic (or 'one stuff only') materialism. However, in the last few decades of the twentieth century, philosophers of mind have returned, if not to embracing, then at least to a persistent flirting with some form of dualism. They have done so in the belief that if there is to remain a real distinction between our mental life and our non-mental life, then there must be some form of dualism. Clear distinctions are very often twofold and so *ipso facto* dualistic. After all, our whole life is coloured by a host of fairly innocuous dualisms brought about by the need to make just such basic, twofold distinctions. We describe parts or aspects of the world as male or female, animate or inanimate, hot or cold, wet or dry, ripe or unripe, sweet or sour, large or small, and so on. Moreover we seem to cope better by dividing the world up into such opposing categories. To take a simple case, we are more likely to get exactly what we want in a shop if we say 'I would like a large, ripe, sweet apple' rather than if we simply asked for an apple. For then we might be disappointed to receive one that was small, unripe and sour. Nevertheless, as we saw, even those modern philosophers of mind who feel the need for some form of dualism disagree about what form this dualism should take. The dualisms that came back into fashion after the identity theory and eliminative materialism were not dualisms of substance but of descriptions or properties. Thus, for example, functionalism distinguished mind from body in terms of two distinct sets of properties and their appropriate descriptions. Our psychological descriptions picked out certain sorts of abstract, functional properties of the human organism. Our neurophysiological descriptions picked out physical properties of the human organism. Others made the mind–body distinction in terms of types of descriptions. Psychological descriptions were intentional descriptions which contained normative or evaluative elements as well as purely descriptive ones. Psychological descriptions were deliberate attempts to regiment human behaviour according to certain norms or values of rationality, coherence, and consistency. Such descriptions were deemed useful or, some argued, necessary, to making sense of humans as organisms with reason-generated purposes and the freedom to carry them out. These psychological descriptions, sometimes called 'intentional descriptions', were to be distinguished from non-intentional descriptions, sometimes called 'extensional descriptions', whose paradigm were the 'pure', value-neutral descriptions of the natural sciences.

In the first half of the twentieth century, the move away from viewing mind and body as a duality of distinct substances to thinking of it as a particular neurophysiological part of one and only one material substance was radical. It was equally radical to look for the mind–body distinction in terms of a much weaker duality, namely of properties and finally descriptions. Since then, there has been yet another radical change in outlook about the duality of mind and body. There has been an explicit call, on the part of at least one influential philosopher, Richard Rorty, to

Figure 6.3 Richard Rorty who believes that many of the problems of modern philosophy of mind stem from the still influential legacy of Descartes, Locke and Kant.

jettison altogether the search for a distinction between mind and body, and thereby to give up the traditional concept of mind. He reasoned that to adopt such a concept is already to drift back into the old ways of seeing mind as something that only exists in contrast with the body. If the universe underwent no changes of temperature, then we would not experience hot or cold. We would have no concepts of hot or cold. Similarly, Rorty seems to be urging upon us the view that the human organism should be viewed as metaphysically seamless, so that it is a distortion to break it down into the polar opposites of mind and body. Rorty believes that the mind versus body picture, and in consequence the whole dualism versus monism debate, is a mistake foisted upon us by our taking Descartes, or at least Cartesianism, as the starting point in modern philosophy of mind.

In his bracing, iconoclastic work of 1980, *Philosophy and the Mirror of Nature*, Richard Rorty presented himself as influenced in this outlook by the later work of Wittgenstein, the German existentialist philosopher Martin Heidegger (1889–1976), and the American pragmatist philosopher John Dewey (1859–1952). He also presented himself as turning against a series of assumptions that philosophy had accepted more or less unchallenged from the seventeenth century. He pointed out that, in the areas of philosophy of mind and epistemology, implicitly or explicitly, modern philosophy had accepted some form of dualism of mind and body because it had retained elements of 'the notion of "the mind" common to Descartes, Locke, and Kant – as a special subject of study, located in inner space, containing elements or processes which make knowledge possible'.[19] More trenchantly, he asserted that one of the aims of his book was 'to undermine the reader's confidence in "the mind" as something about which one should have a "philosophical" view',[20] for he believed that the mind–body problem was a pseudo-problem brought about by our having inherited our view of the mind from Cartesian substance dualism. We look for 'a mind' which is sharply demarcated from the body because that is how Descartes set up the ground rules for the original search.[21]

The important lesson to be learned here may be a less stark and uncompromising one than that suggested by Rorty. The lesson may be not to give up completely on the concept of mind, but to admit that no single form of dualism, whether of substance or property or description or anything else, could possibly capture the distinction between the mental and non-mental life of humans. The main reason for this, easily underestimated, is simply that the mental life of humans itself takes such a large number of different forms. Our mental life is an eclectic gathering of disparate capacities, abilities and skills and the activities that stem from these. A swift glance at the contents pages of any current textbook of psychology will confirm this. It will be divided into chapters on such things as consciousness and perception; development and learning; memory, imagination and thinking; motivation and emotion; personality and individuality; stress, psychopathology, and therapy; and social behaviour.[22] Thus among the items in our mental stock-taking there will be, for example, conscious mental acts as well as subconscious mental acts. There will also be mental states, such as feelings, which are simple, and mental states, such as emotions, which are complex and involve, besides feelings, also cognitive and appetitive states, physiological events, facial expressions and behaviour. In addition there will be behavioural dispositions, to which we give mental descriptions, such as, for example, being irascible or shy, and there will be the behavioural acts which are the upshot of those dispositions being activated, to which we also give mental descriptions, such as, for example, being now in a rage or being now embarrassed. There will be achievements, in tasks or tests, which merit psychological commendation, such as being intelligent or musical, and there will be failures, which merit psychological condemnation, such as being a dunce or having a tin ear.

Our mental life is so complex that it would be simply astounding if there were some reasonably simple and single concept and term, which referred to a reasonably simple and single ingredient, which could be used as a way of picking out the different items that make up our mental life. It would also be astonishing if, by reference to this ingredient, we were able to produce a neat and sharp contrast with our non-mental life, so as to produce a plausible and employable dualism of mind and body.

The fundamental lesson here seems to be that philosophers of mind need to adopt an account of the nature of mind which is sensitive to the history of the debate about mind and body, especially over the twentieth century. They need to adopt an account which recognises, first, that our theorising about the mind has been constrained in two ways. First, it has been constrained by the way in which the agenda of the modern mind–body debate was set long ago by Descartes. Then it has been constrained by various models that were borrowed from those parts of natural science that were fashionable or in the vanguard at the time. Discovering the nature of mind, or our mental life, is not going to be a matter of finding an essential ingredient, such as consciousness or thought or anything else, which distinguishes the mental from the physical. To look for such an ingredient is to be misled by the way the mind–body debate came into being. What presently we count as mental turns out by and large to be just those capacities, abilities and skills which Descartes packed into the soul part of the human organism, and so those things which could be considered as 'higher' and worthy of immortality. It follows that 'mind' and 'mental life' were never purely descriptive terms but terms that were shot through with evaluative and normative considerations. In the next section, I will examine these matters further.

Minds, and who may have them

In Chapter 2, when discussing logical (philosophical) behaviourism, I mentioned Gilbert Ryle's well-known story by means of which he illustrated the logic of the concept of a category mistake, namely the mistake of incorrectly assigning some word to one logico-linguistic category or type when in fact it should be assigned to another. Ryle in turn had defined a category as the set of ways in which it is logically legitimate to operate with a word.

Ryle's well-known story was about a foreigner who visits Oxford or Cambridge for the first time and is shown around the university. Having completed the tour of the university, and so having seen all the colleges, libraries, offices, lecture rooms, laboratories, museums, galleries and playing fields, the visitor then asks, 'But where is the university?' The foreigner mistakenly takes the word 'university' to be on a par with words such as 'library', 'laboratory' and 'museum', when in fact the word 'university' is not a simple labelling word like these but a term that operates in a quite complex, multifaceted manner. Ryle was not interested, in that context, in how exactly the term 'university' does operate. The story was merely intended to illustrate the concept of a category mistake, or category confusion, as Ryle sometimes called it.

My purpose in referring once again to Ryle's story about the visitor misunderstanding the use of the term 'university' is three-fold. First, I am going to investigate in some detail the way the multifaceted and complex term 'university' operates. Second, I am going to suggest that the word 'mind' operates in important respects like the term 'university'. Finally, and somewhat para-doxically, I am going to suggest that while psychology and philosophy of mind form part of *scientia* (as explained in the section 'Substituting *scientia* for science' of this chapter), the word 'mind' itself is not a term of *scientia* but, given its genesis, merely a term of historical convenience.

It is time to get down to detail. The word 'university' is a complex, multifaceted term. To say that so-and-so is a university implies that so-and-so comprises at least a selection of buildings from the usual assortment of libraries, offices, laboratories, playing fields and everything else that includes the physical assets or plant of a university. In that sense, the word 'university' does imply the existence of buildings, at least for the present. There may come a time, in the future, when there is an internet plus e-mail university. But, even so, the current use of the word 'university' is not just as a sort of super-labelling term which labels the whole collection of buildings, individually labelled as 'library', 'laboratory', 'museum' and so on, which make up the

Figure 6.4
Oxford
University – it
is much more
than just a
group of
buildings

physical plant of a university. It has much more to its use. For a
start, to merit the title 'university', the so-and-so in question
must also have people in it, and have these people assigned to
specific roles with attendant duties and obligations. The human
constituents of a university are divided up, very roughly, into
teachers, students, research workers, technicians, administrators,
caterers, cleaners, and security staff. The terms for these human
constituents, such as, for example, 'teacher' and 'student', will
imply functional relations between themselves and other human
or non-human constituents of the university. A university teacher
has, for example, duties to advise, instruct and examine students.
The students at a university also have duties, such as to attend
lectures and tutorials, read course materials, complete assign-
ments, sit examinations and, in general, to seek to learn about
various subjects.

The suggestion so far is that a correct use of the term 'university' will imply that what has been so described will comprise various buildings or areas as well as have various types of staff and students with various duties. This might be called the *descriptive* element in the term 'university'. Contrasted with that descriptive element is what might be called the *normative* element. This means that to be a university, the human and non-human components (lectures, courses, staff, students, buildings and so on) must aim at certain standards. Being a university imposes an obligation to meet certain standards, for example, in regard to the holdings of the libraries, the equipment of the laboratories, the nature of the courses and the mode of instruction for them. For instance, the courses should be at third-level and so more up-to-date, specialised and demanding than courses at secondary- or primary-school level. The manner of teaching should not involve, say, mere rote learning or mere inculcation of facts but should aim to inculcate the ability to assess critically the course material, to bring about a real understanding of it and to encourage creative projects in regard to it.

To complicate matters further, there is at least a third facet to the use of the term 'university'. It has not merely descriptive and normative elements but also an *authorisation* element. To be a university, at least in most countries, you have to be declared to be one by an authority that has the power and right to do so. Most often this authority is the sovereign or some government minister, such as the Minister for Education, or some governmental department or committee, such as the Higher Education Authority. To be a university, there needs to be some authority that declares that the complex unity of physical plant and human assets meets the required standards of third-level education. The authority would probably also need assurances that the candidate university has sufficient sources of finance for the future and a likelihood of continuing to attract sufficient numbers of students within its walls. Then and only then, when the authority is satisfied, will the candidate university be authorised as a university.

The point of this long excursus into the use of the term 'university' lies in my belief that the direction of recent debates in philosophy of mind is towards the view that the term 'mind' operates in a somewhat similar manner. The term 'mind' is multifaceted in having descriptive, normative and authorisation facets or elements. First, some general remarks before I draw out

these elements. Consider the occasion when we hear someone
(such as some Oxford don grading an undergraduate student's
viva voce examination) remark that Miss Danvers has a first-
class mind. What is implied by this remark is that Miss Danvers
has performed in the *viva voce* examination in such a way that
she has displayed certain abilities and in doing so has achieved
certain standards in the display of those abilities. In consequence
the don and the group of examiners with him or her has authorised the award of First Class Honours to Miss Danvers. Let us
say that Miss Danvers has just been given a *viva voce* examination in philosophy of mind. Her performance merited the grade
of First Class Honours because she displayed a range of abilities
or skills looked for by examiners in philosophy. She displayed
such skills and abilities as clarity and originality of exposition,
depth and detail in her understanding of relevant material, and
rigour in her production of arguments. The descriptive element
in her performance is the list of abilities and skills upon which
she was judged. The normative element is the high standard
which she reached when exercising those abilities and skills. The
authorisation element is the declaration by legitimate authority
that she displayed those abilities and skills which are deemed
by that authority as relevant in philosophy and did so to the
standard ordained by that same authority.

Now, with a little pushing and pulling about, it will be seen
that the word 'mind' itself is used in this multifaceted way as
well. When, for example, we say that humans but not earthworms
have a mind, we are in the first place making some descriptive
claims. We are saying that humans but not earthworms display a
a certain set of capacities, abilities and skills. These latter terms
are not being used as synonyms. Humans have a capacity to
breathe with lungs. A capacity is something inbuilt in human
biology and physiology. Humans do not have to strive to exhibit it. An ability on the other hand is something a person can do
successfully or otherwise. For example, some humans have the
ability to hold their breath for a whole minute. A skill is an
ability which requires expertise that is gained only after training
or practice. A few humans have the skill of whistling the whole
of a Bach flute sonata. Thus, when we say that humans but not
earthworms have a mind, we are implying that humans have,
for example, the capacity to be conscious, the ability to learn a
natural language, and, very often, the skill of arithmetical calculation. We say that earthworms do not have a mind because,

while they might share in the capacity for consciousness, at least in some minimal way, they certainly do not have any language and will never be able to learn arithmetic.

The normative element in the use of the term 'mind' arises from the fact that in the history of our employment of the term 'mind', humans have at least tacitly set standards of achievement which must be attained if someone is to have a mind. Just being conscious, for example, is not enough. For birds and bats are conscious, and perhaps even eels and earthworms. One test for consciousness is whether or not the organism in question shows signs of experiencing pain or not, for pain is a paradigm of that type of conscious experience that we call a feeling. Moreover it is a form of consciousness that does not need to make use of concepts and so language. If you are conscious of a sharp darting pain in your gut, the feeling is the total content of your consciousness at that time; you are not *ipso facto* conscious in any conceptual way, for example, thinking that something or other is the cause of the pain. If some vile character kicks a cat in the stomach, the unfortunate cat presumably feels something like a sharp, darting pain in its gut. It certainly would react as if it did and a cat certainly does not know how to dissimulate or pretend to those sorts of feelings. On the other hand an eel or a worm probably does not have feelings of pain. Charles Darwin, however, put forward a more fundamental criterion for the presence of consciousness. He held that any organism that had senses, *ipso facto* had the capacity to be conscious. Accordingly he would have been happy to think of a gymnotid eel as being conscious and so as having qualia because it possesses a sensitivity to interference to its self-generated magnetic field and has a primitive nervous system underpinning it. After all Darwin believed that even planaria or flatworms were conscious. In his 'Old and Useless Notes', of 1838–9, Darwin remarked that,

16. A Planaria must be looked at as animal, with consciousness, it choosing food – crawling from light. –[23]

Even having the ability to reason and thereby solve problems is also not considered a sufficient ground for meriting the phrase 'having a mind'. Many animals clearly reason very well, often better than humans in certain contexts. While we may allow that they share this mental ability with us, we do not usually allow that thereby they must have minds. Again Darwin was in no doubt that at least many animals engaged in inductive reasoning,

Figure 6.5
Charles Darwin
– the great
English
naturalist and
co-inventor of
the theory of
the evolution
of species by
natural
selection is
having an
ever-increasing
effect upon
modern
philosophy of
mind.

that is, exhibited the ability to predict a future event by noting and remembering its being consistently preceded by a certain prior event. For example, I might realise that you are about to leave the department because you have just packed up your papers, put your pen into your inside jacket pocket and rung your husband up on the telephone: a routine you always follow just before you leave the department. Darwin was in no doubt that his favourite dog, Polly, could reason in just that way. The following passage, illustrating this ability of Polly's, is taken from 'Reminiscences of my father's everyday life' by Darwin's son, Francis, and published in 1883, the year following Darwin's death:

> But the dog most closely associated with my father was the above-mentioned Polly, a rough, white fox-terrier. She was a sharp-witted, affectionate dog; when her master was going away on a journey, she always discovered the fact by the signs of packing going on in the study, and became low-spirited accordingly. She began, too, to be excited by seeing the study prepared for his return home. She was a cunning little creature, and used to tremble or put on an air of misery when my father passed, while she was waiting for dinner, just as if she knew that he would say (as he did often say) that 'she was famishing'.[24]

Darwin gave an additional ground for thinking that animals can reason. This additional ground, besides their ability to exhibit skills of inductive reasoning, is their possession of memory. This passage is from Darwin's 'Notebook N' and written sometime around the years 1838–40:

> 90 . . . I suspect [a] very strong argument might be advanced, that animals have reasons, because they have memory. – what use this faculty if not reason. – or does this reasoning apply chiefly to recollection. [Y]et a dog hunting for a bone shows he has recollection.[25]

It is clear from this passage that the argument that animals must have the power or ability to reason, because they exhibit the capacity for memory, is tied in with an animal's ability to engage in inductive reasoning. Polly the dog reasons that she must have buried the bone over there by the oak tree because she has a memory of burying bones by the oak tree in the past. It is her regular boneyard. In effect the argument is that animals could only have the ability to reason inductively if they also had the prior capacity for memory. The next step is less logically secure, for it seems to amount to the suggestion that since animals have memory, then they must also have the ability to deploy it in inductive reasoning, otherwise memory would have evolved for no purpose.

Nevertheless, while we grant that Polly can reason, we do not say that Polly can think, because we seem to reserve the term

Figure 6.6
An illustration
of a dog from
Darwin's *The
Expression of
the Emotions
in Man and
Animals* –
Darwin had
no doubt that
dogs had
emotions and
could reason
inductively.

'think' for reasoning that makes use of language and so concepts. No one would want to say that Polly ever thought about abstract things, for example, about the nature of inductive reasoning and how it might differ from deductive reasoning.

Unfortunately Polly's remarkable powers of inductive reasoning, which probably include noting clues in contexts to which we humans are blind, will not admit Polly into the ranks of those who have minds. Even though an animal might be both conscious and be able to reason, we demand yet higher standards of mental ability to qualify for the award of 'having a mind'. Even if we add on the capacity to exhibit emotions, which is a mental capacity that animals also share in, many people would still not allow that even the 'higher' animals have minds.

The history of our usage of the term 'mind' has tacitly declared that having a mind must include the ability to employ language and then to deploy it in higher or conceptual thought. Just as it is conceivable that universities might lower their standards, under pressure, say, to admit more students and so make more money, so it is conceivable in the future that we might lower our standards as regards what it means to have a mind. After all it was probably Descartes who put the emphasis on having language as a necessary condition for having a mind when he declared that:

> Now it seems to me very striking that the use of words, so
> defined, is something peculiar to human beings. Montaigne

and Charron may have said that there is more difference between one human being and another than between a human being and an animal; but there has never been known an animal so perfect as to use a sign to make other animals understand something which expressed no passion [i.e. a sign other than the mating and warning cries and cries of rage or fear commonly found among animals]; and there is no human being so imperfect as not to do so, since even deaf-mutes invent special signs to express their thoughts. This seems to me a very strong argument to prove that the reason why animals do not speak as we do is not that they lack the organs [of speech] but that they have no thoughts. It cannot be said that they speak to each other and that we cannot understand them; because since dogs and some other animals express their passions to us, they would express their thoughts also if they had any.[26]

Since animals did not think, and since Descartes held that the essence of mind or soul was thought (that is, a soul was a conscious substance whose function is language-based thinking), then it followed that animals must not have a soul. In turn this lead him to suggest that what animated an animal was not a true *animus* but merely the flow of blood, and to a lesser extent other more subtle bodily fluids, for 'it is these [the blood and other

Figure 6.7 A French stamp depicting Descartes. In Paris there is also a street and a campus of the university of Paris named in his honour. The French have always recognised his importance in philosophy, especially his immense influence upon modern philosophy of mind.

fluids] which move the whole machine of the body as they flow from the arteries through the brain into the nerves and muscles'.[27] In effect dogs, and all other animals, were just physiological machines or automata, without consciousness and so without thought or even feelings. Philosophical wags have suggested that these views of Descartes really resulted from his dislike of dogs. If dogs did not have a soul, then they could not share in an after-life and so could not disturb Descartes's heavenly peace. With more malevolence than jest, anti-Cartesians spread the rumour that the Cartesian philosophers and logicians of the Port-Royal de Champs monastery near Paris, because of their adherence to Descartes's view of animals, engaged freely in vivisection and in particular were cruel to dogs:

> They administered beatings to dogs with perfect indifference, and made fun of those who pitied the creatures, as if they had felt pain. They said that the animals were clocks; that the cries they emitted when struck, were only the noise of a little spring that had been touched, but that the whole body was without feeling.[28]

The authorisation element in our use of the term 'mind' – the authority that says the term should cover this group of capacities, abilities and skills rather than that group – is nothing but the usage of the term itself over time. 'A mind' means whatever, gradually, over time, we have come to mean by it. Clearly the group of capacities, abilities and skills, to which we accord the title 'mind', has not remained absolutely stable over time. It has been added to and subtracted from. In Descartes's view, and for that matter the earlier medieval view, a mind was whatever powers (capacities, abilities and skills), and faculties that were the source of such powers, that it seemed right and proper to assign to a soul rather than to a body. In turn what it was right and proper to assign to a soul was settled, in part, by thinking about what powers and faculties could plausibly outlive the disintegration and death of the body and be part of the life of a pure spirit in heaven, alongside the saints, angels and God himself. In western culture, then, the original blueprint for the human mind was by and large dictated by theological considerations in the Middle Ages. Certainly, over the ensuing centuries, this blueprint has altered. For example, we now allow that certain mental acts and events can be subconscious. Nevertheless the alterations are, by and large, alterations to Descartes's original blueprint. It is still his outline that dominates our view of the mind. Given that history, we should admit that the term 'mind' does not pinpoint a natural organism, such as a rabbit, or a natural organ of such an organism, such as a heart or liver, or even a naturally occurring integrated grouping of organs. We should admit that what the term does, in an inexact way, is group together a disparate collection of human capacities, abilities and skills. A mind is not a discovery of *scientia* but, in a sense similar to the way in which we speak of a university, a product of human history and artifice. It is no wonder that the mind does not lend itself to easy explanation by any natural science.

A Lamarckian valediction

In the history of biology, a word which he himself coined, the French naturalist Jean Baptiste de Lamarck (1744–1829) has fared badly. He has been roundly defeated by Darwin and Wallace in regard to his views on the mechanism of evolution. For Lamarck the mechanism of evolution was wholly environmental. The giraffe in your neighbourhood zoo has a very long neck because its parents, and grandparents, and great grandparents, and great great grandparents, throughout their lives, had strained and so stretched their necks towards the foliage at the very tops of the trees in their continual search for food in inhospitable terrain. Thus an ancestral giraffe's neck gained in length during its lifetime and this gain was then passed on to its offspring by simple reproduction. In turn, during the next generation, giraffe necks were further lengthened, and so on down the generations till we get to the giraffe in your local zoo. Unfortunately, all the evidence was against this view, though, ironically, Darwin himself also believed in the inheritance of at least some acquired characteristics.[29]

However, in the context of the evolution of ideas, Lamarckism is probably the right model. Thus, in all probability, philosophy of mind in the twenty-first century will be very much the Lamarckian offspring of philosophy of mind in the twentieth century. Philosophers of mind in the twenty-first century will not be able to avoid learning some clear lessons from the last hundred years, much of it about what roads not to take. For example, I doubt whether mainstream analytic philosophy of mind will ever again seriously consider the exaggerated bifurcation of substance dualism, or the resolute anti-dualism-of-any-kind that

was characteristic of behaviourism, the identity theory or eliminative materialism, as possible solutions to the mind–body
problem. For, with that hubris that comes with hindsight, these
'solutions' to the mind–body problem now seem unsubtle and
unattuned to the complexity of our mental life and to the complexity of our psychological vocabulary, and to the complexity
of the history of that vocabulary, and so destined for the
philosophical scrap-heap. Yet it was the daring of these same
'solutions', and in some respects their partial success, that taught
us to acknowledge those very complexities.

Notes

1: The Twilight of the 'Two Worlds' View

1. Gilchrist, 1863, p. 59. I am indebted to my colleague in the English Department at Trinity College, Professor Terence Brown, for drawing my attention to this passage in Gilchrist. Another colleague in the English Department, Joseph Pheifer, drew my attention to the fact that this passage in Gilchrist is echoed in W. B. Yeats's poem *Sailing to Byzantium*, II, 1–3.

2. Descartes's name on his Latin texts was written as *Renatus Cartesius*, hence the adjective 'Cartesian'.

3. Descartes, 1954, pp. 31–2.

4. These objections, or at least the most famous ones made by Descartes's contemporary, the English philosopher, Hobbes, together with Descartes's replies to them, are nowadays almost always published along with the original text of the *Meditations*. The full title of the *Meditations* is *Meditations on First Philosophy*, and it was published in 1641.

5. Ryle, 1949, ch. 1, pp. 11–12.

6. McDougall, 1911, pp. xiii–xiv. Compare this with Descartes's own remark, in his letter dedicating his *Meditations* to the Sorbonne, 'Few people would prefer what is right to what is expedient if they did not fear God or have the expectation of an after-life' (see Descartes, 1984, p. 3).

7. Plato, 1974, Bk I, sect. 3; Nietzsche, 1933, Prologue, and Nietzsche, 1990, pp. 126–7.

8. Laird, 1925; the three quoted extracts appear on pp. 112–13, 113, and 117 respectively. See also, Jones, 1915, pp. 463–4, and Kneale, 1962, pp. 7–8, and 56.

9. While the first German edition of Wundt's *Lectures on Human and Animal Psychology* appeared in 1862, I am referring to the quite heavily revised second English edition of 1896.

10. Wundt, 1896; the two quotations appear on pp. 451 and 453 respectively.

11. The term 'metaphysics' arose, in a catalogue of Aristotle's works by Andronicus of Rhodes, as the title for a group of Aristotle's texts that came after another text of his called *The Physics*, for 'meta' is a Greek prefix for 'after'. Because the content of that

group of texts was a series of discussions about certain fundamental aspects of reality itself, such as motion, change and causality, 'an enquiry into fundamental aspects of reality' became the first meaning of the term 'metaphysics'. Subsequently, especially after the early nineteenth-century positivism of Comte and others, 'metaphysics' acquired in many quarters the pejorative meaning of 'speculative conclusions unjustified, and probably unjustifiable, by any known facts'. Wundt is clearly using the word 'metaphysics' in this latter pejorative sense.

12. McDougall, 1911, p. 365. See also McDougall, 1929, for, in the Preface, he states that this book, *Modern Materialism and Emergent Evolution*, is, in effect, 'a supplement' to McDougall, 1911, as it seeks mainly to provide a new and stronger argument for the main thesis of the earlier book.

13. Stout, 1913, ch.1, p. 17.

14. The phrase 'coextensive with our conscious life' needs a little more explanation to be perfectly accurate. G. F. Stout, in his textbook, *Manual of Psychology* (Stout, 1913, ch.1, sect. 6), would have employed the phrase 'coextensive with our conscious life or with any mental dispositions to exhibit episodes in our conscious life'. For Stout a 'mental disposition' was the state of being disposed to do something conscious when and if the circumstances were propitious. Thus, when I am trying to think of the name of the student who was meant to give me her essay today, I am disposed to think of her name but, so far, I cannot quite dredge it up into consciousness. Eventually, most likely, it will come to mind, that is, come into my consciousness. The disposition, in other words, will be activated. However, Stout then went on to talk of this shadowy world where dispositions reside as a world of 'mental structures' which are made of 'psychical' stuff. So he could be interpreted as saying that the mind was coextensive with consciousness or its shadowy mental underpinning, a sort of subconscious.

15. The resonant phrase 'stream of consciousness' was an invention of that most literate of the early psychologists, William James. His fullest account is in Volume 1, Chapter 9, of his monumental two-volume work, *The Principles of Psychology*, 1890. In using that phrase, James wanted to stress that he viewed consciousness as continuously in flux, as an uninterrupted 'flight'. Our referring in any static way to distinct objects or events in consciousness, that is to say, in the course of those 'flights' any reference to our 'discovery' of 'perchings', as James himself put it, was, strictly speaking, a product of our attempts, conceptually, to grasp and express the ever fluid contents of that stream.

16. Further explanation of the term 'empirical' might be needed. In general, an empirical claim is one that is based, at least ultimately,

upon the experience of some object, property or event mediated by one of the senses. Thus, to take an example, my smelling the rotten eggs when I open the fridge is philosophically describable as an empirical experience (even if it be more commonly referred to as simply disgusting), and the subsequent verbal claim, 'There is a smell of rotting eggs in my fridge', is describable as an empirical claim. In more recent times, the term 'empirical' has been associated with the experimental methods of the natural sciences. Strictly speaking, given its derivation, it should not.

17. The German philosopher Franz Brentano (1838–1917) could be said to be the progenitor of that distinction. In his text, *Psychology from an Empirical Standpoint*, 1874, which had a strong influence upon early psychology as well as upon so-called Continental philosophy from Husserl onwards, Brentano distinguished between 'inner *perception*' (*Wahrnehmung*) and 'inner *observation*' (*Beobachtung*). (See Brentano, 1973, Bk 1, sect. 2.2, p. 29.) Unlike subsequent introspectionist psychology, Brentano felt that the employment of 'inner observation' (or introspection) for scientific purposes involved a number of insuperable problems so that 'inner perception', for all its drawbacks, was what empirical psychology should employ.

18. As Wundt himself realised, introspection was not a useful way of investigating a number of areas in psychology, such as developmental and social psychology. For, in the first case, one had to observe a child developing over time and a child is incapable of introspection (or at least 'laboratory quality' introspection). In the second case, humans interacting socially cannot easily, if at all, be subjected to the disciplines of a laboratory. Besides, social psychology was best carried on by observation of a looser sort and by field work, in much the same way as social anthropology. Between 1900 and his death in 1920, Wundt himself wrote a ten-volume comprehensive psychology of culture, *Völkerpsychologie* (*Folk Psychology*). There is a much more accessible, short version of the *Völkerpsychologie*, in English, in Wundt, 1916.

19. See, for example, Myers, 1909, ch. 1.

20. The following example might make the concept of an 'afterimage' clearer. When you have been reading in bed for some time and you decide to go to sleep, you might reach across and turn off the bedside lamp. For a few moments after you have turned off the lamp, you will experience, seared, so to speak, on your stream of consciousness, a reddish-orange flash. That 'flash' is an afterimage resulting from having looked at the light bulb just as you were turning off the light.

21. English, 1921, pp. 406–10.

22. James, 1950, I, pp. 192–3.

23. Descartes lived in Holland from 1628 to the year before his death in 1650. He moved to Sweden, in that final fatal year, at the invitation of one of his patrons, Queen Christina of Sweden. A combination of a Swedish winter and Queen Christina's habit of requiring him to give her tutorials in philosophy at five o'clock in the morning almost certainly hastened his death from pneumonia.

24. By 'bodily spirits' physiologists of the time meant 'very subtle fluids', for they believed that the human nervous system probably operated by means of the wave motion of fluids which resided more or less imperceptibly in the miniscule hollow ducts situated inside nerves. As we now know the brain operates in an electrochemical way, with transmission along the nerve fibres being in terms of electrical impulses aided or impeded at certain junctions by chemical action and reaction.

25. Descartes, 1981, p. 136.

26. Sprott, 1937, for example, explains, under the heading 'pineal gland', that 'little is known of the function of this gland' (p. 418). Nowadays, like our appendix, it is sometimes 'written off' as an organ that has lost its function (see Young, 1978, pp. 65–9).

27. Descartes, 1981, p. 140.

28. Freud, 1962, p. 43. Freud also wrote about a 'group unconscious', such as a tribe or a group of children might possess. Interestingly, Freud also drew comparisons between the formation of social groups and the way a 'social bond' is formed between the hypnotist and his subject. (See Freud, 1971.) Freud, of course, was not the first person to write about the unconscious. In 1869, for example, the German philosopher Eduard von Hartmann published his book *Philosophy of the Unconscious*, which subsequently went through many editions. What Freud did was suggest ways in which one might study the unconscious.

29. I often wonder whether experimental psychologists are, or should be, worried by the number of times they must dissemble their real intentions when conducting experiments with humans.

30. Auditory sensitivity (or ability to hear a sound), leaving aside levels of partial deafness in an individual, depends on the loudness (or amplitude of the oscillations) and especially the pitch (or frequency) of pressure waves in the air (or some other medium). A subliminally received auditory message will be one where ordinary sound frequencies will be used but the message will be very brief as regards its content, presented for a very short time, and presented at a very low level of loudness.

31. For details of this sort of experiment, see, for example, Lackner and Garrett, 1973. For details of this sort of experiment when related to the Freudian notion of the unconscious, see, for example, Geisler, 1986.

32. Fernald, 1997, pp. 98–9.

33. We should recall that Wundt himself, unlike many of his followers (especially those in the laboratories founded by his one-time pupil Oswald Külpe), did not think that introspection was a suitable method for studying most areas of human thought. He held that most of human thought could only be explored adequately by the non-experimental methods of social psychology, which in turn would employ the methods of social anthropology and sociology. (In particular, see Wundt, 1907. For an overview of Wundt's psychology, see Miller, 1966, ch. 2).

34. In making this point, William James (see James, 1950, I, p. 189) was in fact responding to an objection made long before by Auguste Comte (see Comte, 1830–42, I, pp. 34–8). For the full story, see Lyons, 1986, ch.1, pp. 10–16.

35. Lyons, 1986, pp. 6–16.

36. See James, 1950, I, pp. 196–8, on 'the psychologist's fallacy'. For James's definition of psychology as the 'Science of Mental Life', see James, 1950, I, p. 1.

37. See Humphrey, 1951, ch. 4.

38. See Watson, 1995, p. 30.

39. See Watson, 1930, ch. 1.

40. Watson, 1930, p. 5.

41. For example, in his 'Letter to Herodotus', Epicurus maintained that 'the whole of being consists of bodies and space'. (See Gaskin, 1995, p. 14.) In Descartes's own time, Hobbes bravely put forward an uncompromisingly materialist view. In his masterpiece, *Leviathan*, Hobbes wrote that 'the *universe*, that is, the whole mass of things that are, is corporeal, that is to say, body; and hath the dimensions of magnitude, namely, length, breadth, and depth: also every part of body, is likewise body, and hath the like dimensions; and consequently every part of the universe, is body, and that which is not body, is no part of the universe: and because the universe is all, that which is no part of it, is *nothing*; and consequently *nowhere*'. (Hobbes, 1996, ch. 46, sect. 15.) Given the religious tenor of those times, Hobbes's view was never going to receive much of a hearing.

2: Observing the Human Animal

1. Watson, 1995, p. 24.

2. The brief biographical details are from Cohen, 1979.

3. By the term 'philosophical psychology', in this context, I mean psychological topics, such as consciousness or memory or perception, studied and taught in a more theoretical and non-experimental way.

4. While Ralph Waldo Emerson also appears on an American postage stamp, by means of the simple test of whether or not he appears in most of the popular, single-volume, paperback dictionaries of philosophy, he does not count as a philosopher.

5. Watson gave an overview of his work on animal psychology in Watson, 1910.

6. These quotations are from Watson, 1995, pp. 32–4 (i.e. his manifesto article originally published in 1913). Watson considered his article, 'Image and Affection in Behavior' (Watson, 1913) to be the sequel of his manifesto article of 1913.

7. There is a version of this dilemma argument in E. B. Titchener's famous reponse, at a meeting of the American Philosophical Society in Philadelphia in April 1914, to Watson's manifesto article of 1913 (see Titchener, 1914, esp. pp. 15–17).

8. The Greek word 'psyche', from which our word 'psychology' is derived, meant 'animating principle, spirit, soul, mind, reason . . .'

9. Probably a reference to the British psychologist Godfrey H. Thomson (1881–1955), who was eminent in the field of educational psychology.

10. Watson, 1920, p. 94. See also Jones, 1915, which is a commentary on Watson, 1995 (1913). The American philosopher Alfred Harrison Jones obtained his Ph.D. in philosophy from Cornell University in 1912, was an Assistant Professor at Brown University (1912–19), and then an Associate Professor at Cornell (1919–26).

11. Mead, 1934, pp. 2–3. At least one of Watson's disciples had anticipated him. A particularly uncompromising rejection of consciousness occurs in Elliot Park Frost's article, 'Cannot Psychology Dispense with Consciousness?' (Frost, 1914).

12. Watson, 1930, pp. 9–10.

13. Skinner, 1974, p. 117.

14. In regard to Sartre, see Cohen-Solal, 1987, pp. 444–9. Sartre's reason was not, as is usually claimed, because the Nobel Prize was bourgeois but because 'the writer must refuse to let himself be transformed by institutions'. In regard to the birth of analytic philosophy, see also note 17 below.

15. Neurath, with Hahn and Carnap, 1973.

16. After the Circle was broken up, the title of the journal was changed yet again to the more openly logical positivist title, *The Journal of Unified Science*, and published in the Netherlands.

17. Ayer, 1959, pp. 6–7. Alfred Jules Ayer was the author of *Language, Truth and Logic*, a book which is considered by many to be the best short introduction in English or any other language to the views and outlook of the Vienna Circle, though Ayer himself (Ayer, 1977, p. 154) gives a richer source for the book: 'Except in a few details, the thoughts [in *Language, Truth and Logic*] were not

original. They were a blend of the positivism of the Vienna Circle, which I also ascribed to Wittgenstein, the reductive empiricism which I had taken from Hume and Russell, and the analytical approach of Moore and his disciples, with a dash of C. I. Lewis's and Ramsey's pragmatism.' That mixture could also serve as an account of the mixture which has given rise to current analytic philosophy.

18. Comte is also credited with inventing both the subject and the term 'sociology'. The extended account of his ideas was first promulgated in a series of lectures delivered in Paris in 1826. The written version of these lectures is his daunting, six-volume treatise, *Cours de Philosophie Positive* (see Comte, 1830–42).

19. Wittgenstein, 1961, p. 49.

20. The decimal numbering was not invented by Wittgenstein but can be found, for example, in Russell and Whitehead's *Principia Mathematica*, with which Wittgenstein was familiar.

21. Wittgenstein, 1961, p. 49.

22. I am altering the reference of Comte's phrase. By the 'religion of humanity', Comte meant not science itself, but a new secular ethics of scientific orientation which he hoped to invent and substitute for the old religions.

23. Carnap, 1995, p. 46.

24. Carnap, 1995, p. 43.

25. I note that the paperback *Encyclopedia of Psychology* (Eysenck, Arnold and Meili, 1975, I, pp. 423–6) states that graphological claims have a 'low level of accuracy', though it also records that 'graphology is [still] taught at some German and Dutch universities as a branch of academic psychology'.

26. See Ayer, 1959.

27. Ryle, 1971, p. 61.

28. The label 'ordinary language philosophy' is more accurately placed upon the work of the Oxford philosopher, J. L. Austin (1911–60), and his disciples, but the label was often used more loosely to apply to British philosophy in the middle decades of the twentieth century.

29. The reviewer was J. L. Austin, see previous note. One result of Ryle's deliberate adoption of an unacademic style was his complete omission of both notes and bibliography from *The Concept of Mind*.

30. Ryle, 1949, p. 8. Ryle acknowledged that his account of categories and category mistakes was indebted to Bertrand Russell's 'Theory of Types'. The 'Theory of Types' is built around the idea that there are, for example, different levels or types of statements, arranged in a heirarchy, such that to confuse these levels or to subvert the hierarchy will result in 'type errors' and thereby produce

paradoxes. Thus the statement 'All Cretans are liars' is perfectly alright. However, if this statement is made by a Cretan, a paradox is produced. For if the utterer of the statement is a Cretan, then the statement must be taken to be untrue (a lie), for all Cretans are liars. However, if the statement is untrue, then it follows that not all Cretans are liars, and the statement made by this Cretan might not after all be untrue. The way out of this logico-linguistic merry-go-round is to rule out of court those statements where the truth-affirming nature of the *act of uttering* is subverted by the truth-denying *utterance* itself, because the latter includes the utterer and his act of utterance within its scope. To fail to proscribe in this way would be to fail to distinguish between these two levels or types of truth (untruth).

31. I owe this example to Professor J. C. A. Gaskin, who was a pupil of Ryle.
32. Ryle, 1949, p. 155.
33. Ryle, 1949, p. 8.
34. Strictly speaking the term 'university' is much more complex in its usage. For it is not purely a descriptive term, as it might first appear. It has normative and evaluative elements in it. For, besides the buildings, and staff and students, and an account of various teaching and research functions, you would have to mention that the level of education is 'third level' or 'part of higher education', and also that the term 'university' has been sanctioned by the granting of a charter by a government or some relevant ratifying body, and probably many other things as well. See ch. 6.
35. Skinner and Holland, 1961, p. 213.
36. Skinner and Holland, 1961, p. 214.
37. The reader should note that, in the psychological literature, the term 'appraisal' is often substituted for the term 'evaluation'. More generally, there are discussions of behaviourist accounts of emotion, the debate in the 1960s and 1970s about the nature of emotion, and the subsequent turning away from behaviourist accounts to cognitive accounts, in Lyons, 1980.
38. See James, 1884, and James, 1950, vol. 2, ch. 25.
39. See Lyons, 1980, pp. 17–21.
40. Titchener, 1914, pp. 11–12.
41. Watson, 1920. This article was originally a contribution to the Symposium presented at the Congress of Philosophy in Oxford, September 1920. Watson's friend and fellow behaviourist at Johns Hopkins, the neurologist Karl Lashley, produced what might be called a 'follow-up' to Watson's 1920 paper, namely the celebrated two-part article in the *Psychological Review* of 1923, entitled 'The Behavioristic Interpretation of Consciousness'. (See Lashley, 1923.)
42. Watson, 1920, p. 89.

43. Woodworth and Schlosberg, 1955, pp. 816–17.
44. Skinner, 1965, sect. 3.
45. Skinner, 1965, p. 263.
46. See Lyons, 1984, pp. 635–6, and Skinner, 1984, p. 659.
47. Magee, 1973, pp. 144–5.
48. Magee, 1973, p. 145.
49. Chomsky, 1980, p. 52.

3: *Nothing but the Brain*

1. Galvani, 1953, p. 24. Luigi Galvani's commentary on electricity first appeared in a scientific journal, the seventh volume of the proceedings of the Bologna Academy and Institute of Sciences and Arts, in an issue of 27 March 1791. References to figures in the text have been removed from the quotation.
2. Galvani, 1953, pp. 96–7. This extract is from a letter, of 1792, from Galvani to Professor Don Bassano Carminati, a translation of which is appended to this 1953 edition of Galvani's commentary. Carminati was Professor of Medicine at the University of Pavia. The letter was first published in the Italian scientific journal *Giornale Fisico-medico* in 1792.
3. The pioneers in electroencephalography were the British physiologist Richard Caton (1842–1926) and the German psychiatrist Hans Berger (1873–1941), who coined the term 'EEG'.
4. Golgi and Cajal were jointly awarded the Nobel Prize in Physiology or Medicine in 1906.
5. Sherrington and Edgar Douglas (Lord) Adrian were jointly awarded the Nobel Prize for Physiology or Medicine in 1932.
6. Penfield, 1958, pp. 21–2. I have introduced some punctuation, as Penfield seemed to eschew such pedestrian things.
7. Some of Sperry's many papers on commissurotomy are Sperry, 1964, 1968 and 1977. In 1981 Sperry received the Nobel Prize for his work on identifying the specialised functions of each hemisphere of the human brain. The papers of Michael Gazzaniga, who worked with Sperry, are also of great interest; see, especially, Gazzaniga, 1967.
8. Sperry, 1968, p. 724.
9. Sperry, 1968, p. 724.
10. Lashley, 1923, II, p. 343.
11. Skinner, 1956, p. 227.
12. E. G. Boring, at the time, was Edgar Pierce Professor of Psychology at Harvard University. Boring, who was the introspectionist psychologist Titchener's most famous pupil, had already won distinction with the publication of his *History of Experimental Psychology* in 1929. Though it should be pointed out that, in

recent years, Boring's history (Boring, 1929) has come under critical fire for being historically inaccurate. See, for example, Danziger, 1980.

13. While acknowledging in that book his debt to the work of the neurologist and behaviourist Karl Lashley, Boring accused him of, ultimately, being 'cautious and conservative'. The implication was that Lashley was conservative because he did not, in the light of the remarkable recent advances in neuroscience, embrace 'an identity hypothesis of the relation of "mind" to "body"'. (Boring, 1933, pp. vi and viii.)

14. Boring, 1933, p. 14.

15. Place, 1990, p. 20.

16. The most accessible version of this is Feigl, 1953.

17. Place, 1995, pp. 106–7.

18. Smart, 1995, p. 130.

19. Smart, 1995, p. 118.

20. A more accessible introduction to Armstrong's views is Armstrong, 1995.

21. Armstrong, 1995, p. 179.

22. Armstrong, 1995, p. 178.

23. Kurt Baier, an American, was for a time the Professor of Philosophy in the School of General Studies at the Australian National University. Subsequently he took up a senior post in the Philosophy Department at the University of Pittsburgh in Pennsylvania.

24. Smart, 1963, p. 99.

25. In short, as the philosophical jargon has it, with a weaker, token–token identity claim there is only a claim of 'multiple realisability' (or 'multiple forms of incarnation') of a particular mental state as brain states or processes. With a type–type identity claim there is a claim of 'single realisability' (or 'a single form of incarnation'). As we shall see, in the next chapter, functionalism claims only a token–token identity and 'multiple realisability'.

26. Sperry, 1952, p. 292.

27. Sperry, 1952, p. 296. The reference to Sherrington is to Sherrington, 1933. Sperry himself suggested, towards the end of his 1952 article, that the brain of humans, as well as animals, might better be conceived as primarily a machine for coordinating 'perceptual input' (or information received through one of the senses) and 'motor output' (or behaviour). If the relation between our mental life and our brains was to be explained, it would need to be explained in that context. However, he did not go much further than the bare expression of this enigmatic suggestion.

28. Edelman, 1985, p. 4.

29. Edelman, 1985, pp. 4–5.

30. I should make it clear that there are still plenty of neurophysiologists who would not go as far as Edelman in dismissing the identity theory of mind and brain. Many would still see it as 'an open question' (see, for example, Fischbach,1992). I admit, however, to finding Edelman's arguments very cogent.

31. Feyerabend produced a typically idiosyncratic autobiography, *Killing Time* (Feyerabend, 1995.)

32. Feyerabend, 1981, p. 167. Feyerabend's best-known book is *Against Method* (1975).

33. Rorty, 1965, pp. 28–9.

34. Rorty, 1965, p. 30.

35. Rorty, 1965, pp. 31–2.

36. Churchland, Paul, 1995, p. 237.

37. Churchland, Patricia, 1986, p. 482.

38. Russell, 1957, pp. 26–7.

39. Wittgenstein, 1958, Pt I, sect. 1. (The quotation is from *Confessions*, I.8.)

40. Wittgenstein, 1958, Pt I, sect. 43. Cf. Horace *Art of Poetry*, 71, 2.

41. Wittgenstein, 1958, Pt I, sect. 257.

42. Wittgenstein, 1958, Pt I, sect. 293.

4: *Computers to the Rescue*

1. Herman Goldstine suggests that a candidate for being the inventor of the mechanical calculator is the German Wilhelm Schickard (1592–1635), who was Professor of Astronomy, Mathematics and Hebrew at the University of Tübingen. The only knowledge we have of Schickard's invention of a calculating machine is a description, with sketches, in some of his letters to the great German astronomer Johann Kepler (1571–1630). (See Goldstine, 1993, p. 6.) I suppose that another candidate for being the first computer might be the Chinese abacus, which would predate Pascal's machine by some thousands of years. But perhaps it does not really merit the title 'machine'.

2. 'Calculating box' was the name given to Pascal's calculator by Leibniz. Leibniz also generously described Pascal's invention of his calculating machine as 'an example of the most fortunate genius'.

3. Hollingdale and Tootill, 1975, p. 35.

4. Babbage, 1994, pp. 30–1.

5. Hollingdale and Tootill, 1975, pp. 42–3.

6. Babbage, 1994, ch. VIII.

7. Goldstine, 1993, p. 67.

8. Goldstine, 1993, p. 112.

9. The logarithm of a number, x, is that number expressed as the power of another number, the 'base number', usually 10. Thus if x

$= 10^n$, then n is the logarithm of x (strictly speaking, 'the logarithm of x to the base 10').

10. The *sine* and *cosine* of an angle x, to take just two examples, are ratios concerning two of the sides of the right-angled triangle in which x is found. The branch of mathematics that makes use of these ratios is called *trigonometry* because it makes use of the fact that, when three (or *tri*) parts of a triangle's values are known (e.g. the length of two sides plus the degrees of one of the angles), then the rest of the values relating to that triangle can be calculated by means of these trigonometrical ratios. Other such trigonometrical ratios are the *tangent, secant, cotangent* and *cosecant*.

11. Dunn, 1989, p. 376.

12. A *transistor* is an electronic, semiconductor device that does the work which was previously done by a traditional diode or thermionic valve, namely of amplifying or rectifying a current. (To rectify a current is to transform an alternating current into a direct current.) A *semiconductor* is an electrical conductor made of materials, such as silicon or germanium, whose resistance, and this is the reverse of most conducting materials, can be raised in a controlled way by a rise in temperature or by the deliberate introduction of 'impurities'. It is called a *semi*conductor because it is intermediate or *halfway* between a good conductor and a complete non-conductor or insulator. A *diode* is any two-electrode or *di-electrode* (cathode/anode) electronic system. The advantages of a transistor over a thermionic valve include the former being less fragile, much smaller, requiring lower voltage and no initial warming up.

13. Early programming languages were close to the electronic engineer's machine language of the 'this switch to be opened, that one to be closed' type. Later programming languages were at a higher level, or greater remove from the machine languages, and were deliberately made much easier to use. They were easier to use because, between them and the 'machine languages', there were 'compilers' which were programs for translating a higher, easier-to-use, 'source' language into the lower-level, complex, electrical engineer's 'machine' language.

14. Keene, Buzan and Goodman, 1997, pp. 110–14.

15. Menabrea (1809–96) had heard Babbage himself describe and explain his Analytical Engine when they met at Turin in 1840. Menabrea's account, praised by Babbage himself, was published as 'Notions sur la machine analytique de M. Charles Babbage' in the *Bibliothèque Universelle de Genève*, t. xli, October 1842 (see Babbage, 1994, p. 102).

16. Hollingdale and Tootill, 1975, 112; emphasis in the original. There is now a programming language, designed by the US Department

of Defense, called 'Ada', named after Ada Lovelace.

17. Craik, 1967, pp. 120–1.

18. The *Entscheidungsproblem* or 'decision problem', for the first-order predicate calculus (the symbolic logic which formalises the relations between subject-predicate sentences, such as 'All tortoise-shell cats are female. This is a tortoiseshell cat. Therefore this is a female cat'), was a problem described by the German mathematician David Hilbert (1862–1943). In simplistic terms it might be described as a meta-problem about what problems were and were not decidable in an algorithmic way, i.e. in terms of a finite set of computable steps. This problem is associated subsequently especially with Turing and his equally gifted, one-time teacher-collaborator at Princeton, the philosopher and logician Alonzo Church. (See, for example, Turing, 1936–7.)

19. In effect Turing had outlined the essential features of the Turing Machine in 1936, in his early, quite technical paper on computable numbers (see Turing, 1936–7, esp. sects 1–3).

20. See, especially, Copeland, 1998.

21. Turing, 1950, p. 434.

22. Putnam, 1975, pp. 372–3. In this chapter, by implication, I have suggested that the main source of functionalism in modern philosophy of mind was the computer, which in turn, via the work of Craik and Turing, led to the early computer-functionalism of Putnam. I think that this suggestion is correct. However I should mention that there were other, lesser influences on philosophical functionalism. One that deserves a mention here is the analysis of mental concepts by such identity theorists as David Armstrong and David Lewis. Armstrong and Lewis suggested that mental concepts were to be analysed *in terms of inner states with causal roles* and, for additional reasons, suggested that these internal states, exercising these causal roles, were then to be identified with brain states and processes. A belief, for example, was to be analysed as *some inner state* (which, strictly speaking, might be realised in any sort of stuff, whether material or spiritual) that was *apt for being caused by* certain (usually external) events and *apt for causing* certain sorts of actions or reactions, usually certain sorts of behaviour, including verbal behaviour. Given that account, it is not a giant step to move from the concept of something's 'having a causal role' to the concept of its 'having a function'. See especially Armstrong, 1968, and Lewis, 1966.

23. Fodor, 1981b, p. 124. (I suspect that Fodor's point would have been clearer if the last phrase of the quotation read 'on how the stuff functions' rather than 'on how the stuff is put together'.)

24. Fodor, 1981b, p. 131.

25. Fodor, 1987, pp. 18–19.

26. Fodor, 1987, p. xii.
27. Block, 1980, p. 276.
28. The original version of Searle, 1981, contained an initial batch of objections embedded in Searle's own text plus another, larger batch, printed as an appendix to that article. See also Searle, 1990.
29. Fodor, 1981b, p. 130. It is interesting to note that, ten years later (see Fodor, 1991), Fodor was reiterating this point, this time in the context of cognitive science as a whole. He writes that 'the cognitive science movement has been research-in-progress for about thirty years now. In consequence, we know a little about language, a little about perception, very little about cognitive development, practically nothing about thought, and, as far as I can tell, nothing at all about consciousness. The problems about consciousness, in particular, have proved intractable in a very unsettling sort of way. We not only can't solve them, we don't even seem to be able to state them in a form that suggests a research programme.'
30. Kim, 1996, p. 114.
31. This device, of merely wearing an apparatus that expresses colour discriminations in terms of bleeps, needs to be distinguished from another sort of device whereby the wearer does have some sight restored. This latter device was developed by Professor William Dobelle and his research team at the Dobelle Institute and the Columbia-Presbyterian Medical Centre in New York. It involves a miniature video camera and range finder mounted on spectacles which in turn, via a portable computer programmed to detect outlines and an array of 68 platinum electrodes operating as an artificial optic nerve, send electrical signals to the surface of the brain's visual cortex. In that case the previously blind person now apparently sees, that is to say, has visual sensations with qualia, even if these qualia are not the usual ones and are very primitive in form. 'The 62-year-old man was able to see well enough to find his way around a city's underground system, read two-inch tall letters and even watch television and surf the Internet . . . If he is walking down a hall, the doorway appears as a white frame on a dark background . . . The electrical impulses sent from the device's computer stimulate the visual cortex region of the brain which creates the sensation of dots of light' (Connor, 2000, p. 5).
32. See especially Weiskrantz, 1986, and Pöppel, Frost and Held, 1973.
33. See Tallis, 1999, ch. 2.
34. See, for example, Glover, 1989, pp. 60–1, where Jonathan Glover writes that 'Because "person" is a concept with boundaries that are blurred or disputed, there may be no satisfactory single answer to the question "What is a person?" I want to suggest that a prime feature of personhood is self-consciousness. A person is someone

who can have thoughts, whose natural expression uses the word
"I". This seems to capture one central strand in our idea of a
person . . . It is suggested, then, that to be a person is to have a
single stream of I-thoughts.'

5: The Bogey of Consciousness

1. The brain stem, in more technical terms, comprises the *mesen-
   cephalon* (or midbrain), the *pons* (from the Latin word for bridge,
   as it is an area where large groups of afferent and efferent nerves
   pass through), and the *medulla oblongata* (sometimes called 'the
   bulb' but, literally, in Latin, 'oblong-shaped, innermost part' – a
   regulatory centre for basic life-maintaining processes, and perhaps
   the most important of the three main parts of the brain stem from
   the point of view of the maintenance of consciousness).
2. *The Independent* (UK), 23 November 1991, p. 34.
3. *The Independent* (UK), 23 November 1991, p. 34.
4. Holmes, 1993, p. 198.
5. Nagel, 1995, p. 159.
6. Nagel, 1995, p. 160.
7. An eel's detection of interference in its electromagnetic field is
   assumed to be conscious because the detection of the interference
   is associated with what zoologists refer to as a sense organ in the
   eel (that is to say, it has physiological similarities to the conscious-
   ness-producing sense organs in other species), and because the eel
   is not so far down the evolutionary tree that we would think of
   them as obviously lacking in consciousness. (See McFarland, 1987,
   pp. 148–9.) Of course, if a gymnotid eel is in no way conscious,
   then I cannot use this example to make Nagel's point. See also
   Dretske, 1994, ch. 3, sect. 4.
8. McInerney, 1993, p. 101. I am grateful to Patrick O'Sullivan for
   drawing my attention to McInerney's novel.
9. James, 1950, 1, pp. 375–6, fn. James in fact misquotes Adolf
   Strümpell. The sentence should read, 'Wenn ich nicht sehen kann,
   dann bin ich gar nicht'.
10. Dahl, 1979, p. 152ff.
11. Nagel, 1995, p. 169.
12. Barrett et al., 1987, p. 618.
13. Barrett et al., 1987, p. 638.
14. Huxley, 1866, Lesson VIII, sect. 3, p. 193. It is interesting to note
    that, by the 4th edition of 1885, the reference to Aladdin and his
    lamp had been excised.
15. Chalmers, 1996, p. xi.
16. Chalmers, 1995a, p. 63.

17. As he readily acknowledges, Chalmers borrows this thought-experiment from Jackson, 1986. Indeed, this thought-experiment is sometimes referred to in the literature as Jackson's 'Mary' argument. See also Jackson, 1982.

18. At Chalmers, 1995b, pp. 210 and 217, Chalmers does seem ready to swallow this alternative.

19. In what follows I give a fairly loose interpretation of McGinn's position rather than a strict paraphrase.

20. McGinn, 1995, p. 272.

21. 'A type of mind M is cognitively closed with respect to a property P (or theory T) if and only if the concept-forming procedures at M's disposal cannot extend to a grasp of P (or an understanding of T).' McGinn, 1995, p. 273.

22. McGinn, 1995, p. 272.

23. Strictly speaking, there are at least three forms of *Knowing How*, namely *Knowing How To Do Something* (e.g. knowing how to swim), *Knowing How To Make Something* (e.g. knowing how to make cheesecake) and *Knowing How Something Works* (e.g. knowing how a sundial tells the time).

24. *The Independent* (UK), 23 September 1997, p. 8.

25. Hume, 1902, Pt I, sect. IV, p. 31.

6: *The Pit and the Pendulum*

1. See, for example, William James who, in volume 1 of *The Principles* writes that 'If, then, by the seat of the mind [by which he meant, in this context, consciousness] is meant nothing more than the locality with which it stands in immediate dynamic relations, we are certain to be right in saying that its seat is somewhere in the cortex of the brain' (James, 1950, vol.1, p. 214). On the other hand, since for James consciousness or mind was not physical, he did want to distinguish this sense of locality from mere position or location in space.

2. Dennett, 1995.

3. See Davidson, 1980 and 1995.

4. For a more comprehensive account of a cognitive view of emotions, see Lyons, 1980.

5. Quine, 1981, p. 93; emphasis mine.

6. Quine, 1981, p. 98.

7. Brown, 1993, vol. 2, p. 2717.

8. Johnson, 1828, p. 1034.

9. Johnson, 1828, p. 315.

10. Aristotle, 1954, Bk. 1, ch. 7, lines 1098a27–35.

11. Greenfield, 1996, p. 158. The entry on 'being aware' also admits that 'consciousness is remarkably difficult to define'.

12. The most famous proponent of panpsychism is probably Baruch de Spinoza (1632–77), a Jew of Portuguese origin who emigrated to Holland to avoid religious persecution but was then expelled from his synagogue for heterodox views. His best-known work is his posthumously published *Ethics*.

13. See, for example, Searle, 1994, pp. 25–6.

14. Libet, 1994, esp. pp. 120–1.

15. Searle, 1994, p. 25.

16. Shapere, 1998, p. 196. Roger Penrose, mathematician and theoretical physicist, puts a similar if interestingly different slant on this matter, 'We know that at the sub-microscopic level of things the quantum laws do hold sway; but at the level of cricket balls, it is classical physics. Somewhere in between, I would maintain, we need to understand the new law, in order to see how the quantum world merges with the classical. I believe, also, that we shall need this new law if we are ever to understand minds! For all this we must, I believe, look for new clues' (Penrose, 1990, p. 386.) See also Unger, 1998.

17. I have removed from the text the names, which were in brackets, of the individual actors who played each part.

18. Chapman, et al., 1989, pp. 109–10.

19. Rorty, 1980, p. 6.

20. Rorty, 1980, p. 7.

21. See Rorty, 1980, ch. 1, esp. sect. 6, 'Dualism and "Mind–Stuff"'.

22. I took the contents list from Rita L. Atkinson et al., 1996, and modified it in the light of other psychology textbooks.

23. Barrett et al., 1987, p. 604. The unusual grammar and punctuation are Darwin's.

24. Francis Darwin, 1958, p. 74.

25. Barrett et al., 1987, p. 588. Darwin also felt that animals might have free will. He wrote, in 'Notebook M', of 1838, that 'with respect to free will, seeing a puppy playing cannot doubt that they have free will, if so all animals . . .' (Barrett et al., 1987, p. 604).

26. Letter of Descartes to the Marquess of Newcastle, 23 November 1646, in Descartes, 1981, p. 207. The reference to Montaigne is to Michel Eyquem de Montaigne (1533–92), French essayist and sage, best known for his *Essays*, first published in 1580. The reference to Charron is to Montaigne's contemporary and disciple, the French theologian Pierre Charron (1541–1603), whose best-known work is his *De la sagesse*, which went through thirty-two editions between its first publication in 1601 and 1664.

27. Letter of Descartes to Buitendijck of 1643; Descartes, 1981, p. 146.

28. Spink, 1960, p. 227 n. 2. Spink is quoting N. Fontaine, *Mémoires pour servir à l'histoire de Port-Royal* (1736).

29. In *The Origin of Species*, Darwin says: 'I think there is little doubt that use in our domestic animals strengthens and enlarges certain parts, and disuse diminishes them; and that such modifications are inherited' (Darwin, 1968, p. 175).

Bibliography

Aristotle (1954), *The Nicomachean Ethics* (c. 330 BC), trans. and intro. by Sir David Ross, The World's Classics (Oxford, Oxford University Press).

Armstrong, David (1995), 'The Causal Theory of Mind' [1977], in Lyons (1995).

Armstrong, David (1968), *A Materialist Theory of the Mind*, International Library of Philosophy and Scientific Method (London, Routledge & Kegan Paul).

Atkinson, Rita L., Atkinson, Richard C., Smith, Edward E., Bem, Daryl J., and Nolen-Hoeksema, Susan (1996), *Hilgard's Introduction to Psychology*, 12th edn (Fort Worth, Texas, Harcourt Brace).

Ayer, A. J. (1977), *Part of My Life* (London, Collins).

Ayer, A. J. (ed.) (1959), *Logical Positivism*, The Library of Philosophical Movements, gen. ed. Paul Edwards (New York, The Free Press).

Ayer, A. J. (1946), *Language, Truth and Logic* (1936) (New York, Dover).

Babbage, Charles (1994), *Passages from the Life of a Philosopher* [1864], ed. with new intro. by Martin Campbell-Kelly (London, William Pickering).

Babbage, Charles (1993), *On the Economy of Machinery and Manufactures* [1835] (London, Routledge-Thoemmes Press).

Baldwin, James Mark (1913), *History of Psychology: A Sketch and an Interpretation* (London, Watts & Co.), ii.

Barrett, Paul H.; Gautrey, Peter J.; Herbert, Sandra; Kohn, David, and Smith, Sydney (eds) (1987), *Charles Darwin's Notebooks, 1836–1844: Geology, Transmutation of Species, Metaphysical Enquiries*, transcribed and ed. Barrett et al. (London, British Museum – Natural History and Cambridge, Cambridge University Press).

Blanning, T. C. W. (1996), *The Oxford Illustrated History of Modern Europe* (Oxford and New York, Oxford University Press).

Block, Ned (1980), 'Troubles with Functionalism' [1978], in Ned Block (ed.) *Readings in Philosophy of Psychology*, The Language of Thought Series (Cambridge, MA, Harvard University Press), i.

Boring, Edwin G. (1933), *The Physical Dimensions of Consciousness*, The Century Psychology Series, ed. Richard M. Elliott (New York, Century, and London, Appleton).

Boring, Edwin G. (1929), *A History of Experimental Psychology* (New York, Appleton-Century).

Brentano, Franz (1973), *Psychology from an Empirical Standpoint* [1874], eds Oskar Kraus and Linda McAlister, trans. A. C. Rancurello, D. B. Terrell and L. L. McAlister, International Library of Philosophy and Scientific Method (London, Routledge & Kegan Paul).

Brown, Lesley (ed.) (1993), *The New Shorter Oxford English Dictionary, on Historical Principles* [1933], 2 vols (Oxford, Clarendon Press).

Carnap, Rudolf (1995), 'Psychology in the Language of Physics' [1931], trans. Niamh Ní Bhleithín, Fionnula Meehan and Daniel Steuer, in Lyons (1995).

Chalmers, David J. (1996), *The Conscious Mind: In Search of a Fundamental Theory* (Oxford and New York, Oxford University Press).

Chalmers, David J. (1995a), 'The Puzzle of Conscious Experience', *Scientific American*, 273/6.

Chalmers, David J. (1995b), 'Facing up to the Problem of Consciousness', *Journal of Consciousness Studies*, 2/3.

Chapman, Graham; Cleese, John; Gilliam, Terry; Idle, Eric; Jones, Terry, and Palin, Michael (1989), *Monty Python's Flying Circus: Just the Words* (London, Methuen), i.

Chomsky, Noam (1980), 'A Review of B. F. Skinner's *Verbal Behavior*' [1959], in Ned Block (ed.), *Readings in Philosophy of Psychology*, The Language of Thought Series (Cambridge, MA, Harvard University Press), i.

Churchland, Patricia Smith (1986), *Neurophilosophy: Toward a Unified Science of the Mind–Brain* (Cambridge, MA, MIT Press).

Churchland, Paul (1995), 'Eliminative Materialism and the Propositional Attitudes' [1981], in Lyons (1995).

Cohen, David (1979), *J. B. Watson: The Founder of Behaviourism – A Biography* (London, Routledge & Kegan Paul).

Cohen-Solal, Annie (1987), *Sartre: A Life* (London, Heinemann).

Comte, Auguste (1830–42), *Cours de philosophie positive*, 6 vols (Paris, Bachelier).

Connor, Steve (2000), 'Implants in brain let blind man "see"', *The Independent* (UK), 18 January.

Copeland, B. Jack (1998), 'Turing's O-machines, Searle, Penrose and the Brain', *Analysis*, 58.

Cottingham, John (1995), 'Cartesianism', in Ted Honderich (ed.) *The Oxford Companion to Philosophy*, Oxford and New York, Oxford University Press.

Craik, Kenneth J. W. (1967), *The Nature of Explanation* [1943] (Cambridge, Cambridge University Press).

Dahl, Roald (1979), *Tales of the Unexpected* (Harmondsworth, Middlesex, Penguin).

Danziger, Kurt (1980), 'The History of Introspection Reconsidered', *Journal of the History of the Behavioral Sciences*, 16.

Darwin, Charles (1968), *The Origin of Species by Means of Natural*

Selection or The Preservation of Favoured Races in the Struggle for Life [1859], ed. and intro. J. W. Burrow (Harmondsworth, Middlesex, Penguin).

Darwin, Francis (ed.) (1958), *The Autobiography of Charles Darwin and Selected Letters* [1892] (New York, Dover).

Davidson, Donald (1995), 'Psychology as Philosophy' [1971], in Lyons (1995).

Davidson, Donald (1980), 'Mental Events' [1970] in Donald Davidson, *Essays on Actions and Events* (Oxford, Clarendon Press).

Dennett, Daniel (1995), 'Intentional Systems' [1971], in Lyons (1995).

Descartes, René (1984), *The Philosophical Writings of Descartes*, vol. II, trans. J. Cottingham, R. Stoothoff and D. Murdoch (Cambridge, Cambridge University Press).

Descartes, René (1981), *Philosophical Letters*, trans. and ed. Anthony Kenny (Oxford, Blackwell).

Descartes, René (1954), *Discourse on the Method of Rightly Directing One's Reason and of Seeking the Truth in the Sciences* [1637], in trans. and ed. E. Anscombe and P. T. Geach, intro. A. Koyré, Descartes: *Philosophical Writings* (Edinburgh, Nelson).

Dretske, Fred (1995), *Naturalizing the Mind*, the 1994 Jean Nicod Lectures (Cambridge, MA, MIT Press).

Dretske, Fred (1988), *Explaining Behavior: Reasons in a World of Causes* (Cambridge, MA, MIT Press).

Dretske, Fred (1981), *Knowledge and the Flow of Information* (Cambridge, MA, MIT Press).

Dunn, Donald (1989), 'Computer: History', in E. Barnouw, G. Gerbner, W. Schramm, T. L. Worth and L. Gross (eds), *International Encyclopedia of Communications* (New York and Oxford, Oxford University Press), i.

Edelman, Gerald (1985), 'Neural Darwinism: Population Thinking and Higher Brain Function', in Michael Shafto (ed.), *How We Know* (San Francisco, Harper & Row).

English, H. B. (1921), 'In Aid of Introspection', *American Journal of Psychology*, 32.

Evans, David C. (1966), 'Computer Logic and Memory', *Scientific American*, 215/3.

Eysenck, H. J.; Arnold, W. J. and Meili, R. (eds) (1975), *Encyclopedia of Psychology*, 2 vols (London, Fontana-Collins).

Feigl, Herbert (1953), 'The Mind–Body Problem in the Development of Logical Empiricism', in Herbert Feigl and May Brodbeck (eds), *Readings in the Philosophy of Science* (New York, Appleton-Century-Crofts).

Fernald, Dodge (1997), *Psychology* (New Jersey, Prentice-Hall).

Feyerabend, Paul (1995), *Killing Time* (Chicago, University of Chicago Press).

Feyerabend, Paul (1981), 'Materialism and the Mind–Body Problem' [1963], in Paul K. Feyerabend, *Realism, Rationalism and Scientific Method: Philosophical Papers* (Cambridge, Cambridge University Press), i.

Feyerabend, Paul (1975), *Against Method* (London and New York, New Left Books).

Fischbach, Gerald D. (1992), 'Mind and Brain', *Scientific American*, 267/3.

Fodor, Jerry A. (1991), 'The Problem of Consciousness', Letters to the Editor, *The Times Literary Supplement*, no. 4601, June.

Fodor, Jerry A. (1987), *Psychosemantics: The Problem of Meaning in the Philosophy of Mind* (Cambridge, MA, MIT Press).

Fodor, Jerry A. (1983), *The Modularity of Mind: An Essay on Faculty Psychology* (Cambridge, MA, MIT Press).

Fodor, Jerry A. (1981a), *Representations: Philosophical Essays on the Foundations of Cognitive Science* (Cambridge, MA, MIT Press).

Fodor, Jerry A. (1981b), 'The Mind–Body Problem', *Scientific American*, 244/1.

Fodor, Jerry A. (1975), *The Language of Thought*, Language of Thought Series (New York, Crowell).

Freud, Sigmund (1971), *Group Psychology and the Analysis of the Ego* [1922], trans. James Strachey, intro. Franz Alexander (New York, Bantam).

Freud, Sigmund (1962), *Two Short Accounts of Psycho-Analysis: Five Lectures on Psycho-Analysis* [1910] and *The Question of Lay Analysis* [1929], trans. and ed. James Strachey (Harmondsworth, Middlesex, Penguin).

Frost, Elliot Park (1914), 'Cannot Psychology Dispense with Consciousness?', *The Psychological Review*, 21.

Galvani, Luigi (1953), *Commentary on the Effect of Electricity on Muscular Motion* [1791], trans. and ed. Robert Montraville Green (Cambridge, MA, Elizabeth Licht).

Gaskin, John (ed.) (1995), *The Epicurean Philosophers*, trans. C. Bailey, R. D. Hicks and J. C. A. Gaskin (Everyman – London, J. M. Dent; Vermont, Charles E. Tuttle).

Gazzaniga, Michael S. (1989), 'Organization of the Human Brain', *Science*, 245.

Gazzaniga, Michael S. (1967), 'The Split-Brain in Man', *Scientific American*, 217.

Geisler, C. (1986), 'The Use of Subliminal Psychodynamic Activation in the Study of Depression', *Journal of Personality and Social Psychology*, 51.

Gilchrist, Alexander (1863), *Life of William Blake, 'Pictor Ignotus', with Selections from his Poems and Other Writings*, 2 vols (London and Cambridge, Macmillan).

Glover, Jonathan (1989), *I: The Philosophy and Psychology of Personal Identity* [1988] (Harmondsworth, Middlesex, Penguin Books).

Goldstine, Herman H. (1993), *The Computer: From Pascal to von Neumann* [1972] (Princeton, New Jersey, Princeton University Press).

Greenfield, Susan A. (ed.) (1996), *The Human Mind Explained: An Owner's Guide to the Mysteries of the Mind*, a Henry Holt Reference Book (New York, Henry Holt).

Hobbes, Thomas (1996), *Leviathan* [1651], ed. with intro. J. C. A. Gaskin, The World's Classics (Oxford, Oxford University Press).

Hollingdale, S. H. and Toothill, G. C. (1975), *Electronic Computers* [1965] (Harmondsworth, Middlesex, Penguin).

Holmes, Oliver (1993), *Human Neurophysiology: A Student Text*, 2nd edn (London, Chapman & Hall).

Hume, David (1902), *Enquiries Concerning Human Understanding and Concerning the Principles of Morals* [1777], ed. L. A. Selby-Bigge (Oxford, Clarendon Press).

Humphrey, George (1951), *Thinking: An Introduction to its Experimental Psychology* (London, Methuen, and New York, Wiley).

Huxley, Thomas H. (1866), *Lessons in Elementary Physiology* (London, Macmillan).

Jackson, Frank (1986), 'What Mary didn't know', *Journal of Philosophy*, 83.

Jackson, Frank (1982), 'Epiphenomenal Qualia', *Philosophical Quarterly*, 32.

James, William (1950), *The Principles of Psychology* [1890], 2 vols (New York, Dover).

James, William (1884), 'What is an Emotion?', *Mind*, 9.

Johnson, Samuel (1828), *Dictionary of the English Language* [1773] (London, Joseph Ogle Robinson).

Jones, A. H. (1915), 'The Method of Psychology', *Journal of Philosophy, Psychology and Scientific Methods*, 12.

Keene, Raymond; Buzan, Tony, with Goodman, David (1997), *Man versus Machine: Kasparov versus Deep Blue* (Poole, Dorset, Buzan Centres).

Kim, Jaegwon (1996), *Philosophy of Mind*, Dimensions of Philosophy Series (Boulder, Colorado, and Oxford, England, Westview Press).

Kneale, William (1962), 'On Having a Mind', The Arthur Stanley Eddington Memorial Lecture (Cambridge, Cambridge University Press).

Lackner, J. R. and Garrett, M. F. (1973), 'Resolving Ambiguity: Effects of Biasing Context in the Unattended Ear', *Cognition*, 1.

Laird, John (1925), *Our Minds and Their Bodies* (London, Oxford University Press).

Lashley, Karl (1929), *Brain Mechanisms and Intelligence* (Chicago, Chicago University Press).

Lashley, Karl (1923), 'The Behavioristic Interpretation of Consciousness', I and II, *Psychological Review*, 30/4 and 5.

Lewis, D. K. (1966), 'An Argument for the Identity Theory', *Journal of Philosophy*, 63.

Libet, Benjamin (1994), 'A Testable Field Theory of Mind–Body Interaction', *Journal of Consciousness Studies*, 1/1.

Lichtheim, George (1972), *Europe in the Twentieth Century* (London, Weidenfeld and Nicolson).

Lyons, William (ed.) (1995), *Modern Philosophy of Mind* (Everyman – London, J. M. Dent; Vermont, Charles E. Tuttle).

Lyons, William (1986), *The Disappearance of Introspection* (Cambridge, MA, MIT Press).

Lyons, William (1984), 'Behaviorism and "The Problem of Privacy"', *Behavioral and Brain Sciences*, 7/4.

Lyons, William (1980), *Emotion*, Cambridge Studies in Philosophy (Cambridge, Cambridge University Press).

McCarthy, John (1966), 'Information', *Scientific American*, 215/3.

McDougall, William (1929), *Modern Materialism and Emergent Evolution* (London, Methuen).

McDougall, William (1911), *Body and Mind: A History and a Defence of Animism* (London, Methuen).

McFarland, David (ed.) (1987), *The Oxford Companion to Animal Behaviour* (Oxford and New York, Oxford University Press).

McGinn, Colin (1995), 'Can We Solve the Mind–Body Problem?' [1989], in Lyons (1995).

McGinn, Colin (1993), *Problems in Philosophy: The Limits of Enquiry* (Oxford, Blackwell).

McGinn, Colin (1991), *The Problem of Consciousness: Essays Towards a Resolution* (Oxford, Blackwell).

McInerney, Jay (1993), *Bright Lights, Big City* [1984] (Harmondsworth, Middlesex, Penguin).

Magee, Bryan (1973), *Modern British Philosophy* (St. Albans, Hertfordshire, Paladin).

Mead, G. H. (1934), *Mind, Self and Society: From the Standpoint of a Social Behaviourist*, ed. C. W. Morris (Cambridge, Cambridge University Press).

Menabrea, Luigi (1842), 'Notions sur la machine analytique de M. Charles Babbage', *Bibliothèque Universelle de Genève*, xli.

Mill, John Stuart (1882), *Auguste Comte and Positivism* [1865], 3rd edn (London, Trubner).

Miller, George A. (1966), *Psychology: The Science of Mental Life* (Harmondsworth, Middlesex, Penguin).

Minsky, Marvin L. (1966), 'Artificial Intelligence', *Scientific American*, 215/3.

Myers, Charles S. (1909), *A Text-Book of Experimental Psychology* (London, Edward Arnold).

Nagel, Thomas (1995), 'What is it Like to be a Bat?' [1974], in Lyons (1995).

Neurath, Otto, with Hahn, Hans and Carnap, Rudolf (1973), *Wissen-schaftliche Weltauffassung: Der Wiener Kreis* [The Scientific Conception of the World: The Vienna Circle] [1929], in trans. and eds. Marie Neurath and Robert S. Cohen, *Empiricism and Sociology* (Dordrecht and Boston, D. Reidel).

Nietzsche, Friedrich (1990), *Twilight of the Idols* [1889] and *The Anti-Christ* [1895], trans. R. J. Hollingdale and intro. Michael Tanner (Harmondsworth, Middlesex, Penguin).

Nietzsche, Friedrich (1933), *Thus Spake Zarathustra* [1883–92] (London, Everyman – J. M. Dent, and New York, Everyman – E. P. Dutton).

Penfield, Wilder (1958), *The Excitable Cortex in Conscious Man*, The Sherrington Lectures V (Liverpool, Liverpool University Press).

Penrose, Roger (1990), *The Emperor's New Mind: Concerning Computers, Minds, and the Laws of Physics* (London, Vintage).

Place, U. T. (1995), 'Is Consciousness a Brain Process?' [1956], in Lyons (1995).

Place, U. T. (1990), 'E. G. Boring and the Mind–Brain Identity Theory', *The British Psychological Society, History and Philosophy of Science Section: Newsletter*, 11.

Plato (1974), *The Republic* [c. 375 BC], trans. and intro. Desmond Lee, 2nd edn (Harmondsworth, Middlesex, Penguin).

Pöppel, E.; Frost, D., and Held, R. (1973), 'Residual Visual Function after Brain Wounds involving the Central Visual Pathways in Man', *Nature*, 243.

Putnam, Hilary (1995), 'Philosophy and Our Mental Life' [1973], in Lyons (1995).

Putnam, Hilary (1975), 'Minds and Machines' [1960], in Hilary Putnam, *Mind, Language and Reality: Philosophical Papers* (Cambridge, Cambridge University Press), ii.

Quine, W. V. O. (1981), *Theories and Things* (Cambridge, MA, The Belnap Press).

Rorty, Richard (1980), *Philosophy and the Mirror of Nature* (Oxford, Blackwell).

Rorty, Richard (1965), 'Mind–Body Identity, Privacy and Categories', *Review of Metaphysics*, 19.

Russell, Bertrand (1957), *Portraits from Memory* (London, Allen & Unwin).

Ryle, Gilbert (1971), *Collected Papers: Volume II, Collected Essays 1929–1968* (London, Hutchinson).

Ryle, Gilbert (1949), *The Concept of Mind* (London, Hutchinson).

Schultz, Duane P. and Schultz, Sydney Ellen (1996), *A History of Modern Psychology* [1969], 6th edn (Fort Worth, Texas, Harcourt Brace).

Searle, John R. (1994), *The Rediscovery of the Mind* [1992] (Cambridge, MA, MIT Press).

Searle, John R. (1990), 'Is the Brain a Digital Computer?', Presidential Address to the Pacific Division of the APA, March 1990, *American Philosophical Association Proceedings*, 64/3.

Searle, John (1981), 'Minds, Brains and Programs' [1980], in Douglas R. Hofstadter and Daniel Dennett (eds), *The Mind's I: Fantasies and Reflections on Self and Soul* (Brighton, Sussex, Harvester Press).

Shapere, Dudley (1998), 'Matter', in Edward Craig (gen. ed.), *Routledge Encyclopedia of Philosophy*, 6 (London, Routledge).

Sherrington, C. S. (1933), *The Brain and its Mechanisms* (Cambridge, Cambridge University Press).

Sherwood, Stephen L. (ed.) (1966), *The Nature of Psychology: A Selection of Papers, Essays and Other Writings by the late Kenneth J. W. Craik* (Cambridge, Cambridge University Press).

Skinner, B. F. (1984), 'Author's Response: Representations and Misrepresentations', *Behavioral and Brain Sciences*, 7/4.

Skinner, B. F. (1974), *About Behaviorism* (London, Jonathan Cape).

Skinner, B. F. (1965), *Science and Human Behavior* [1953] (New York, Macmillan – The Free Press, and London, Collier Macmillan).

Skinner, B. F. (1957), *Verbal Behavior* (New York, Appleton-Century-Crofts).

Skinner, B. F. (1956), 'A Case History in Scientific Method', *American Psychologist*, 11.

Skinner, B. F. and Holland, J. G. (1961), *The Analysis of Behavior* (New York, McGraw-Hill).

Smart, J. J. C. (1995), 'Sensations and Brain Processes' [1959], in Lyons (1995).

Smart, J. J. C. (1963), *Philosophy and Scientific Realism*, International Library of Philosophy and Scientific Method, ed. A. J. Ayer (London, Routledge & Kegan Paul).

Sperry, R. W. (1988), 'Psychology's Mentalist Paradigm and the Religion/Science Tension', *American Psychologist*, 43.

Sperry, R. W. (1977), 'Forebrain Commissurotomy and Conscious Awareness', *Journal of Medicine and Philosophy*, 2/2.

Sperry, R. W. (1968), 'Hemisphere Deconnection and Unity in Conscious Awareness', *American Psychologist*, 23.

Sperry, R. W. (1964), 'The Great Cerebral Commissure', *Scientific American*, 210.

Sperry, R. W. (1952), 'Neurology and the Mind–Brain Problem', *American Scientist*, 40.

Spink, J. S. (1960), *French Free-Thought from Gassendi to Voltaire* (London, Athlone Press).

Spinoza, Baruch de (1988), *Ethics* [1677], in ed. and trans. E. Curley, *The Collected Works of Spinoza* (New Jersey, Princeton University Press), i.

Sprott, W. J. H. (1937), *General Psychology* (London, Longmans, Green).

Stout, G. F. (1913), *A Manual of Psychology* [1898], 3rd edn (London, University Tutorial Press).

Strümpell, Adolf (1878), 'Beobachtungen über ausgebreitete Anästhesien und deren Folgen für die willkürliche Bewegung und das Bewusstsein', *Deutsches Archiv Für Klinikich Medizin*, 22.

Tallis, Raymond (1999), *The Explicit Animal: A Defence of Human Consciousness* [1991] (London, Macmillan – New York, St Martin's Press).

Titchener, E. B. (1914), 'On "Psychology as the Behaviorist Views It"', *Proceedings of the American Philosophical Society*, 53/213.

Turing, Alan (c. 2000), 'A Lecture and Two Radio Broadcasts on Machine Intelligence' [1951–52] in B. J. Copeland (ed.), *Machine Intelligence*, forthcoming.

Turing, A. M. (1950), 'Computing Machinery and Intelligence', *Mind*, 59.

Turing, A. M. (1936–7), 'On Computable Numbers, with an Application to the *Entscheidungsproblem*', *Proceedings of the London Mathematical Society*, series 2, 42 (with corrections in 43).

Unger, Peter (1998), 'The Mystery of the Physical and the Matter of Qualities: A Paper for Professor Shaffer', *Midwest Studies in Philosophy*, 22.

Uvarov, E. B., Chapman, D. R. and Isaacs, Alan (1977), *The Penguin Dictionary of Science*, 4th edn (London, Allen Lane).

Watson, J. B. (1995), 'Psychology as the Behaviourist Views It' [1913], in Lyons (1995).

Watson, J. B. (1930), *Behaviorism* [1924], 2nd edn (Chicago, Phoenix-University of Chicago Press).

Watson, J. B. (1920), 'Is Thinking merely the Action of Language Mechanisms?', *British Journal of Psychology*, 11.

Watson, J. B. (1913), 'Image and Affection in Behavior', *Journal of Philosophy, Psychology and Scientific Methods*, 10/16.

Watson, J. B. (1910), 'The New Science of Animal Behavior', *Harper's*, March.

Watson, J. B. (1908), 'Imitation in Monkeys', *Psychological Bulletin*, 5.

Watson, J. B. (1907), 'Condition of Noddy and Sooty Tern Colony, Bird Key, Tortugas, Fla.', *Bird Lore*, 9.

Watson, J. B. (1906), 'The Need of an Experimental Station for the Study of Certain Problems in Animal Behavior', *Psychological Bulletin*, 3.

Watson, J. B. (1905), 'The Effect of the Bearing of Young upon the Body-Weight and the Weight of the Central Nervous System of the Female White Rat', *Journal of Comparative Neurology and Psychology*, 15.

Watson, J. B. (1903), *Animal Education: Experimental Study of the Psychical Development of the White Rat, Correlated with the*

Growth of its Nervous System, a dissertation submitted to the Faculty of the Graduate School of Arts and Literature, in candidacy for the degree of Doctor of Philosophy (Chicago, Chicago University Press).

Weiskrantz, Lawrence (1986), *Blindsight: A Case Study and Implications* (Oxford, Oxford University Press).

Wittgenstein, Ludwig (1961), *Tractatus Logico-Philosophicus* [1921], trans. D. F. Pears and B. F. McGuinness, intro. Bertrand Russell (London, Routledge & Kegan Paul).

Wittgenstein, Ludwig (1958), *Philosophical Investigations* [1953], trans. G. E. M. Anscombe (Oxford, Blackwell).

Woodworth, Robert S. and Schlosberg, Harold (1955), *Experimental Psychology*, 3rd edn (London, Methuen).

Wundt, Wilhelm (1900–20), *Völkerpsychologie: Eine Untersuchung der Entwicklungsgesetze von Sprache, Mythus und Sitte*, 20 vols (Leipzig, Wilhelm Engelmann).

Wundt, Wilhelm (1916), *Elements of Folk Psychology: Outlines of a Psychological History of Mankind*, trans. E. L. Schaub (London, George Allen & Unwin, and New York, Macmillan).

Wundt, Wilhelm (1907), 'On the *Ausfrage* Experiments and on the Methods of the Psychology of Thinking', *Psychologische Studien*, 3.

Wundt, Wilhelm (1896), *Lectures on Human and Animal Psychology*, 2nd English edn, trans. J. E. Creighton and E. B. Titchener (London, Swann Sonnenschein, and New York, Macmillan).

Young, J. Z. (1978), *Programs of the Brain: Based on the Gifford Lectures, 1975–7* (Oxford, Oxford University Press).

Index

Page references in *italic* refer to illustrations.